W9-APW-711

CURRENCY TRADING

How to Access and Trade the World's Biggest Market

Philip Gotthelf

John Wiley & Sons, Inc.

Copyright © 2003 by Philip Gotthelf. All rights reserved.

Published by John Wiley & Sons, Inc., Hoboken, New Jersey
Published simultaneously in Canada

No part of this publication may be reproduced, stored in a retrieval system, or transmitted in any form or by any means, electronic, mechanical, photocopying, recording, scanning, or otherwise, except as permitted under Section 107 or 108 of the 1976 United States copyright Act, without either the prior written permission of the Publisher, or authorization through payment of the appropriate per-copy fee to the Copyright Clearance Center, Inc., 222 Rosewood Drive, Danvers, MA 01923, 978-750-8400, fax 978-750-4470, or on the web at www.copyright.com. Requests to the Publisher for permission should be addressed to the Permissions Department, John Wiley & Sons, Inc., 111 River Street, Hoboken, NJ 07030, 201-748-6011, fax 201-748-6008, e-mail: permcoordinator@wiley.com.

Limit of Liability/Disclaimer of Warranty: While the publisher and author have used their best efforts in preparing this book, they make no representations or warranties with respect to the accuracy or completeness of the contents of this book and specifically disclaim any implied warranties of merchantability or fitness for a particular purpose. No warranty may be created or extended by sales representatives or written sales materials. The advice and strategies contained herein may not be suitable for your situation. You should consult with a professional where appropriate. Neither the publisher nor author shall be liable for any loss of profit or any other commercial damages, including but not limited to special, incidental, consequential, or other damages.

For general information on our other products and services, or technical support, please contact our Customer Care Department within the United States at 800-762-2974, outside the United States at 317-572-3993 or fax 317-572-4002.

Wiley also publishes its books in a variety of electronic formats. Some content that appears in print may not be available in electronic books.

For more information about Wiley products, visit our web site at www.wiley.com.

Library of Congress Cataloging-in-Publication Data
Gotthelf, Philip.
   Currency trading: how to access and trade the world's biggest market / Philip Gotthelf.
      p.cm.--(wiley trading)
   Includes index.
   ISBN 0-471-21554-6 (alk. paper)
   1. Foreign exchange futures. 2. Foreign exchange market. I. title. II. Series.
HG3853.G68 2003
332.45--dc21   2002190743

Printed in the United States of America

10 9 8 7 6 5 4 3 2 1

This book is dedicated to my wife, Paula and my daughters, Jenna and Rikki. Their permission to write instead of play is responsible for this book.

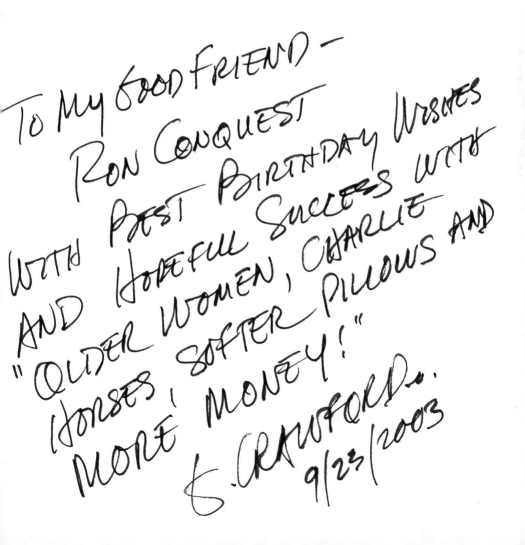

TO MY GOOD FRIEND —
RON CONQUEST
WITH BEST BIRTHDAY WISHES
AND HOPEFUL SUCCESS WITH
"OLDER WOMEN, CHARLIE
HORSES, SOFTER PILLOWS AND
MORE MONEY!"
C. CRAWFORD...
9/23/2003

Founded in 1807, John Wiley & Sons is the oldest independent publishing company in the United States. With offices in North America, Europe, Australia and Asia, Wiley is globally committed to developing and marketing print and electronic products and services to our customers' professional and personal knowledge and understanding.

The Wiley Trading series features books by traders who have survived the market's ever changing temperament and have prospered—some by reinventing systems, others by getting back to basics. Whether a novice trader, professional or somewhere in-between, these books will provide the advice and strategies needed to prosper today and well into he future.

For a list of available titles, please visit our Web site at *www.WileyFinance.com*.

ACKNOWLEDGMENTS

Special thanks are extended to those who helped compile facts, figures, and assisted in linguistic constructs that readers should be able to understand. I thank my wife, Paula for her patience and editing skills. I am sure her comments improved the quality of this book. Thanks to my associates Ron Goodis and Martin C. Niemi for working out trading examples and helping to acquire facts and graphic figures. I am forever grateful to Robert W. Hafer who provided access to charts and data while he was with Bridge/ Commodity Research Bureau. I want to thank the many individuals at the International Monetary Market (IMM) of the Chicago Mercantile Exchange and my friends at FINEX for providing contract specifications and access to international monetary statistics. Thanks are extended to various Refco FX Associates and Bruce Pollack for providing screen shots and permission to use them.

Special acknowledgement is extended to Edward M. Bernstein, Esq. whose diligent efforts provided me with the time to complete another text. In turn, Ed and I thank Robert LoBue, Esq. and Stuart Karl, Esq. for their persistence and perseverance that aided in the growth of my nest egg and helped me pursue more extensive trading endeavors.

Finally, I want to acknowledge a very special individual, Ariel Jacobs, who lost his life during the September 11th 2001 terrorist attack upon the World Trade Center. Ari worked for FutureSource as Senior Vice President/National Sales Director. Ari provided the original permission to include FutureSource data and statistics in this book. He left this world on his birthday and just prior to the birth of his first child. Those who knew him appreciated his youthful energy and sincerity. He was an asset to his company and his customers. He will be missed.

TABLE OF CONTENTS

INTRODUCTION

In 1972, my father, the late Edward B. Gotthelf, met with Everett Harris, President of the Chicago Mercantile Exchange, to discuss promoting their new International Monetary Market (IMM). Major world currencies were being floated against the dollar under a new Smithsonian Agreement consummated in December 1971. The exchange was working swiftly to create foreign currency futures that would take advantage of an expanded fluctuation band from 1 to 4.5 percent. Although this was hardly the kind of dramatic swing seen in some agricultural markets, this evolutionary development represented the potential for a 9 percent trading range from top to bottom. Approximately 4 months later, western Europe formulated their European Joint Float, which permitted a 2.5 percent intermember parity fluctuation labeled *the snake* and a 4.5 percent band against the dollar called *the tunnel.* Again, the implied range against the greenback was 9 percent.

If memory serves me correctly, a gentleman named Mark Powers was involved in making currency futures a reality. This bold plan represented the birth of financial futures and a new era of derivative trading. Founders of currency futures appropriately reasoned that a 1 to 10 percent margin would magnify a 9 percent trading range by several hundred percent. Consider that a 5 percent move against the dollar translates into a nickel. If you only need .01 to .001¢ to accomplish this trade, your potential profit is 500 to 5,000 percent.

Fortunately, no insider trading restrictions applied to commodity markets. When I visited home from college, my father excitedly explained the enormous profit potentials represented by these new markets. He pointed out that certain currencies such as the Japanese yen and Mexican peso were being revalued against the dollar. However, IMM contracts hadn't reflected the anticipated changes.

It was my first official venture into commodity trading. Using money earned through summer jobs and guitar perform- ances in coffee houses, I funded my first currency trading ven- ture. With less than $1,000, I took positions destined for realignment. Within a few months, a few hundred dollars in mar- gin ballooned into a whopping $7,000. Although this was not as impressive as Hillary Clinton's alleged gains in soybeans and cat- tle, keep in mind that these were 1970's dollars. I immediately took my newly found riches and went car shopping. For those familiar with cars of the 1970s, my choice narrowed down to the Alfa Romeo Berliner at $2,800 and the BMW 2002 Tii at $3,200. Imagine such prices! The remainder of my profits went toward paying taxes, tuition, and (of course) party expenses.

Although the BMW represented *the* car at the time, I remem- ber thinking, "$400! How can I afford the extra $400?" As of this writing, $400 buys a modest New York dinner for four with a decent wine, very few drinks, and perhaps dessert. I bought the Alfa and admit that I drove that car for 17 years—until I married my wife Paula, who refused to push-start the vehicle on cold winter days. After all, we were married and she didn't have to play *that game* anymore!

Of course, the point of this introductory story is threefold. First, it exemplifies the enormous amplification a 9 percent max- imum trading range had when combined with a 1 percent initial margin requirement. In effect, 9 percent became almost 900 per- cent. By the 1990s, currencies bounced against each other in multiple percentages. Daily volume grew to average an astound- ing $1 trillion. World-renowned financier/investor George Soros realized more than $1 billion over a few days when currencies were *adjusted* in the fall of 1992. In addition, the story adds an often forgotten perspective of changing currency value—the effects of inflation. Most importantly, it demonstrates a funda- mental transition in world currency structures from monetary standards to commodities.Why is this important? Too fre- quently, we overlook differences between monetary standards and commodity valuation. For example, a dollar fixed to gold eliminates gold's speculative potential. Simply put, gold's price cannot fluctuate. The dollar effectively becomes gold and gold becomes the dollar. Unlink gold and you have a commodity with price fluctuation potential. Indeed, gold was disassociated with the dollar and President Nixon closed the U.S. Gold Window early in the 1970s.

Modern Currency Speculation

When currencies were permitted to fluctuate more freely against a dollar standard, modern currency speculation was born. Some believe the new world of floating currencies is a prelude to disaster. Without a physical standard such as gold, governments are free to violate the public trust and play with the money supply. Sooner or later, public confidence may be stretched to its limit and the world might experience a confidence crisis. Such an event would lead to a monetary meltdown that might make the Great Depression seem like a minor interlude.

Parity

In a previous book I authored entitled *The New Precious Metals Market,* I called attention to the relationships between physical standards such as gold and silver and commodity standards that rely upon relationships called *parity*. Interestingly, the parity concept and term is conspicuously missing from modern currency trading vernacular and recently written texts. Being somewhat of a traditionalist, I return to the use of parity in this book as a term of art and vital currency trading principle. Today's currency traders can focus too closely upon the money. What is the British pound doing today, this hour, minute, or even second? A narrow focus misses the big picture. Currency buys commodities and services. Currency has a value or standing relative to commodities and services. This is parity. It is expressed as a ratio or a price.

Parity is where modern currency trading becomes exceptionally exciting and broad. For the moment, we have global commodity markets trading in various currencies on an almost continuous basis. Coffee quoted in pounds is also bid in dollars. Oil traded in dollars may also require payment in euro currency. Any time a commodity is valued in more than one currency, there is an automatic cross-parity potential. This is commonly

called *arbitrage*. Anytime a currency has multiple-parity relationships, there is arbitrage. However, the significance of cross-
parity is far greater than quick profit opportunities. The entire
structure of an emerging and changing global economic system
relies on maintaining parity.

Equally intriguing are technological and structural changes
in trading forums and mechanisms. Electronic tracking, order
execution, and accounting permit more precise and less dangerous arbitrage, as discussed in later chapters. Paths to riches are
diverse and expanding.

As readers will see, parity is obvious, but obscure. The principle put forth by the mediaeval philosopher William of Occam
states, *"non sunt multiplicanda entia praeter necessitatem,"*
which means "things (such as, data, relationships, and observations) should not be multiplied (expanded) beyond their requirements or necessities." This is known as *Occam's Razor* or *the
principle of parsimony.* Parity is simplicity. We can pile up
trends, cycles, waves, neural net predictive equations, relative
strength, stochastic measurements, and a host of technical or
fundamental methodologies. In the end, we seek to define parity
and its possible change. Keeping it simple should be a universal
objective. Within the simple lies the secret to enormous wealth!

Efficient Market Theory

This raises another question often presented by skeptics who
insist markets are efficient and there are no realistic opportunities to achieve consistent trading success. Efficient Market
Theory states that markets almost instantly discount price-influ-
encing news. Thus, anything publicly known cannot generate a
profit. Again, referencing my earlier book on precious metals, I
predicted a rise in palladium beyond $1,000 per ounce and plat-
inum above $600, and a fall in silver below $4.50 and gold well
under $300. At the same time, I stated that the gold sector would
continue providing security and stock appreciation. These documented predictions were not divined or lucky guesses. They
were logically deduced from publicly known information well in
advance of the eventual price move. In fact, the behavior of the
group of four metals (gold, silver, platinum, and palladium) was

generally predicted within the book using simple approaches that have been market-proven before and since the publication date.

The Goal of This Book

The purpose of this text is to provide an understanding of foreign exchange trading. Although I may reference historic changes in the international currency system, the past does not necessarily reflect the future because the entire concept of foreign exchange has changed and continues to change. The Bretton Woods Accord is interesting, but irrelevant to today's market. Debating a gold standard is an interesting intellectual exercise, but may have no bearing on how currencies are valued today.

Therefore, the ultimate objective is to get down to the business of trading currencies to earn huge returns. I say huge because it is an appropriate description. Just since the introduction of the euro currency, the U.S. Dollar Index moved 16 percent while the euro currency futures plunged from 1.2200 to 0.8245 against the greenback—a whopping 32 percent. Using leveraged futures or options, the profit potential magnifies more than 100 times. Perhaps calling this huge is an understatement. Before that interim trend concluded, there was a 50 percent appreciation in the dollar relative to European currencies. After the terrorist attacks on September 11th, the dollar finally reversed. Amazing profit opportunities became available in 2002 by selling dollars or buying the euro, yen, Australian dollar, and even the pound.

Of course, anyone can relate past movements. The key is learning how *you* can participate. Along such lines, you must know how *you* can trade in these exciting markets. There are texts describing how professional currency traders and brokers trade or how institutions use various markets and strategies to deal with adverse currency fluctuations. However, one question remains: How do you make money? If this is your question, read on! Learn how various currency markets like futures, options, Interbank, and forwards work. Discover why currencies change value (parity) and see how market theory has been altered by innovations such as interest rate futures, derivatives, and synthetic transactions. What do international trade balances do to currencies? How do interest rates correlate with currency values?

You'll want to know which markets are best for you. Should you use the Interbank, futures, or options? What are the new electronic markets and how can you take part? What are the risks and exposures? After answering these basic questions, we'll explore predictive skills and methodologies. What are the time-proven trading approaches? How can you potentially build unimaginable wealth? Can you enjoy the excitement and fast action?

There is also the concern about panics and monetary meltdowns. How real are the possibilities and what can you do to protect yourself against such events? All too often, we assume good times are here indefinitely. However, history demonstrates there are economic and social cycles that can alter perception and cripple public confidence. After all, the money you carry is no more than paper with sophisticated printing. This paper may be exchanged for tangible goods and services because you and your counter party have faith in the paper's value. But it's just paper—more now than ever. What happens if we lose faith?

The Rapid Evolution of Modern Currency Markets

This is a truly exciting time for investors and evolving currency markets. Over the next several decades, monetary systems and methods of exchange and valuation *will change.* The consolidation of individual western European currencies is only one example. Electronic transactions represent an entirely new world of opportunities. Globalization is an unknown phenomenon that will surely reshape monetary systems and structures.

Before delving into how you can profit from trading currencies, we must develop an appreciation for the speed with which our world is changing. Technological advances are accelerating at a nearly exponential rate. As an example, Gordon Moore observed that the performance of transistor-based computer chips was exhibiting a pattern of doubling capacity every 18 to 24 months. His observation was subsequently expressed as Moore's Law and has been supported by the data since his revelation in 1965. Indeed, computer chip advancement has been exponential and there are powerful indications that the trend will remain in place for many decades, if not centuries. With this advancement in raw computing power, the human knowledge base is exploding at an equally impressive rate. The possibility of mapping the human genome was sheer fantasy just a few decades ago. Now, the race to complete this formerly impossible project is nearing completion.

Interestingly, as science moves us forward at a whirlwind pace, the science of economics crawls forward at less than a snail's pace. Money has essentially remained the same for thousands of years. It has only been since the 1970s that the fundamental concepts and construct of money have been changing. Central banks are brand new in comparison with the history of money. Gold and silver were briefly the basis for all global valuation.

Yes, there have been new monetary ideas, products, and services. We might liken the credit card to the first semiconductor or transistor. How far have we come since then? However, there are signs that more rapid monetary and money evolution *is* taking place. Electronic cash may replace bills and coins. The euro currency is indicative of a monetary consolidation. The development and growth in foreign exchange trading suggests a new paradigm. As such, even the life span of this text may be brief as the role of money, currency, and foreign exchange evolves and changes.

Many of us recognize the enormous profit potential associated with evolving monetary systems and foreign exchange. Just as Bill Gates seized on the phenomenon expressed as Moore's Law by augmenting hardware with software, individual investors (like you and me) can grasp present and future wealth building opportunities in the foreign exchange markets. Simply put, you must be prepared if you want to profit. That's what this is all about.

Chapter 1

MONEY, CURRENCY, AND FOREIGN EXCHANGE (FOREX)

The most basic questions and concepts we must address involve the differences between money, currency, and foreign exchange (FOREX). All too often these terms are interchanged. With equal frequency, the differences are blurred and misconceptions are developed. Aren't the three terms one and the same? The answer is no.

The Barter Process and the Evolution of Money

Money is the primal evolution of barter. It was developed as a convenient means for exchanging goods and services. If my education correctly serves me, the first recorded book entries date back 5,000 years ago to the Sumerians who were defined as the first society. Book entries could only become a reality as numeric systems were developed. This is how money allegedly originated.

Certainly, there were methods to exchange goods and services before the Sumerians. The barter process appears in cave wall drawings and remains widely used today. However, barter lacks efficiency because it inevitably involves considerable negotiation to consummate a transaction. Value must be determined through a process of bidding and offering. Sound familiar? For example, suppose an ancient tribesman trapped a few beavers while a fellow tribesman caught several fish. Not needing all the beavers or all the fish, the two may decide to exchange beaver for fish. Depending on the perceived value of beaver pelts in the mind of the fisherman versus the relative hunger of the trapper, some ratio of beaver to fish would be agreed upon.

Understandably, perceived values will change. The first inkling of seasonality can be deduced from the previous example by overlaying the need for warmth during the winter onto the nonseasonal requirement for food. Logically, pelts should fetch more fish as temperatures cool. The trapper is likely to fatten up during winter, but go hungry in the summer. This suggests that the trapper will expand his product line to include meat as well as pelts. This overcomes seasonal problems. Both the trapper and fisherman must spend the better part of their day accumulating their bounties. Perhaps neither has time to build or maintain shelter. However, another tribesman discovers that his lack of skills as hunter or fisherman is offset by his ability to construct sturdy huts.

The hut builder introduces the concept of cyclical supply and demand as well as an underlying seasonal influence. He must build huts when the weather is mild and there is easy access to the ground. His unique challenge derives from his product's durability coupled with seasonal supply. He develops a prolonged barter whereby he swaps a hut for a year's supply of fish or meat. Thus, the hut builder's commitment to exchange today is carried forward in payments. Heavens! Was this the first mortgage?

The model grows more complex when the hut builder discovers that the value of his trade exceeds his requirements for fish and meat. Since he cannot consume all he has bartered for, he decides to use his excess to acquire a wagon from the wagon maker to transport his building materials and increase his efficiency. Perhaps he also exchanges fish and meat for tools. The increased efficiency only brings the hut builder more fish and meat. He decides to train other hut builders with the understanding that they will work for him and receive a portion of his meat and fish. The first real-estate tycoon is made. In all likelihood, he doesn't even pay for the land!

We see an economic system emerging from barter. All the while, however, transactions and relative values must be negotiated. Eventually, the hut builder's tradesmen may decide to go off on their own. Suddenly, there is competition in the real-estate market. With equal certainty, the tribe will have many fishermen, hunters, wagon builders, toolmakers, and other tradesmen. If competition becomes heated, arguments can develop, and, alas, we see the makings of war.

This is not necessarily a historically correct portrayal. The metaphor simply illustrates how a barter economy develops and functions. Reviewing and understanding this fundamental economic system is important when we seek to determine FOREX trading strategies based upon relative values for global goods and services. With the decline of colonization, nations have become regional. Since global resources are highly regional, national wealth becomes a function of location, population, and sophistication. In turn, national wealth determines a currency's relative strength or weakness.

Although this concept will be covered in later chapters, I won't hold you in total suspense. Some basic examples can be illustrated by Middle East oil or South African gold and platinum. These natural and valuable resources provide foundations for national economic security. They also fuel currency exchange. Japan relies upon ingenuity to efficiently convert raw materials into finished goods. The yen's value rises and falls relative to Japan's innovation and related exports. Each nation relies upon particular resources to derive wealth. As we will see, this wealth is a driving force behind fluctuating currency values. However, it is not the only driving force.

Returning to our barter example, we can identify a need for a more efficient method of exchange. A toolmaker observes that some metal materials have a mysterious attraction. A shiny yellow metal is far heavier than the harder bronze he uses for an ax or hammer. His neighbor takes a fancy to the yellow metal and offers to exchange his skills as an artisan for a portion of the shiny yellow metal. Incredibly, the entire tribe, as well as other tribes, finds this yellow metal universally attractive. Of course, this metal is gold. After a sufficient quantity of gold becomes available, tribal members decide to mold it into uniform pieces called coins. They examine a fundamental product like fish and see that one fish fetches two beaver pelts. If they set the value of one fish equal to one gold coin, then one gold coin buys two beaver pelts. Thus, the value of a gold coin is established as a ratio to a common barter product with a relatively stable perceived value.

This example of converting gold into money does not take seasonal or cyclical values into consideration. It is only a way to explain the probable transition from barter to money. You are probably saying, "Tell me something I don't know." I emphasize that basic concepts translate into a more precise understanding of how FOREX works.

In reality, gold is a convenient example rather than a historically accurate account of how money emerged. Gold and even silver were too scarce to be effective forms of money. This is why the Phoenicians resorted to shells, while other cultures minted copper, tin, and iron or used glass, beads, and stones. This does not imply that gold and silver were not used for exchange. However, gold and silver's widespread use for day-to-day transactions was not common until far more sophisticated economies evolved.

As we will see, gold and silver were symbols of wealth and *stores of value*. These metals were used for more substantial transactions often involving exchange between kings or noblemen. These metals represented the first significant form of FOREX. Equally important, gold and silver were used to measure overall and relative wealth. You may say, "Wealth is wealth." This truism stands; however, there is a concept of relative wealth that plays an important role in determining modern international currency trends.

The Family Tree of Money, Currency, and FOREX

Most of us are familiar with trading cards. Whether trading baseball or Pokémon cards, children probably develop their first sense of value and negotiating skills by swapping trading cards. Indeed, some of us learned through this same primal exercise in FOREX. We can analyze card swapping in three ways. We can assume each card represents a form of currency whereby a specific card is likened to the yen while another symbolizes the dollar. We immediately comprehend that the card's value is directly associated with its scarcity relative to demand. Children instinctively know that the more rare the card, the more valuable it becomes relative to other cards or simply for outright purchase.

By the same token, children grasp the concept of storing value when they refuse to relinquish extremely valuable cards regardless of the offer. Of course, this is where children may appear irrational. After all, every card should have a price, right? Interestingly, adults and, more significantly, entire societies can enter periods of irrational savings. The concept of storing value, regardless of alternatives, can be seen as a confidence crisis. In the child's case, he or she lacks confidence that he or she will secure a replacement card. Suddenly, this card is the only such card in the child's mind—a *must have* or *must keep*. When socioeconomic panic sets in, history suggests we fall back on primal wealth symbolism like gold, property, or essential assets. Today, we call this a flight to quality.

Experienced currency traders might legitimately disagree with equating each unique card with a unique currency. It is not necessarily the case that the scarcest currency fetches the highest price or attains the greatest perceived value. In fact, the most abundant currency, like the dollar, is frequently viewed as the most valuable. Therefore, another viewpoint is that each playing card represents a unit of currency similar to the $1, $5, $10, and $20 bills going up to the highest denomination. In this example, the trading card becomes *money* rather than *currency*. What's the difference?

Simply put, money represents the means of exchange within its country of origin. When we think of money, we immediately resort to the bills and coins in our pockets or purses. We rarely conjure up an image of equalizing values between our pocket cash and the money of western Europe or the Pacific Rim. The difference is subtle, but consider that money has a fixed value within its place of origin. If baseball cards had a fixed value, they would not be negotiated. You would simply trade a known X number of cards for a known Y quantity of cards. In turn, the ratio of cards to each other permits different mixes of cards to buy goods and services. Observation tells us this is not the case. Trading cards change value in accordance with the inventories of those making the bids and offers.

Today, money, currency, and FOREX are like a family tree. Currency is money once removed. They are similar, yet they operate in different forums for different purposes. Another way to view trading cards expounds upon the market concept of the bid and offer. At any given moment, groups of children sporting different card inventories gather in separate markets to set their relative card values. Depending upon the inventories available within each market, the same cards will take on different values. Given the sophistication and indulgence of our newest generations, kids might plan to be in different markets at the same time by communicating bids and offers via cell phone or email. Behold, children participating in arbitrage!

When card values are exchanged in broad markets, we see a metaphoric example of FOREX. Taking this forward another step, money is used to buy local goods and services. Assume a bushel of soybeans is worth $6. We know that a $1 bill and $5 bill will purchase a bushel of beans. If we use a $10 bill, we receive $4 in change. A drought may drive soybeans higher, whereas good weather may lower prices. If the price is stable at $6, what is the same bushel worth in pounds (£)? The answer lies in the relative value of pounds to dollars. Consider that if the pound loses value against the dollar, U.S. soybeans become more expensive in the United Kingdom, but remain the same price in dollars. This is another way to differentiate money from currency. Recognize that this example uses a single commodity priced in two currencies. When soybeans are sold in the United Kingdom, local influences may make the price in pounds higher or lower. Thus, local supply and demand prevails to set local prices.

It does not take a great deal of perception to know where the example culminates. If we remove the soybeans and simply trade pounds against dollars, we are dealing in FOREX. In the FOREX market, the supply and demand for different currencies at any given moment establishes an exchange value—hence the expression *foreign exchange*. When you trade FOREX, you attempt to anticipate fluctuations in relative currency values. More often than not, you are not concerned with the price of local goods and services in local monies. There is an obvious link between local currency strength and weakness that is associated with inflation and deflation. If the dollar is inflating while the pound is not, there is a very good chance the pound will appreciate against the dollar. Unfortunately, FOREX relationships have become highly anticipatory. This means that today's inflation might be discounted by tomorrow's anticipated price correction. The subtle aspects of forecasting will be explained in later chapters. For now, keep this concept in the back of your mind as we move forward.

The Mechanisms of Money, Currency, and FOREX

With a modest understanding of money, currency, and FOREX, the next step in building a trading strategy involves breaking each component down into its mechanism. Here, distinctions between money and currency tend to blur. With concentration, we can maintain differentiation to develop more profound interpretations of intermarket events. Today's money consists of cash and book entries. Both use common denominations or units. U.S. money begins with the unit of currency called the *dollar*. This is fractionalized or multiplied as required to refine purchase prices. The fractions are on a base-10 system beginning with $1/100^{th}$ of $1 called the cent (¢). The physical representation of 1¢ cent is the penny. Cent is the unit, whereas penny is the coin. Five cents is coined as the nickel. We are still dealing with the cent, but our physical money can be either 5 pennies or 1 nickel. Of course, 10¢ is a dime, 25¢ is a quarter, and, oddly, 50¢ is a 50-cent piece.

I indulge in this elementary-level exercise because it is exceedingly important to make the leap from fractional units to currency units. The entire process of FOREX trading is based upon common fractional values known as *pips*. A pip is the common denominator between currencies much like the cent is the denominator for the dollar. While writing this text, I could only identify one U.S. product where domestic prices were quoted in fractions of a penny. Perhaps you can identify more. What is it? For some strange reason, U.S. retail gasoline is priced ending in nine-tenths of a cent. I've always wondered why this is always rounded up to the nearest cent. Who is keeping all those one-tenths?

Those familiar with Charles Dickens' novel *Great Expectations* might associate the word *pip* with that book's central character. We less-literary folk must direct our attention to the last significant decimal of a quoted currency. Again, this seemingly simple definition takes on monumental importance because pips determine the most common intraday and interday spreads and are also used to price transactions. The spread in pips can be the market maker's commission and, thus, your trading cost. As we will discuss in further detail, the pip is used when currencies are quoted against each other in the cash, Interbank, or electronic spot FOREX markets. When the reciprocal is correlated to the dollar in U.S. futures and options, the pip disappears. Each marketplace has its own language and structure. Once you understand each market's operations, including its advantages and disadvantages, you can make an educated decision about how and where to participate.

When conducting seminars on FOREX trading, I often draw the parallel between components like money or currency and quantum physics versus cosmetology. Admittedly, this correlation is a scientific stretch and is not intended to infringe upon the territorial imperative of our most brilliant academicians. FOREX trading does not require the CERN particle accelerator to identify its inner most workings. However, the perspectives are similar to emphasize a FOREX trader's required multiplicity. The tiniest particles within our universe were born out of the greatest cosmological event presumed to be the Big Bang.

Money is derived from the most fundamental human premise—faith. This faith that money is, in fact, valuable must be governed by multiple facilities that include government treasuries, central banks, commercial banks, consumer banks, specialty banks (savings and loans, credit unions, government lending institutions like Fannie Mae and Freddie Mac, and so on), the International Monetary Fund, and international currency markets. In addition, each sovereign's taxing authority plays a role in the amount of money citizens have available to spend and the amount governments have to spend or waste as they see fit. Each link in money's governing chain plays a role in determining value. Relationships between money institutions such as banks, coupled with the monetary policy of the governing institutions like the Federal Reserve or Treasury, determine the money supply. When correlated with demand, money establishes its value relative to domestic goods and services as well as its value as international currency.

The Regulation of Money Supply

As you can see, our very simple explanations of money, currency, and FOREX begin to become more complex. The amount of money we have is primarily regulated by interest rates and transactions commonly called *open market operations*. In the United States and many other nations, money supply is also a function of reserve requirements. The focus on money and related banking mechanisms alone can fill a book. Indeed, many texts have been written on the subject. A basic understanding of how money supply is regulated is another essential piece of the FOREX trader's strategic puzzle. This is because money becomes a commodity for FOREX trading. Money translates into currencies that can be exchanged at rapidly fluctuating values to generate a profit or, heaven forbid, a loss.

Three Expressions of Money Supply in the United States

In the United States, money supply is expressed as three numbers referenced as M1, M2, and M3. These three expressions have different presumed transaction velocities. M1 is cash in circulation plus primary bank deposits called *demand deposits*. M2 takes savings deposits into consideration. Following the U.S. Savings and Loan Crisis, many analysts discounted M2 as a relic because banking structurally changed to give savings deposits more flexibility. With check-drawing privileges, saving accounts are almost the same as demand deposits with the exception that they pay nominal interest. The advent of money market accounts required a third category encompassed in M3. Together, these three measures of supply comprise the total amount of local currency capable of circulating within the United States.

During the 1970s through the 1980s, FOREX traders keenly focused on money supply. It was a Friday ritual to bet on the change in M1 and M2, and therefore the change in U.S. currency value relative to other currencies. The premise was simple. If M1 and M2 grew appreciably, the dollar should weaken against other currencies —all things being equal. If the supply of U.S. currency shrank while demand remained stable, the dollar's value should increase. Also, flooding the money supply implied increasing inflation. Inflation meant devaluation.

The Facilities and Principles for Regulating Fluctuation

The classic formula for determining domestic price levels postulates that the price level is equal to the velocity of money multiplied by the money supply. Referencing college texts such as the famous 1948 book *Economics* by Paul Samuelson:

$$P = MV$$
$$\text{Price} = \text{Money Supply} \times \text{Transaction Velocity}$$

More money in circulation chasing the same number of goods at an increasing velocity leads to inflation (a rising price level). Of course, this is a market truism, too! The price of any commodity is a function of how much money we throw at it and how fast we throw it. This is easy to understand if we imagine an auction. If the room is crowded with people holding fists full of cash, it's a good assumption the value of auctioned items will be high. If a small crowd with lousy credit shows up, it is unlikely auctioned items will reach their upset prices.

As FOREX trading became more popular and sophisticated, pricing models grew more anticipatory. In other words, traders wanted to get the jump on money supply by examining the underlying elements driving M1 and M2. Interest rates are first in line. Central banks have the authority to change lending rates between themselves and commercial banks as well as the loan rates between commercial banks. Lower rates permit more borrowing that, in turn, increases cash in circulation. The more cash there is circulating, the greater the demand for goods and services. As demand grows, the economy grows.

Of course, too much cash creates excessive demand. When too much cash chases a static supply of goods and services, prices are forced higher. This is the most fundamental market dynamic. The relationship between price and money supply has a role in determining relative currency value. Money in circulation represents currency.

The Federal Reserve's ability to increase money supply is complemented by tools to limit money supply. The most obvious tool is the capacity to raise interest rates to discourage borrowing. This drains cash in circulation with the objective of limiting demand for goods and services.

It is essential to understand that these actions and their associated results are generalizations that have subtle or even blunt harmonics. For example, increasing interest rates also entice savings. Saving money removes it from circulation. Our central bank has a solution to this potential problem. In addition to setting interest rates, the Federal Reserve can change the ratio of deposits to loans through an adjustment in the reserve requirement. The reserve requirement is the amount of cash that a bank must hold to cover immediate withdrawal demands.

The mixture of reserves and interest rates becomes a complex economic elixir as we examine the theoretical and actual effects of altering reserves and interest rates. If a bank is permitted to loan a portion of its deposits, the amount of money expands by the reserve ratio. This is called the *multiplier* because the reserve requirement actually multiplies the amount of cash in circulation.

Although this book is not intended to be a text on money and banking, the subject is inseparable from understanding what makes FOREX fluctuate. If you learn anything about modern FOREX, it should be that it is part of a regulatory mechanism. For all practical purposes, money as it is created today is a fiction. Assets backing much of the world's currency do not actually exist, although government authorities will beg to differ! Whether we examine operations of the U.S. Federal Reserve (affectionately called the FED),or look at western European central banks operating under the Maastricht Treaty, the principles and facilities are designed to achieve the same results—regulate money in circulation.

Efficient Economic Theory in Modern Currency Trading

Recall our first discussion of barter and the evolution of money. We know monetary value is associated with the ratio of a unit of currency such as $1 and the amount it can buy. What is the amount it can buy? Obviously, we must know the reference commodity. Is it an amount of gold or sugar? Assume it is sugar. Suppose $1 can buy 10 pounds of white sugar. Assume £1 can buy 20 pounds of sugar. It stands to reason that £1 will have a value of $2. It is simple algebra.

This simplistic algebraic relationship was expressed by Navarro Martin de Azpilcueta who lived during the time of Christopher Columbus (1492–1586). He postulated that the values of the same goods in different countries created a ratio for the relative value of different currencies. In its original expression, the theory was simple and suggested the relationship was absolute. The concept of purchasing power parity was remarkable for Azpilcueta's time since it came at the leading edge of the Age of Mercantilism. Of course, his assumption lacked economic sophistication because it presumed that goods within each country were the same. As mercantilism evolved into international commerce, it became clear that divergent goods exclusively available from certain countries drove currency parity. Similar goods might be used to define an approximate currency relationship. Thus, an ounce of gold could be used as a standard to determine the relative value between currencies. However, the forces that determined the gold ratio were independent.

Silk and spices came from the Orient. Weapons, ships, and mechanical devices came from Europe. How can these dissimilar goods be reconciled? History students know that mercantilism was a primary catalyst for colonialism. Nations simply took over resources in foreign lands. Thus, foreign products could be valued in local currencies.

How does this apply to modern currency trading? The foundation of any nation's wealth was previously established by its natural resources. Thus, if silk were an exclusive product of China, then China's wealth would be defined by demand for silk from nonproducing nations. A nation rich in gold would be rich if other nations relied upon a gold standard. This empiric conclusion was challenged during the 1980s and 1990s. A phenomenon labeled *Japan Inc.* suggested that a nation could become wealthy based upon its ability to convert another nation's raw materials into finished products.

This will be covered in greater detail later. However, the evolution of efficient economic theory actually altered the way currencies fluctuated. Most notably, post World War II Germany took full advantage of a consumer economy to build wealth and drain gold reserves from other nations. Japan also capitalized on being prohibited from building or maintaining a war machine. Radios, TVs, and cars became the measure of the yen and deutsche mark. Explosive economic growth followed both World Wars. By the 1960s, Western economies were becoming more diversified and complex. Growth was being restricted by monetary standards, primarily gold.

Learning from the Great Depression, U.S. and European monetary policy looked for an alternative to asset-backed currency. Eventually, gold was abandoned as a standard. Floating currencies took gold's place. Some proponents of asset-backed currency insist we must return to a gold standard. Although gold appears to be demonetized, it continues to play a role in cross-parity calculations. As we will see, gold remains a hidden reserve asset and potential monetary measuring stick.

The Ongoing Evolution of FOREX

It is often said that the more things change, the more they remain the same. Currency markets demonstrate that this is partially true. Although the concept of money has evolved to include paper bills, coins, checks, credit and debits cards, and electronic book entries, the essential function remains the same. Although international currencies have progressed from asset-backed valuation to floating parities, currency is still distinguishable from region to region. However, FOREX has changed its methods and philosophies many times over the past few decades. Indeed, by the time you finish this book, there are likely to be a dozen new twists to FOREX. From strategies to trading forums, FOREX is a moving target with massive profit possibilities. That is why FOREX is emerging as the most exciting and fastest moving market in the world!

Chapter 2

UNDERSTANDING PARITY

Parity may easily be the most important economic and investment principle. Unfortunately, it is so primal and fundamental that we rarely spend the time to comprehend the enormity of its role and influence. The term *parity* has practically disappeared from currency trader vocabulary. You don't see it mentioned in newspapers or on television. Parity is simply nowhere to be found.

Consider that every fluctuation in every market is based on some form of parity. For example, the very move of a stock price reflects parity between the stock and the currency of valuation. Within a few minutes, the parity between dollars and IBM equity can change a fraction of a percent. When an ice cream store raises the price of a scoop, it is changing parity between money and ice cream. So, what does this mean?

Simply put, you want to master parity rules and relationships to participate in profit potentials. Whether it is foreign exchange (FOREX) trading or negotiating the price of a new car, understanding parity is critical to your success. Equally important, parity is not a standalone term. It is progressive because there is cross-parity, multiple parity, or compound parity. The comforting thing about parity is that the basic principle is easy to understand.

The Basics of Parity

An adjunct phrase for parity is *ratio of equality*. Parity is a ratio between items that always equals or resolves to one. One share of stock equals so many dollars or yen (¥). We want to know what ratio between two or more items consummates *one* transaction. When are these items considered equal in value and therefore exchangeable? Determining parity is actually the market process. It is a series of tests between buyers and sellers that result in a deal.

Interestingly, this process is reflected in modern technical trading techniques. Most notably, a price chart is a picture of historical parity based on successful tests between buyers and sellers. Assume you are seeking a new house. The first step would be to look for listings or offers by sellers who own homes with the right criteria. Suppose a house that catches your attention is listed for sale at $635,000. What do you do? After reasonable consideration, the usual step is to make an offer under the listed price, such as $550,000. Your broker presents your bid and the seller is likely to counter with another price. The process continues until you and the seller agree on a final deal. You and the seller have found a ratio of dollars to one house or parity. Each time you make an offer and the seller counters, you are testing to find parity. It's that simple. In the end, one house sells for a fixed dollar amount.

Technically, none of these tests appears on a chart because they are unsuccessful. Only the final transaction shows up. During the course of many transactions, a pattern appears that tells where successful parities have been found. In turn, we assume these charts have predictive values because we see patterns of rising, falling, or static parity. In real estate, buyers, sellers, and brokers look at prior sales to determine value. In FOREX, traders examine the same information and patterns. I am sure you have encountered the statement that the real-estate market is rising or falling. At any given moment, there are price patterns that substantiate this observation. However, if you were speculating in real estate, you would want to know if prices will continue rising or falling and the possible influences that could make a difference.

Obviously, the same objectives serve the currency trader. Along such lines, parity is defined by multiple relationships. In the first chapter, we covered the relationship between what a country produces and the value of its currency. In addition, we touched on price-parity theory that assumes currency values will be tied to the value of the same goods or services. This theory sets the stage for a basic understanding of parity, yet it fails to describe the real world. In particular, it fails to consider the modern world and how currencies and transactions are changing.

Cross-Parity and Fixed Value

This leads us to the theory of cross-parity and fixed values. Recall the brief discussion of gold and asset-backed currency. Prior to the dissolution of a global gold standard, currency values were tied to an ounce of gold. Here, the equation was simple. Although goods and services could be highly diversified from country to country, gold was viewed as immutable and fixed in value. Thus, if an ounce of gold were fixed at $40, while 20 pounds (£) fetched the same ounce, the dollar/pound parity would be 2 to 1, also expressed as 2:1. The pound would be worth $2. This parity system has some very obvious advantages starting with its simplicity. In fact, the most supportive argument for bringing back a gold or silver standard rests in the consensus that if all else fails, asset-backed currency has always worked.

A more substantial argument is that asset-backed currency is inherently more stable and less subject to inflation. Certainly, backing currency with gold accomplishes two things. First, it removes the ability to speculate in gold because gold's price cannot change. Second, it assuredly puts a crimp in currency trading because FOREX becomes a strict function of trade balances. Thus, those who argue in favor of a gold standard would eliminate profit potentials from fluctuating gold and currency values.

For the moment, we know currencies are not fixed to precious metals. Still, the basic parity relationship remains. Suppose the dollar/pound is at 2:1. Add in the Japanese yen at a dollar/yen parity of 1:50. What would be the assumed cross-parity between the pound and the yen? Since we know the pound equals $2 and the dollar equals ¥50, algebra tells us the pound is worth ¥100. This assumption of cross-parity is a basis for an arbitrage. If you are sufficiently nimble, you might identify a situation where the pound is trading for $2 and ¥100. At the same time, the yen is trading at 55 to the dollar. If you buy ¥110 for $2 and sell ¥100 for £1, you can immediately convert the pound back into $2 and realize a ¥10 profit.

Since several FOREX market forums are available such as the Interbank, futures, and electronic cash systems, this type of aberration can and does occur. In fact, professional traders use sophisticated computer programs to monitor cross-parity and automatically execute trades when opportunities are identified. A small but notable example is the FINEX U.S. Dollar Index futures contract. This index is comprised of the major western European currencies and the yen in varying proportions. Arbitrageurs take cash positions in the index currencies and trade against the index. Speculators are able to trade against these arbitrageurs who essentially make a market.

Cross-Parity between Commodities and Currencies

Equally intriguing are cross-commodity parity differentials. International commodities such as coffee, sugar, cocoa, and metals are quoted in different markets and currencies. Even crude oil is subject to valuation in dollars as well as the euro currency. What happens if there are differentials between commodity prices relative to different currencies?

Although this book is about currency trading, keep in mind that the objective is to lead you to profit potentials. Thus, cross-parity between commodities and currencies is particularly intriguing. For example, assume coffee is trading for $1 per pound in the U.S. futures market, while it is bid at £.45 to the pound in London. At the same time, you observe that dollar/pound parity is 2:1—$2 for £1. As with the cross-currency arbitrage, you can buy coffee in pounds cheaper than you can in dollars. Therefore, coffee provides a vehicle for trading against dollars and pounds. This same logic applies for any commodity simultaneously traded in more than one currency.

When Iraq announced it wanted payment for oil in euros rather than dollars, cheers were heard throughout currency and energy trading rooms. At last, one of the largest cash commodities that has always been valued in dollars was about to present an enormous cross-parity market. As with coffee, oil might trade

the Treasury Web site a few minutes early. Nonetheless, December T-Bond futures chart soared three full points in a single session. Long-term yields plunged and billions evaporated in less than a day. By the same token, billions were available for those who were on the right side of the dollar or debt. Anyone involved in compound transactions was certainly stimulated by this event.

Equally, if not more impressive, was the reaction following the discontinuation of T-Bonds as illustrated on the December 2001 T-Bond futures chart. As seen in Figure 2.1, principal value took a nosedive from 112'19 on November 1, 2001 to 99'08 by December 17, 2001. Consider the enormity of this move. In approximately $1^1/_2$ months, futures exhibited a $13,343.75 range, representing a profit for anyone who was short from top to bottom. With an approximate margin of $2,100.00, the return on a single position amounted to an astounding 635 percent in 33 trading days.

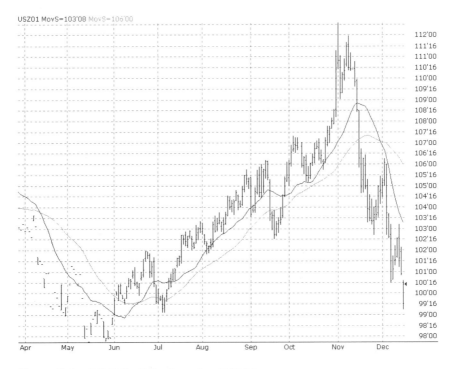

Figure 2.1   U.S. Dollar Index December 2001 futures.

By the same measure, currency volatility has steadily increased to the point where parity can change by 5 to 10 percent and more in a few weeks. Consider the yen during the last half of 2001. From September 21, 2001 through December 17, 2001, the cash yen plunged 12.38 percent from 1.1201 (.8927 to the dollar) to 1.2784 (.7822 to the dollar). Putting this move into profit perspective, the annualized rate of return would be 779 percent. Using futures on a leveraged basis, the margin was approximately $2,000.00 with a profit potential of $13,812.50 on this interim move—a 690 percent return on the initial margin. See Figure 2.2.

To say that parity change among the major world currencies is dramatic is an understatement at best. These wide swings are not established in a vacuum. As we will see when we examine fundamentals, volatility has expanded in virtually all investment and speculative forums. Certainly, the meteoric rise in high-tech

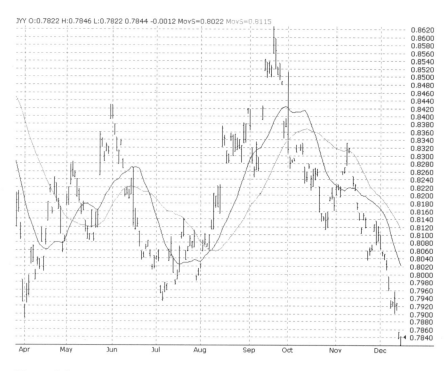

Figure 2.2   2001 Japanese yen cash.

stocks from 1998 through March 2000 illustrates the incredible exaggeration attainable in equity valuation. Price earnings ratios went through the roof and beyond with ratios of 200 and 300. Still, investors bought. Equally incredible was the plunge from March highs as more than $6 trillion in wealth vanished from U.S. equity markets alone—not to mention Japan and Europe.

Market Volatility and Parity Fluctuation

Market volatility begets tangential volatility. If we consider currency tangent to equities and interest rates, huge interim ranges of 5 percent to more than 10 percent are easily understandable. More importantly, they are tradable for spectacular gains. Clearly, there are secondary and even tertiary parity considerations. Ratios between interest rates and currency value have also been referenced as *interest rate parity*. Ratios between stock values and currency have also been called *equity parity*.

Simply put, suppose the U.S. 30-day Treasury bill (T-Bill) rate was 3 percent annualized, whereas the Japanese 30-day equivalent was 1 percent. The appreciation of $1 million in yen relative to $1 million in dollars would be 2 percent less. Thus, the dollar should be worth 2 percent more than the yen within 30 days, assuming a fixed interest rate. Other factors influencing this direct ratio would be inflation and potential yield fluctuations. In fact, forward currency pricing is based on this ratio logic.

The spread between today's currency parity and the anticipated value within 30 days is called the *forward spread*. Using the basic parity logic, components consist of the comparable interest rates and the currency parity.

Consider:

$$I_1 = \text{Domestic interest rate}$$
$$I_2 = \text{Foreign interest rate}$$
$$P_1 = \text{Domestic parity}$$
$$P_2 = \text{Foreign parity}$$
$$Y_1 = \text{Domestic cash yield}$$
$$Y_2 = \text{Foreign cash yield}$$
$$T = \text{Term to maturity}$$

$$Y_1 = I_1 \times P_1 \times (T/365)$$
$$Y_2 = I_2 \times P_2 \times (T/365)$$

$Y1 - Y2 =$ Yield differential or spread

This formula assumes constant or stable currency and interest rate parity. In reality, there will be a bid and offer for both. Thus, the equation must be calculated for the bid and the offer to derive a bid or offer spread for the currency based on present interest rates. At any given moment, major and minor currencies have multiple I, P, and Y relationships. These ratios drive the spot cash markets, forward cash markets, futures, and related options.

The rules and practices for each FOREX market are considerably different. At any given moment, the spot exchange rate is the basis or building block for derivative transactions in other forums. The spot market settles within two business days. Maturities in the forward market are variable.

Once understood, there is frequently an urge to experiment with the math using real-world examples. Caution is in order when you discover the numbers are not represented by the bid and ask spread. First, the math is used for making an approximation. In addition to interest rates and parity, traders must instantly deal with the immediate availability of one or more currencies as well as factoring inflation into the equation.

Therein lies the difficulty in successfully forecasting the future value of a currency or set of currencies. Economists and currency theorists have made careers and fortunes out of estimating, formulating, guesstimating, and prognosticating everything from interest rates to inflation rates and consumer spending. My review of models, guesswork, and crystal ball gazing suggests that these exercises are helpful in developing an understanding of the fundamental forces influencing currency parity, but accuracy is another matter.

This leads to one of the most important axioms of FOREX trading you will learn in this text. *There are no exact relationships.* I should add a qualifier. No exact relationships exist that I am aware of other than the consummation of each sequential transaction. Does this sound like techno-speak? It means that the print on the chart or quotation screen is the only exact relationship. You will find more meaning in this statement when we subsequently examine fundamental and technical analysis.

A perfect example is illustrated in the September 11th ter-rorist attacks on the United States. Certainly, the perpetrators knew of the events. However, the rest of the world remained ignorant until the explosions were identified. The influence on currency parity that followed represented a knee-jerk reaction unrelated to previous formulas. You simply cannot put cata-strophic intervention into an equation.

U.S. interest rates initially plunged in response to the con-sensus that the Federal Reserve would ease to accommodate the economic devastation associated with a major blow to the finan-cial industry. Indeed, the Fed continued easing rates. As previ-ously mentioned, the Treasury joined in with the decision to discontinue the long bond (30-year bond). The entire yield curve shifted a few notches downward. Examine the chart. Although the long bond was rising in conjunction with falling rates, the U.S. Dollar Index was also rising. During this period, foreign interest rates were static. This implies that the perception that the dollar was more secure overrode the formula that suggests traders should seek out the higher yield.

Interestingly, by mid-November, long-bond yields dramati-cally jumped, as seen by the decline in principal value shown in Figure 2.3. Notice that the U.S. Dollar Index remained relatively stable in contrast with an expectation for rising parity well into December. Where are the rules? More importantly, how could anyone comfortably buy or sell currencies forward without an ironclad hedge against adverse fluctuations?

While this circus was proceeding, financial columns in major newspapers raised the specter of renewed inflation. The general rule is that low interest rates fuel inflation. This rela-tionship is expressed in the Fisher Effect equation that combines real interest rates with the inflation rate to derive a nominal inflation rate. This is an empiric approach based on the clear observation that inflation impacts commodity parity. Refer-encing our previous discussion, inflation devalues a currency relative to goods and services. A pound of sugar that was 5¢ might rise to 10¢. Assuming this was purely the result of infla-tion, other commodity prices would rise proportionately. Priced in a different currency that was not inflating, the sugar price would remain the same in that currency. Of course, the value of the inflating currency would decline relative to the stable currency.

Figure 2.3 U.S. Dollar Index versus U.S. 30-year bond.

If the inflating currency had a very high associated interest rate, this would potentially decrease the inflationary impact on invested money. A rise from 5¢ to 10¢ represents 100 percent. This might be exceptionally high for any realistic interest rate. However, an 8.33 percent monthly yield could conceivably compensate for 100 percent annual inflation. Any interest rate model that factors inflation into the formula makes a questionable assumption that the currency has a yield. However, unless it is invested, currency has no income potential. Again, any formula is more of an explanation than an actual solution.

Inflation, Parity, and the Global Economy

Inflation is the universal parity determinant within the country of origin. The amorphous nature of modern international currency management is perhaps the most impressive aspect of modern parity determination outside a country of origin. The Fisher Effect simply suggests that a 5 percent annual inflation coupled with a 5 percent real interest rate produces a zero rate of return or a zero real inflation. The relationship was stated before derivative transactions could provide an offsetting hedge or, better still, a profit potential. We combine this with the theory that the general price level is a function of the velocity of money multiplied by the amount in circulation, as previously mentioned. This raises several important points about money, currency markets, and FOREX trading. Clearly, fundamental relationships that previously determined parity between money, goods, and services have changed. Consider a rather far-fetched concept of modern delivery mechanisms including the Internet and phone systems for services and transaction processing, Federal Express, Airborn Express, and other overnight couriers for goods, and modern container lines for bulk transportation. All of these have contributed to a global economy. Globalization, in turn, provides far more means of exchange. This has changed the way the world uses money and currency.

Perhaps the first indication that parity would forever be altered came when Nixon closed the Gold Window, forcing the world away from fixed exchange rates. The world suddenly lost the foundation for a substantial portion of modern economic theory. For example, the 1970s produced an unforeseen phenomenon appropriately labeled *stagflation*. Against all economic models, we saw it was possible to have very high inflation with low productivity and employment. The cause was rooted in a remnant of old thinking that distinguished two types of inflation. One was caused by an increase in money supply relative to the supply of goods and services. This was called *demand pull*. Essentially, a larger or increasing money supply was thought to be chasing the same amount of goods and services. Relying on our understanding of parity, it should be easy to see that the ratio of money to goods and services changes. Hence, the value of money is altered.

The second form of inflation was associated with a decrease in supply relative to demand. The implications are somewhat similar since you experience the same disproportionate or altered ratio between the supply of goods and service and the demand generated by the amount of money available. The difference is that an extrinsic event can selectively impact one or more essential commodities. The scarcity of this single commodity can ignite an inflationary cycle.

A perfect example of cost-push inflation relates to oil and the OPEC oligopoly. After the Yom Kippur War in 1973, Arab nations aligned in the infamous 1970s oil embargo. The resulting supply squeeze threw Western economies into a tailspin of deteriorating productivity and rocketing prices. Virtually every facet of our economy was linked to energy, from the cost of driving a car to heating and cooling homes and offices. Production costs, transportation, construction, commutation, plastics, chemicals, fertilizers, tar, and asphalt all drew their price from crude oil.

When you have such a severe commodity dislocation, the old rules or assumptions do not necessarily apply. The government instituted a massive conservation effort to little avail. Then came the revelation that deregulating domestic pricing could provide enough self-sufficiency to partially offset the OPEC squeeze, eventually challenging the embargo's effectiveness. Energy was not the exclusive cost-push influence during the early 1970s. In addition, a near food crisis pushed the world dangerously close to catastrophe.

Some may recall that the United States was the world's breadbasket. As the largest food producer and exporter, countries like Russia heavily relied on U.S. production to supplement domestic deficiencies. In 1971, the United States experienced a serious corn leaf blight that dangerously reduced corn supplies for the 1972 carryover. The next year brought an unusually severe El Niño weather phenomenon that virtually wiped out the Peruvian fishmeal crop that Russia relied on to supplement soybean and corn feed. The 1972 Russian wheat crop failed and the famous Russian Wheat Deal was consummated, which took U.S. grain prices to their highest levels of the century. Of course, OPEC countries were large buyers of U.S. food. Thus, their extraordinary oil profits were somewhat offset by their need to purchase U.S. food.

If you're not getting the picture, it's simply that the 1970s were a tumultuous time of unprecedented economic change.

Within a single decade, the world monetary system was changed forever. However, driving forces that brought about change were the same as those that previously determined monetary parity and national wealth. A great deal has been written about the Bretton Woods Accord and its stabilizing influence on the global monetary system. The accord pegged western European currencies to the dollar, while the dollar was linked to gold at a parity of $35 to the ounce. If a currency moved outside of a 1 percent range from the predetermined exchange rate (or parity) with the dollar, the central bank had to intervene.

The Bretton Woods Accord eventually failed because it did not accommodate more rapid economic expansion, nor did it compensate for disproportionate resources among member nations. Why is this important to understand when analyzing today's currency markets? The history lesson serves to demonstrate why currency markets evolved into commodities and how they can undergo a metamorphosis. Economists and political counterparts never experienced a cost-push inflation as severe and surprising. This is not to say that the 1970s encountered the worst inflation. It was not comparable to Germany's post World War I hyperinflation. However, economists were dealing with new and different potential tools for delivering us from economic uncertainty.

Demand-pull inflation was combated using monetary constraint instituted by the Federal Reserve or foreign equivalent. Cost-push was less responsive to monetary intervention because raising the cost of money (interest rates) only added to the overall cost of production and potentially restricted capital expansion. To restrict capital expansion was to exacerbate potential shortages. The answer was to allow currencies to radically adjust parity.

This transition was not an easy one, but rather an enormous learning curve that world leaders continue to ride today. In addition, it is a process that is unlikely to stop within the foreseeable future. It is important to grasp a solid understanding of parity and forces that influence ratios between currencies and between money, goods, and services. With this knowledge, you can make decisions about the potential for change among major and minor currencies. You can gain a sophisticated feel for fundamentals and their influence on your speculative ventures.

As we move into an explanation of fundamental and technical analysis, think about the possible scenarios and try to draw your own conclusions. Do not always rely on experts. In this complex world, incentives are often self-serving. Experts usually voice their opinion in conjunction with their own profit motives. This is true of analysts, government representatives, and even economic statistics. Have confidence in your ability to perceive the big picture and extrapolate an appropriate course of action. In today's FOREX markets, anything can happen!

Chapter 3

THE WEALTH OF NATIONS

Perhaps the earliest form of currency speculation occurred in ancient times when caravans transported and exchanged regional goods. Scarcity determined relative value as long as there was a demand for the regional items. Whether it was cloth, glass, foods, or metals, there was an ebb and flow of trade based on fluctuating product values. If spices suddenly fell out of favor, there was a strong likelihood their producing region would suffer. If glass making was confined to a specific area, its value would regionalize. Thus, the economic fate of one region or another rested with the relative value of its goods. Entire economies and even whole civilizations disappeared when misfortune took away the means of production or the demand for regional products.

Even the Bible teaches about economic planning and interregional trade. Wealth was measured by a family's means of production. This included flocks and herds, arable land, and material possessions such as silver and gold. In addition, family size was an extremely important yardstick of wealth. This is why there was such an emphasis on bearing children. How does this relate to modern foreign exchange (FOREX) fundamentals? When taken one at a time, regional global wealth is still measured by the means of production. Countries that have highly diversified resources tend to have the strongest economies and, therefore, currencies. Look at some examples.

The United States

The United States spans four time zones and latitudes from the Tropics to the Arctic. An exceptionally varied climate provides the extreme good fortune of vast temperate arable land. Although it is not a self-sufficient mineral or energy producer, enough supplies are available to provide for more than 25 percent of domestic requirements. The United States is blessed with a diversified population that has enormous human resourcefulness and energy. With modest redirection, the United States could become independent in most natural resources including energy and strategic metals. The United States remains the most technologically advanced nation in the world.

Although a subject of considerable debate, the United States still has relatively open borders. This has maintained a consistent working class that generally benefits the economy. However, social policies interfered with some of the benefits as portions of immigrant populations are supported by government subsidy programs. Still, the United States tends to inherit the world's enthusiasm as people move in to realize the American dream.

Since the 1970s, the United States has basically run a trade deficit. This means that more goods are imported than exported. Although theory suggests this should weaken a currency, the dollar has maintained immunity to adverse effects of a trade deficit into the new millennium. The United States imports coffee, cocoa, sugar, and energy—just to name a few raw commodities. The bulk of U.S. imports are finished goods such as automobiles, electronics, and clothing.

From the 1800s through the first two-thirds of the twentieth century, U.S. manufacturing was a dominant global force. The propensity for industrial mobilization has been credited with victories in the World Wars and the explosive mechanization that swept the globe from 1900 through 2000. However, the U.S. economy experienced a massive transformation that few would ever have anticipated. During a 30-year span from 1950 through 1980, the United States exported its manufacturing capacity and formed a service-based economic foundation.

This is not to say that U.S. manufacturing does not play a major role in the overall Gross Domestic Product (GDP). It simply demonstrates how quickly economic characteristics and roles can change. There was a saying during this time: "What's good for Detroit is good for the country." This statement was based on the huge economic influence U.S. automobile manufacturing had on the entire economy from the 1940s through 1975. Detroit's production trickled down to every economic sector because so many materials went into auto manufacturing. Metals, leather, rubber, vinyl, glass, plastics, fabrics, paint, motors, fasteners, and a host of other materials were made into cars. Did I mention labor? The influence was obvious.

As foreign cars made inroads into the United States and new industries like the computer sector took hold, the saying that Detroit determined the fate of the U.S. economy was relegated to the museum of old clichés. Indeed, it seemed that Microsoft was determining economic health through the 1990s and into the twenty-first century.

This brief description and historical overview serves as the foundation of a currency that has dominated modern societies and economies. The strength of the dollar has been based on U.S. resources. As we described in Chapter 1, national wealth has been a function of natural resources for thousands of years. From the biblical perspective, population is likened to family size. Family size determines how much a family can produce. Tribal population relates to production and maintaining a strong defense. Herds and flocks relate to the ability to produce varied foods. Topography determines crops, whereas landmass is strongly correlated to natural resources.

With this in mind, it is important to examine potential contradictions to the premise that resources determine wealth. Indeed, Japan, a nation with virtually no natural resources and a very small landmass, was able to build the second largest world economy. This phenomenon seriously challenged the notion that such a nation could not dominate.

Japan

During the 1980s, Japan turned the label "Made in Japan" from a sign of cheap into a sign of quality. Using Western technology and a unique work ethic, Japan managed to produce everything from electronics to automobiles more efficiently and with ever-increasing standards. This provided a price-to-quality ratio that propelled Japan's economy ahead of more established Western countries like Germany and the United Kingdom to become the second largest economy in the world. At the height of the Japanese juggernaut, U.S. legislatures became frightened that Japanese corporate interests would take over critical U.S. assets that included real-estate, entertainment companies, and the entire electronics industry. States passed laws to limit foreign real-estate accumulation to force land divesture. A panic simmered.

When considering that Japan's post World War II rise took approximately three decades, Japan Inc.'s dominance was brief. Panic over Japanese expansion faded into a remote memory by the close of the second millennium. The roaring yen encountered an incredible downward spiral right along with Japan's overall economy. How was it possible? How could the unstoppable Japanese economy grind to a halt? Worse, how could it slide backward?

Obviously, Japan's economy was primarily based on export. Although there was a push to build international capacity and take advantage of local distribution efficiencies, almost everything Japan used was imported and most of what Japan made was exported. Perhaps it is oversimplifying to claim Japan's fate was obvious. Still, the theory that national wealth is a function of resources appears to solidly apply. The very first ripples in Japan's economic infrastructure were actually visible in 1990 and 1991 when the Gulf War drove energy prices to decade highs. Since Japan does not have internal petroleum resources, rocketing energy prices took a toll on profit margins.

Although logic may dictate that the yen should suffer under such circumstances, Japan moved to strengthen the yen against the dollar. Why? Since oil was priced in dollars, a stronger yen lowered crude oil's value on a cross-parity basis. This action represented a double-edged sword. While energy cross-parity became more favorable, export cross-parity deteriorated. Japanese goods became more expensive in cheaper dollars.

The Success of Japan's Unique Economic Model

Japan provides a somewhat unique study because its economic structure and resources are very different from other major currency nations. Even the United Kingdom, which is also an island nation, has North Sea oil and reasonable agriculture relative to its population. Japan actually broke the traditional mold that presumes wealth can only be established on the back of natural resources. Thus, Japan's success represents a model for other nations with seemingly limited resources.

Like the high-tech frenzy that burst the Nasdaq bubble after March 2000, the Japanese leveraged expansion exposed their entire economy to downturns in other economies. Japan designed an export economy. A fundamental lesson in new currency trading was demonstrated. Entire economies and their currencies have become intimately dependent on the health of the entire global monetary/economic system under certain circumstances.

Books have been written about Japan's incredible economy. For more than a decade, Japan was the model and standard by which other economic systems were judged. Teams of consultants examined Japan's methodology to see if the phenomenon could be duplicated in the United States and western Europe. Even Japanese ideology influenced Western philosophy. Jim Ellis, founder and Chief Executive Officer of Oracle, developed an affinity for Japanese style and methodology. His home was designed after traditional Japanese architecture and lifestyle.

My own experience included a trip to Japan to participate in a think-tank session covering financial engineering. Japanese trading giants branched out into all areas of commodity trading that involved huge financial commitments. I never really grasped the significance of this quest to control commodities until I became more involved in analyzing resource-based accounting. Of course, Japan needed to control commodities. That was the lifeblood of their export economy. The meaning of financial engineering also escaped me. However, several presentations concentrated on leveraging the yen's strength while reducing exposure to adverse exchange rate fluctuations. Financial transactions were engineered to achieve a desired result. This was a fancy way of creating derivative financial vehicles to either enhance returns or increase safety.

These same transactions may have been the precursors to incredible failures and scandals. One such unfortunate event was the Sumitomo copper manipulation. An alleged rogue trader worked with several major U.S. firms to amass price-manipulating copper positions. World prices were driven to more than $1.40 per pound. Pennies were worth more melted than as pocket change.

As a tangential observation, we saw the difference between physical money and its commodity counterpart demonstrated! The Sumitomo situation had an estimated value exceeding $1 billion. This was not an exclusive situation.

At the height of our fascination with Japan's success I wondered if the success could be sustained. Being somewhat of a traditionalist, I could not see how Japan could continue expanding without securing long-term raw material resources. From my perspective, the yen lacked tangible backing. The substitute for gold backing (in my opinion) was and will always be resources. Japan had a formula that gave their economy a competitive edge. Absent from most texts on Japanese ingenuity was their brilliant positioning of the yen. Collective memory always seems to be short. This is generally attributed to the fact that each century is supposed to span four generations. It is an important consideration because each consecutive generation does not share the firsthand experience of the prior generation. In other words, a young 30-year-old currency trader operating in 2005 has no idea of the currency transitions that took place in the 1970s as they were reflected in day-to-day trading. Reading a book and living the experience provide totally different perspectives. In addition, the use of currency strategy to fuel the Japanese economy was not at the forefront of national or global focus. Yet, I assure you it was in the hearts and minds of central bankers.

If we review the currency coverage in *The Wall Street Journal* or *The New York Times* written in the 1980s, we see how the Japanese yen was purposefully kept at a very favorable parity against the dollar and western European currencies. This strategy was designed to inspire a positive export equation that was and remains essential to the Japanese economy. Carefully intertwined with this currency policy were the draconian measures taken to keep foreign participation within the Japanese economy restricted. This created a unique environment of internal isolation. The yen was not subject to internal fluctuations brought about by widely fluctuating imported goods. The only concern was raw material pricing.

Examine Figure 3.1, which depicts the Japanese December 1980 futures contract. Notice that the yen was trading at 0.3950 in April 1980. This means 0.3950¢ per yen—under four-tenths of a cent.

JYZ80 MovS=0.4715 MovS=0.4740

Figure 3.1 December 1980 Japanese yen futures.

Within a decade, the yen had doubled its dollar parity to more than 0.8000, as shown in Figure 3.2. Throughout the yen's climb against the dollar, it maintained an extraordinary balance of trade surplus. However, dollars were understandably building up in Japanese banks.

Follow the logic. A weak yen/dollar parity means raw materials bought in dollars are more expensive relative to the yen. However, the finished products can be more competitively priced in dollars when exported to the United States. The U.S. economy has a powerful seasonal cycle associated with the winter holidays. By developing a buying cycle in conjunction with modest seasonal fluctuations in the yen, Japanese enterprise was able to increase profit margins while decreasing the costs of certain raw materials.

The yen was cheap against the dollar. Trading at 200, the yen averaged approximately 50 percent of its dollar parity when comparing the 1980s with the 1990s. Japan virtually shut down certain electronic sectors in the United States with strategic

JYZ90 MovS=0.7618 MovS=0.7696

Figure 3.2   December 1990 Japanese yen futures.

dumping. Look for a microwave oven stamped "Made in the USA." Check the origins of most consumer electronics and see what you find. Once prominent U.S. names like RCA, Fisher, and Zenith have been eclipsed by Sony, Panasonic, Hitachi, and Mitsubishi. Electronics were not the only casualties of economic war. U.S. steel, automobiles, and heavy machinery also fell victim to Japan's masterful maneuvers.

All the while, countries with equally impressive capabilities were losing ground to Japan. Most notably, Lexus and Infiniti eventually challenged Germany in the high-end auto market. These cars were positioned against Mercedes Benz and BMW rather than Cadillac and the Lincoln. Why? Because the deutsche mark was strong against the dollar relative the yen. Germany was more vulnerable. This is not to say that Toyota positioned the Lexus exclusively based on currency parities. However, at the time Lexus was introduced, the dollar maintained a dominant position among free world currencies.

International Pressure to Open Japan's Economy

Once Japan's tactics were identified, other industrial nations adjusted to meet the challenge. When fundamentally evaluating the yen, it is wise to ask, "What is strength or weakness based on?" This may seem like a foolish exercise because if you know the basis for strength or weakness, you have presumably made your fortune trading the yen. Think again. At any moment during a rally or decline, try to use common sense and observation to answer the question. Your own findings can surprise you.

Conduct a simple historical study. When did Japan's seeming stranglehold on other world economies begin to deteriorate? Correlate the yen's dramatic rise against the dollar and European counterparts with Japan's internal economic woes. See how international pressure forced Japan to open its economy. Some say that the importation of foreign rice, a commodity of spiritual significance, marked the beginning of the end for Japanese domination. A more important consideration is the degree to which Japan exported manufacturing capacity to avoid adverse currency parity, labor costs, and politics. Japan engaged in a new type of colonialism by establishing factories within the importing countries. When the yen pushed beyond the dollar, logic dictated exporting its production capacity. However, this strategy has a mirrored currency exposure when the yen loses ground. Those factories that could have fueled Japan's local economy at the turn of the millennium were supporting foreign labor and capital.

Post-War Economic Consolidation in the European Union

The pages allotted to this text are too limited to analyze each economy and related currency for their potential strengths and weaknesses. Still, brief examinations help form a composite picture that can guide currency traders through the daily maze of currency information. A trader can make money trading FOREX in two ways. One is to take tidbits out of intraday movements or attempt to trade spreads and arbitrage. The other approach is to ride the wave of longer-term currency realignment. Therefore, a trader must select his or her approach and pay attention to those factors that influence the selected timeframe.

For example, Japan, Inc. and U.S. economic dominance set an unthinkable economic consolidation into motion. War after war has been waged throughout Europe and eastern Asia over territory, customs, religion, and politics. If there was one thing everyone could agree on, it was that Europeans could agree on nothing. World War I has been labeled a mistake. World War II was a continuation of the same mistake. The very fact that Germany and Japan rapidly integrated into the free world economy proves the fine line between friend and foe and raises the question, "What was it all about?" Approximately 60 years after the last shots of World War II echoed, Germany, France, Switzerland, and Italy formulated a treaty to merge their economies into a common market with a common currency.

I had an opportunity to speak with some World War II veterans at a Memorial Day gathering in 1999. My curiosity overwhelmed me. Did anyone who lived through that conflagration conceive of a unified western Europe? The universal answer was no. It was more intriguing to hear that most believed the European Union would not last. However, the euro currency was launched in 1999 and became money on January 1, 2002.

Examine the circumstance that drove Europe toward this dramatic structural change. Western European leaders realized that globalization would not tolerate European bickering. To compete with the United States and Japan, western Europe needed to combine resources, production, transportation, and financial systems. Amazingly, wealth became a primordial motivator that overcame political and ideological differences spanning centuries. Currency considerations were likened to prearranged marriages between European royal families that were specifically contrived to preserve the peace.

The United Kingdom

As mentioned, the United Kingdom, like Japan, is an island nation with limited natural resources. Unlike Japan, the United Kingdom has claim to North Sea oil and more diversified agriculture. Years of successful colonialism built solid financial institutions and made England a financial engineering powerhouse in everything from insurance to banking—commodity trading to equity markets. In fact, the United Kingdom's strong global position prevented it from joining in the initial launch of the euro. The British population was too emotionally attached to their pound to wean itself into a more mature euro economy.

The United Kingdom maintained a solid industrial infrastructure moving into the new millennium partially based on the military industrial complex left over from World War II. Although sustaining and maintaining their military represented a financial burden not shared by Germany, it also preserved England's industrial capacity. A powerful working class is still involved in everything from coal and peat mining to automobile manufacturing and Harrier jet production.

England also continued its colonial relationships to the extent that markets continue channeling through London. Traditional assets like seaports enable England to operate as a transportation hub. London is the focal point for coffee, cocoa, sugar, tin, lead, zinc, aluminum, copper, gold, silver, and a host of global raw materials. Like Japan, English trading houses dominate several raw material markets. To this day, the London Gold Fix is the standard that initiates global trading in this precious metal.

A more in-depth perspective of the U.K. economy is apparent in the FTSE 100 Index. This cross section of corporate England reveals the basic economic strengths and weaknesses. It is important to identify and track industries that dominate each nation's economy. Obviously, currency performance can greatly depend on the overall health of such dominant industries.

Germany

Defeated in war and rebuilt by peace, Germany emerged as the cornerstone European economy within three decades of World War II. Like post-war Japan, Germany's rapid recovery and rise to dominance was not coincidental. Germany was also foreclosed from rebuilding its military or participating in military interventions. Without the need to build a war machine, Germany concentrated on consumer goods and services. Germany became the Japan of western Europe. A distinguishing feature of Germany's success was its ability to tap natural resources.

German trade targeted European neighbors more than the United States. After all, proximity offers economic advantages. When the Berlin Wall was dismantled, there was wide speculation that the mark would severely suffer. Absorbing East Germany would cost billions of deutsche marks. However, Germany unified with amazing efficiency and very little destabilization. This formula is similar to the European unification model.

The Economic Impact of Unification

Unification is a tricky concept that will have profound implications for currency trading for many decades, if not centuries. Effective investors know they should think the unthinkable. For example, Germany and Russia were mortal enemies through the first half of the twentieth century. Russia was responsible for splitting East Germany from the West. Germans held a distinct distrust for Russians. Any alliance between these adversaries was, indeed, unthinkable. However, Germany holds the technological key to unlock the massive natural resources controlled by the Commonwealth of Independent States (CIS). By the same token, Russia controls vast natural resources that can fuel Germany's industrial machine.

As with any union, mutual benefits consummate the marriage. These must be balanced. The equation that may economically bind Germany and Russia can change to alter the relative partnership positions. Most notably, Russia has the ability to create the same industrial machine as Germany, yet Germany can never replicate the vast resources controlled by Russia. Alternatively, Russia is part of a commonwealth that fragments the natural resources spanned by 11 time zones. As Russia and the CIS develop, internal dynamics and politics can change. The principal word is *change*. Change is why currency markets fluctuate.

Rapid Change and Globalization

As we move through various regions, pause is appropriate. The very processes that elevated Japan and Germany while sustaining England represent the globalization phenomenon spawned in the twentieth century. This process relies on two developments:

transportation and communication. Transportation is required to move goods and services. Communication is necessary to receive and process transactions. Europe's progressive programs in transportation and communication include the tunnel between France and England, the gas pipeline between Germany and Russia, rapid rail service, and the Internet. All of these accomplishments took place within a very short period. From the time gold was abandoned during the 1970s to the circulation of the euro, there were less than three decades for adjustment. By the time correlations between European currencies were cemented by currency traders, a majority of western European currencies consolidated and the cement had given way to new rules and relationships.

Rapid and dramatic monetary change is a symbol of modern times. Besides some cataclysmic economic meltdown, the metamorphosis of currency systems and relationships will continue. It is likely that a meltdown is the only event that could cause a revolution back to hard-asset monetary systems. Even with such a return, it is probable that currencies will remain consolidated and even continue consolidating. The pattern that has evolved from Japan, Inc., the euro, and emerging capitalism within the former Soviet Bloc suggests that economies are regionalizing. For example, the dollar is associated with the Americas. The yen represents the Pacific Rim with the exception of Australia. The euro reflects western Europe and eastern sections of Asia. The *Big Three* have become the measure for other parity. Thus, the Brazilian real is most frequently associated with the dollar.

As this text was being written, concurrent changes in currency markets were exceptional. Not only was the euro launched as physical money, but China and the CIS were seeking status within the World Trade Organization. Consider the enormous power of these two sovereign entities. Although ruble trading may not be popular as of 2002, it could dominate in future decades. Currency trading requires forward thinking. Keep an open mind and vivid imagination. You never know where the next opportunities will develop.

CIS

As the CIS progresses, it will be important to track how this powerful international player collects new wealth and how it uses newly found riches. Nickel mines in the Norilsk region produce the largest amounts of this strategic metal along with platinum and palladium. Control over these resources translates into control over price. Kazakhstan is home to the largest known oil reserves on the planet (as of this writing). This suggests that this single state can determine world crude oil prices, just as Saudi Arabia has in the past. As is clear from prior Middle East conflicts and energy crises, crude oil is a primal component of economic health and progress. This implies that Russia and its related states are destined to play a pivotal role in global energy for decades to come.

The CIS controls the largest landmass and, most likely, the greatest natural resources. Although communism prevented typical fast-track capitalist-style development, this has changed. Recall that Japan, Inc. took less than 20 years without such natural resources. The former Soviet Union was a head-to-head technological competitor of the United States and western Europe. Its legacy as the number-two superpower has substantially carried over to the CIS. Currently, the CIS is able to build private and public infrastructure using the latest and most efficient combinations of global technology. If the CIS is capable of shifting focus away from past military endeavors in favor of establishing a powerful multifaceted economy, I believe the ruble can become a preeminent currency.

However, an alternate path exists whereby CIS members may embrace the West, permitting the euro to become a de facto currency. Of course, possibilities don't stop with the euro. Anyone familiar with the CIS should remember that the dollar represents the dominant underground currency. When all else fails, trade in the dollar! In fact, when the physical U.S. currency was being converted into its latest iteration, one of the most significant concerns was how it might impact Russia's economy. Billions in old U.S. currency was circulating in Russia as a second and more stable form of money. It was vitally important to keep this underground money in tact through the transition. In conjunction with this concern, the U.S. pledged hundreds of millions in new bills to offset any transition-related decrease in old paper.

The potential three-way tug of war between the ruble, euro, and U.S. dollar represents one of the most exciting profit potentials facing international currency markets. Simply put, we will probably witness the most extraordinary development of totally new economies among CIS members. Politics and power plays will be nothing short of fantastic. Through it all, you should expect incredible parity adjustments and associated profit opportunities. This is not only true for currency markets, but it is also true for the commodities that will be priced in the selected currency or currencies.

I bring this to mind because the most common question asked among speculators is, "Where and when will we see the next really big currency plays?" Short of being clairvoyant, the answer lies in an educated and pragmatic approach. One example is Kazakhstan. By 1990, it was generally known that this CIS member possessed one of the largest crude oil reserves in the world. Initially, the pool of oil stretching forth under the Caspian Sea was believed to rival Saudi Arabia's vast energy resources. By the turn of the century, tests revealed far more oil than originally estimated. This relatively unknown state became repositioned to assume the role of the world *swing producer.*

In the wake of the September 11th terrorist attacks on the United States and the subsequent Operation Freedom in Afghanistan, interesting diplomatic negotiations between the United States and Kazakhstan raised Russian eyebrows. The United States was seeking direct ties with Kazakhstan that moved well beyond the use of borders to facilitate the War on Terror. U.S. energy companies rode the military coattails in an attempt to establish a profound presence in Kazakhstan.

The political sportsmanship is obvious. The person who holds the oil wins, so to speak. However, the currency that prices the oil also wins if that currency is properly controlled by the purchasing entity. In this case, the greenback remained the dominant currency. Thus, it is easy to see that using rubles to price Russian and Kazakhstan crude oil will have a direct impact on ruble/dollar parity. Although the ruble was not a major speculative currency as of the turn of the millennium, you should not foreclose considering this potential rival of dollars and euros over the next several decades. Books on currency trading tend to remain static, whereas currency markets do not. The purpose of drawing attention to Russia and Kazakhstan is to open your mind to the possibilities. What remains in the background today may easily and rapidly move to the foreground tomorrow. For example, the German deutsche mark was the dominant European currency traded on the International Monetary Market (IMM) as futures and options. Shortly after the introduction of the euro, the mark shrank to insignificance.

China

Undoubtedly, China will play an increasing role in currency markets. Although the CIS may possess vast natural resources, China has resources, landmass, and a huge homogeneous population. As China becomes more integrated into the global trading community, the competition will be truly fierce. A great deal is misunderstood about comparative global wealth. We hear that a Chinese farmer may make only $700 per month. The tendency for a western European or American is to ask, "How can you live on that?" Recalling previous examples, the parity of a dollar to Chinese goods is substantially different from the dollar to U.S. goods. The comparison is more diverse than apples to pears. Apples and pears are, at least, fruit. The Chinese yuan and dollar are currencies, but the translation of their parity relative to Chinese farmers and U.S. farmers is not part of the parity equation—yet.

I say yet because the speed of Chinese living standards within various provinces can transform the comparison into apples and apples. When China assumed Hong Kong, it intended to use this reunification as a role model for the mainland. This is the capitalistic model that can be rolled into Chinese socialism. Do not be surprised to see China fast track the transformation. The ultimate goal is to reposition China as a dominant world power. This is extremely important because even as a World Trade Organization member, China does not seem to be a team player. China is competing with the West and even its former ally Russia. Commodity manipulation, product dumping, copyright and patent infringement, and a host of other tactics are fair play for China because it views the prior exclusionary policy of the West as a license to play catch-up without rules.

The fact that the United States and western Europe want to integrate China into the mainstream will not deter disruptive economic behavior. If there was ever a modern economic enigma, it is China. This makes China a potentially destabilizing factor in global currency markets. China is not as hungry for Western integration as the CIS. In fact, China has positioned itself as the controlling entity for the Pacific Rim. Toward that end, China seems willing to go head to head with the West for domination of the East in an effort to spin off three global sectors that include the Americas, western Europe, and the Pacific Rim. Thus, any assumption that currencies will be dominated by the dollar, euro, and yen must be reassessed if China forges forward with its goal of Pacific Rim dominance.

China controls sufficient natural resources to become reasonably self-sufficient. The problem is that there are no all-export economies. If China assumes it can become supplier of all things to the world, expect new waves of protectionism and a consolidation of territories. Protectionism means tariffs, restricted trade, and global tension.

Africa, India, and Pakistan

Finally, we must consider Africa and the subcontinent comprising India and Pakistan. These regions already rely heavily on the West and are highly integrated into Western trade. Dependency and integration will make weaning from Western dominance difficult. Like China, India has vast natural resources and a large homogeneous population. However, adopting capitalist and democratic structures early on top of an ingrained cast social system hinders the single-minded plan for regional domination. China can shape its direction, whereas India and Pakistan are far down the road with too much freedom inherent in structures left over from colonial times.

This is not to say the subcontinent is less significant than China. It only means that China wants independence from the West, whereas the subcontinent desires synergy. China does not view the United States or western Europe as partners. As of the turn of the millennium, China considered both as adversaries. This was apparent to the Bush Administration when U.S. intelligence confirmed that China was aiding and abetting radical Islamic factions. However, China appeared to embrace Western institutions including a vital stock market and incentives for private business that encompassed land ownership.

The Fluctuation of Currency Relationships

The extremely brief overview of global regions and their economic position is an exercise in open-minded analysis. The purpose is to understand the nature of national or regional wealth. The exercise is worthwhile if currency value is eventually determined by fundamental national or regional wealth. The subject of currency fundamentals may appear to be absent from the discussion; however, there is a tendency to jump into attempts to piece data together like relative interest rates, trade figures, monetary numbers, and general economic statistics. Although it is true that such information can determine immediate currency directions, many investors find daily gyrations too rapid and complex to generate profits. Trying to analyze the total balance sheet of a currency includes evaluating underlying regional assets.

What is the source of Middle East wealth? OPEC certainly generates almost all income from oil exports. What form of payment do OPEC producers generally accept? It has been dollars. What happens if OPEC producers seek other currencies for payment or revert to hard-asset payments such as gold? Obviously, it will have a long-term impact on the dollar and the world oil pricing mechanism. Does it make sense to closely follow any developments that might lead to a change in OPEC's payment preference? The answer is yes.

Expand this thinking to include non-OPEC producers. For example, how might changing energy prices or payment policy impact the Mexican peso? Mexico is more closely tied to the United States by a common border. In turn, Mexico shares boarders with South America. The United States borders Canada to the north. What relationships are most likely to form? How will any change in relationships affect currency values? Could we see separate oil cartels develop on a regional basis? For example, is it possible Mexico will align with South American producers, while the United States consolidates with Canada? Will Russia stand alone against the Middle East? Each potential outcome will change currency relationships. Although you may decide these eventualities are far fetched and have little to do with day-by-day trading, it is surprising how quickly relationships can change and transform currency markets.

Forming Currency Alliances—Group of 5 (G5) and Group of 7 (G7)

It was Germany's currency manipulation during the 1960s and early 1970s that forced the United States to call it quits on the Bretton Woods Accord. Of course, this is a rather simplistic view, but Germany was engaged in draining U.S. gold reserves through a process of dollar accumulation and conversion. Using its positive balance of trade, Germany could harvest dollars and go to the Gold Window to reap the precious metal at the established $35 per ounce exchange rate. Without a floating dollar, the United States was at the mercy of the treaty's shortsightedness. The solution was simple. President Nixon closed the Gold Window.

If we closely examine Germany's maneuvering, it is not difficult to conclude that there was a new war being waged. It was economic and used currency exchange as a central weapon. The target was the pre-war alliance. Perhaps Germany and Japan could win the real war of world dominance while having lost the military conflicts that proved so costly. Indeed, look how both nations prevailed in post World War II trade. The development that halted German and Japanese progress may have been the evolution of currency trading. Vast and rapid currency adjustments leveled the playing field to the extent that the five most powerful economies joined in an effort to stabilize the floating monster they had helped to create. The Group of 5 (G5) was formed to negotiate central bank intervention efforts aimed at taking the sting out of adverse exchange rate fluctuations. G5 grew into G7, which kept the same objective. The group quickly discovered that forces driving currencies were significantly stronger than intervention could overcome for the long or even interim term. Interventions invariably cost millions or billions while frequently failing to accomplish any long-range purpose, that is, the meaningful change in parity.

This highlights an important fundamental observation. If central bank intervention is unable to appreciably move currency parity, what does? In reality, intervention does generate an immediate market reaction; however, intervention is usually an attempt to alter the market. All too often, the market proves to be too big for any single effort to change fundamentals. What works? When examining major currency realignment, we invariably discover significant economic shifts that involve trade, interest rates, or economic stability.

Currency Realignment and the Evolution of Currency Trading Theory

Multiple currency valuation is actually the basis for certain global monetary theory. As described earlier, Navarro Martin de Azpilcueta expressed his theory that commodities determine relative currency values. Obviously, today's currency markets are extraordinarily massive compared with simple mercantilism during the fifteenth century. Still, the ebb and flow of raw and finished commodities provides a basis for determining which currencies may be more coveted.

As FOREX trading evolved during the 1970s, the focus was, indeed, on balance of trade. The relationships seemed simple. Countries whose goods were in the greatest demand had the highest currency parity. Ah, life was easy. However, the global economy grew far faster than most had envisioned. In fact, money and currency transformed from exchange mediums to commodities, but with a twist. Once the gold standard was removed, money supply could expand and contract more freely. This set the stage for various revaluations that provided spectacular profit opportunities.

When a country suffered from too much expansion, its central bank usually intervened by raising interest rates. This raised a red flag that the brakes were being applied to avoid inflation. FOREX traders postulated that rising interest rates represented an exit or sell signal. Few wanted to hold a currency that was likely to inflate against other more stable currencies. For a brief time, traders followed this theory. However, the advent of interest rate futures and related options along with derivative transactions altered this logic.

Suddenly, traders realized that they could obtain higher yields by moving into the currency offering better interest rates. The obvious risk was that deteriorating currency value, that is, inflation, would offset the better yield. Of course, ingenuity found a solution. Using currency hedges, a trader could lock in parity while enjoying the better returns. This became extremely popular during the 1980s when countries like Australia issued bonds with rates as high as 20 percent. The transaction involved buying Australian bonds while selling short Australian dollars (AUD). If the AUD lost value against the U.S. dollar, the hedge made up the difference. Thus, the trader could achieve a pure Australian rate of return without currency parity risk.

While this apparent lock on parity appears to make perfect sense, it demonstrates the one cardinal rule in currency trading and, more specifically, currency parity. *There are no rules!* By the 1990s, traders had adopted a completely contradictory logic. Since the demand for higher interest drove traders toward the currency of greatest yield, there was noticeable selling pressure on the low-yield currency and associated buying pressure on the high-yield currency. Thus, a sell hedge on the currency exhibiting higher demand was abandoned. It was an entirely new ball game! This gave rise to the *Currency Portfolio Theory*. By viewing currencies as investment vehicles, the objective is to create a portfolio with the highest yield. The sheer volume of international currency trading obfuscated trade balances. Daily currency transactions dwarfed virtually every other import and export.

The evolution of currency trading theory is vitally important to keep in mind. You must be prepared to change your thinking to track the prevailing cash flow. Regardless of logic or the lack thereof, the rule is always, "Go with the flow." Tremendously sophisticated currency trading models have been developed at great time and expense by universities and financial institutions —not to mention governments. In the final analysis, a simple moving average has been known to beat out the most complicated neural network.

Philosophers have said two paths exist to knowledge. One is fast but long, while the other is slow but short. Both get you to an eventual answer. As investors, we have a propensity to want knowledge fast. However, if we leap into trading before developing a honed skill, the road to riches can be long. If we take our time and prepare for all contingencies with a comprehensive and educated plan, the preparation may be slow, yet the road to riches will be short. A generalization about national wealth is important because our world spins rapidly. Enormous fundamental change can be seen in less than a decade. From technology to political regimes, the world is rapidly changing and currency relationships hinge on this change.

Other Factors That Impact National Wealth

Before covering fundamental analysis, it is wise to touch on one more subject that impacts national wealth. Certain forces are beyond the control of monetary or fiscal policy. Even with resources, 7 years of feast and 7 years of famine applies metaphorically and literally. This is by no means a religious exercise or biblical lesson. The allusion serves to prove that currency fundamentals are as old as the Good Book, and the basics are as true now as they were thousands of years ago. Perhaps it is coincidental that recent scientific studies have determined a correlation between 7 years and cyclical weather changes. It may also be coincidental that sunspots have an approximate 11-year cycle that seems to influence the 7-year swing in El Niño and La Niña shifts in wind and ocean currents. Data has been inconclusive in pinning down precise timing. For currency trading, precision is not necessarily essential. It is enough to know that a shift in global weather can lead to a shift in international trade.

A severe drought, excessive flooding, extreme cold, or unprecedented heat can all exert a profound influence on raw commodity prices. Recall the prospects for cost-push inflation. Single events such as the extraordinary Midwest floods of 1993 can drive food prices for a year and longer. In turn, a potential impact occurs on the dollar and international grain trade. Back-to-back events such as a string of droughts or a series of frigid winters may realign currency parity over several years or in as little as 3 months.

Of course, natural disasters are not the only events that drive secular currency trends. Political agendas, wars, and regional instability are as significant as natural events. In fact, human influences are more easily correlated to immediate price movements and interim trends. An interesting fundamental study traces event-driven trends in gold and currency as the floating foreign exchange system evolved. When the Falkland War broke out, gold prices increased more than $20 in a single session.

When Russia subsequently downed a commercial Korean air-liner, gold's response was far less enthusiastic—proving the link between gold and political uncertainty was dissolving. The Gulf War exploded energy prices. Precious metals took a complete backseat to the yen, dollar, and major European currencies. Japan, the least energy independent nation, suffered the most.

A Brazilian coffee freeze will change the Brazilian real and also affect the pound to the extent that England is one of the world's largest volume coffee-trading nations. Cocoa will influence the Ivory Coast, but also has major implications for the pound for the same reason. The United States continues to rely on grain exports to balance trade. What happens if a drought occurs in the United States while growing conditions in Australia, Argentina, and Brazil are ideal?

So keep your eyes and ears open for information that can influence the relative wealth of nations. You will see that old theories linking resources to national wealth and national wealth to currency parity still hold true.

Chapter 4

SHIFTING SANDS OF FUNDAMENTAL ANALYSIS

Ask a dozen currency traders about fundamental analysis and it is likely you will get 12 different answers. Once considered the scientific approach to forecasting, fundamentals have taken a backseat to technical trading with the advent of increasingly powerful desktop computers and analytical software. Fundamental analysis was always considered quantitative, while technical analysis was viewed as subjective. Since 1970, this consensus, along with other correlative theories, has reversed. This is more the case for currency trading since the basis for currency valuation has substantially and rapidly changed.

Having consumed the topics in preceding chapters, you already have a grasp on the fundamental elements that determine currency value. For example, national wealth is generally mirrored by currency parity. If we consider the United States to be a wealthy nation, it stands to reason that the dollar will consistently maintain high purchasing power parity relative to other currencies. Even with dramatic fluctuations of 5 percent, 10 percent, and more, the dollar remains able to sustain a dominant role among all world currencies.

The same should hold true for the euro currency. The consolidation of major western European currencies represents a unification of the second largest economy in the world as of the turn of the millennium. Thus, even with the same parity fluctuations, the euro will remain a dominant currency in comparison with the Burundi franc or El Salvador colon. This is a basic fundamental principle. However, most discussions about fundamental currency analysis examine specific economic influences. In broad terms, fundamentals fall within six categories:

- Monetary
- Economic
- Political
- Natural
- Seasonal
- Cyclical

Seasonal and cyclical variations are sometimes considered hybrids because they are also referenced as technical factors. Nonetheless, these variations are most definitely fundamental events that can be observed, measured, and analyzed.

The Components of Gross Domestic Product (GDP) Analysis

The importance of these fundamental branches is by no means reflected by the order of listing. As this chapter's title implies, these relationships have shifted and will shift as one category finds favor over another. In the 1970s, economic statistics dominated currency speculation. This is understandable since currency trading was extremely new. Economic output coupled with trade balances provided an essential guideline. Every quarter, the U.S. government releases Gross Domestic Product (GDP) estimates for the previous quarter. This is the statistical "Big Daddy" that encompasses many subcomponents that are given varying degrees of importance depending on the analyst seeking a forecast.

In simple terms, GDP measures:

- Personal consumption
- Private investment
- Business inventories
- Net imports versus exports

- Government spending
- Government investing

   Within these broad categories are subcategories that many of us are familiar with.

- Personal consumption includes:
  - Durable goods—transportation vehicles, furniture and fix-tures, household machinery (washer/dryer, stove, furnace, air conditioner, and so on), and other related goods
  - Nondurable goods—food, apparel, transportation fuels and lubricants (gasoline, diesel, and aviation fuel), home fuels (oil, coal, natural gas, and propane), and other consumables
  - Services—shelter (housing), household operations (mainte-nance), utilities (gas and electric), water, and other house-hold expenses
  - Transportation
  - Medical
  - Other
- Private investment includes:
  - Fixed investment—residential and commercial structures, farms, utilities, mines, factories, and other structures
  - Production capacity (machinery and equipment)—fabrica-tion and assembly lines, information processing (comput-ers), communications, industrial equipment, and transportation equipment including material handling, other machinery, and equipment
  - Residential—single and multifamily homes and residential structures
- Inventory analysis includes:
  - Change in farm inventory
  - Change in nonfarm inventory—manufacturing, wholesale, retail, and recycle/distressed
- Import/export analysis includes:
  - Exports—goods and services such as the previous list, for example, food, animal feeds, industrial supplies/materials, paper goods, capital goods, vehicles, parts, and consumer goods (exclusive of certain automotive categories)
  - Imports—mirror exports adding petroleum and soft goods (sugar, cocoa, coffee, and exotics)

- Government spending includes:
  - Defense
  - Operational
  - Goods and services
  - State and local police, operations, and goods and services
- Catchall:
  - Residual items exclusive of previously referenced items
  - Factor payments and receipts

Quarterly GDP information is available from various financial information service providers, news media, and the government's Department of Labor and Statistics. As the list suggests, there are many numbers. A great deal of emphasis has been placed on GDP analysis. Various institutions and financial firms have proprietary models that analyze separate GDP components as information becomes available in an attempt to approximate quarterly figures. For example, housing permits are a precursor for housing starts. In turn, starts are eventually completes and homes are sold. Tracking each housing component provides insight into the eventual GDP housing component.

The analysis becomes even more intricate and complex. Lumber is a major housing material. Lumber pricing and availability impacts everything from permits to sales. Lumber is a cost component as is copper plumbing, electrical components, and consumer durables such as kitchen appliances, lighting, glass, concrete, drywall, metal studs, and other materials.

Some economic models forecast from the materials forward, whereas others go from demand backward. The question is like the chicken and the egg. Which came first? Do building material prices lead housing or does housing lead material prices? Is demand pushing price or is price controlling demand? It is an interesting debate with roots in two inflation theories called *supply push* and *demand pull*. These are derived from two economic influences: monetary policy and natural supply/demand. As we will see, this debate ties back to national wealth.

Commodity Pricing and the GDP

If we take a closer look at GDP, we see that a good percentage relies on commodity pricing. Assume environmental groups win a major victory and block lumbering of all spotted owl habitats. At the same time, the United States imposes a quota on Canadian lumber. Suddenly, lumber prices shoot up. However, housing may be static. The increasing lumber price forces builders to raise prices in an inelastic housing market. As a result, housing sales fall. We see that lumber prices can influence housing. Therefore, part of our fundamental analysis might be tracking lumber to forecast housing.

However, as housing falls off, so will lumber demand. Eventually, it is fair to assume that the drop in housing will lower lumber prices until some equilibrium between supply and demand is temporarily reached. I say temporarily because a lumber price chart shows us that equilibrium is generally a fleeting condition. This analysis applies in reverse to all housing materials from brick pavers to roofing materials. Each works back into the GDP equation.

Consider transportation. Again, fuel prices can influence automobile sales and the profile of the average new fleet. This was poignantly demonstrated after the energy crisis of the early 1970s. In response to the Arab Oil Embargo, U.S. auto manufacturers were forced to adapt to tight gasoline supplies with smaller, more fuel-efficient cars. The entire automotive philosophy changed within that decade. Muscle cars relinquished to compact vehicles. The *semi-hemi* gave way to Lee Iacocca's K-cars. Not only is the price of oil an important influence in GDP transportation components, it is also a major item in the import/export equation. This suggests that tracking oil prices provide insight into GDP. This correlation carries over into other important parity relationships.

Energy Imports and Exports

Which nations rely on energy imports or exports? The obvious juxtaposition of energy imports to currency value is equally important when making fundamental parity predictions. As mentioned earlier, Japan relies almost exclusively on energy imports. This means that yen parity against the dollar determines how expensive oil imports are in real terms. The expression *real terms* means relative to domestic value. It is a throwback to hard-asset valuation when we could say 10 barrels of oil equaled 1 ounce of gold. Gold was considered the real constant. Regardless of the fluctuation of the currency relative to gold, the assumption was that the 10:1 parity would stand. For oil to change value in real terms, its relationship to gold would have to change. With no single standard, *real terms* becomes somewhat amorphous. Conceptually, it has the same intent to fix value rather than simply price.

When oil prices spike higher, Japan requires more dollars to pay for oil (assuming oil remains priced in dollars). The degree of the price rise determines the influence on yen/dollar parity. A large demand for dollars will bid the dollar higher relative to the yen and decrease yen/dollar parity. However, since Japan tends to run a trade surplus with the United States, there is a possibility for intervention so Japan can preserve the yen's purchasing power. In addition, Japan exports to many other countries. To the extent Japan can buy dollars with other currency, the pressure on the yen is lessened.

It is important to illustrate that logic must be tempered with reality. Figure 4.1 compares the U.S. Dollar Index against the Japanese yen at the beginning of the Gulf War through Operation Desert Storm. Notice the striking divergence. Although oil soared in dollars, the yen actually gained substantial parity against the dollar. Thus, the fundamental holding that Japan's need for dollars would deteriorate yen/dollar parity would have resulted in a disastrous strategy during this extremely volatile period.

The United Kingdom controls North Sea oil. Thus, the pound depends on oil export revenues to help balance trade. The influence of British Petroleum and sister companies goes beyond North Sea production. London trades oil and British affiliates contribute to the local economy. Royal Dutch Shell brings energy revenue into the European community. Here, the oil/pound correlation is as we would expect. Figure 4.2 plots the pound against New York Mercantile Exchange (NYMEX) crude oil futures during the Gulf War period. The pound is valued in dollars (March 1991 futures) to avoid confusion.

Notice how the oil price (in dollars) moves up from July 1990 to mid-October. The pound tracks in tandem. When oil settled into an erratic trading range, the pound flattened and made a top shortly after Desert Storm. When oil collapsed, the pound followed. Logic works correctly for the pound, but not for the yen.

Figure 4.1   December 1990 Japanese yen futures versus the U.S. Dollar Index.

OPEC members benefited from the surge in oil value, but Saudi Arabia came under pressure to lower prices in return for the coalition intervention against Iraq. Further, Saudi Arabia wanted to punish Iraq for the transgression by lowering oil values at a time when Iraq needed currency. Even with permission to pump $3 billion in oil, the equation is value dependent. Lower oil prices and the Saudis will increase the volume Iraq must pump to meet the quota.

As you might suspect, some of the interplay between OPEC and Western consumers falls into political fundamentals. Oil is a mighty political football frequently run up and down the field. Political influences are mostly associated with government currency policy. This includes influencing the central bank, raising or lowering taxes, altering banking and investment regulations, moving from conservative to liberal government control, and a long list of other potential events. We still must understand that commodity price manipulation is a political move that can have political objectives. The Arab Oil Embargo following the 1972 Arab-Israeli conflict was political. The impact was economic.

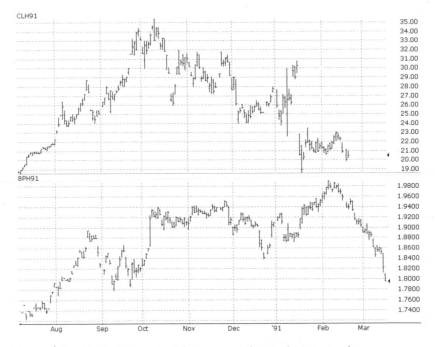

Figure 4.2   March 1991 crude oil futures versus the March 1991 pound.

Memories tend to be short. We look upon the September 11th attacks on the World Trade Center and Pentagon as the first acts of aggression against the United States, discounting the earlier attack on the World Trade Center in 1993. In fact, Arab nations have been waging a quiet and constant war against the West through their oil cartel. We should not ignore the impact OPEC's oil embargo had on the entire industrialized world. As noted, rocketing energy prices altered the entire structure of energy dependent industries. The recession ignited in March 2000 was retrospectively attributed to high energy prices and an imploding stock market.

The Relationship between GDP and Inflation

Aside from oil's relationship to the energy and transportation GDP components and lumber's link to housing and construction, base metals are important as leading indicators for durables, machinery, and industrial infrastructure. Tracking the price of copper, nickel, tin, lead, zinc, and iron add insight into GDP. In a booming economy, these commodities become scarce and tend to inflate. Inflation is another very important aspect of fundamental currency evaluation. The GDP/inflation relationship is becoming more important because traditional assumptions derived through the 1970s and 1980s were challenged by trends in the 1990s and beyond 2000. For approximately 12 years, the U.S. economy handsomely expanded while inflation was kept under control. Employment (another fundamental statistic) remained high without excessive demand-related inflation. Did the equations change?

As the chapter title implies, currency fundamentals are built upon shifting sand. Today's rules are tomorrow's abandonment. Never assume a rule is golden. There are no permanent correlations. There is only relative price movement.

Although U.S. agriculture has been decreasing as a percentage of GDP, food remains one of the largest U.S. exports. Certainly, the world is moving toward regional self-sufficiency. However, the United States is the major global breadbasket. Farm products are a component of GDP. Therefore, tracking U.S. farm policy and exports is a window into future movements of the GDP farming components. This is not to say that soybean prices will correlate to the U.S. Dollar Index. Although at times a negative correlation appears, it is doubtful that the correlation is reliable when considering the frequency of its divergence. Price is not the objective. Influence on GDP is. If GDP is important for dollar parity, then we want to predict the quarterly numbers early enough to take a currency position and profit.

GDP Releases: Surprises and Bombshells

The purpose of the review is to demonstrate that currency traders do not wait for the GDP numbers. They expect the GDP numbers. In fact, upon each quarterly release, most newswires print the high, low, and average expectation along with actual numbers to determine professional consensus accuracy. Immediate reactions to GDP are generally in response to deviations from expectations. Anyone trading currencies will become intimately familiar with two descriptors. The first is called a *surprise*. News might read "There were no surprises . . . ," or "GDP numbers surprised analysts as components for housing came in .5 below expectations . . . " Surprises can cause considerable volatility. It is extremely important to avoid overreaction because small surprises that generate big initial movements tend to quickly fade. The more potent descriptor that is far less frequently encountered is called a *bombshell*. As the name indicates, such deviations cause explosive reactions that can send currencies into extreme and dangerous volatility. Bombshells are not as easy to decipher as we might think. Often, the change is so unexpected that it leaves traders confused. Just how far should the market react to a bombshell? We never really know until the postmortem. By that time, the equity position could be dead.

Gross National Product (GNP)

GDP is considered the foundation of fundamental perspective. This construct was made in the 1980s. Originally, the focus was on Gross National Product (GNP), which is a subset of the newer GDP. As the list of components implies, GDP and its sister GNP concentrate on measuring consumption, investing, government spending, and net trade. First-year economics students are familiar with the concept formulated in the widely used book *Economics* by Dr. Paul Samuelson. His formula states:

$$\text{GNP} = \Sigma\text{consumer spending, investing, government spending, and imports} - \text{exports}$$

GNP reflects a domestic picture. As multinational corporations expanded influence within the United States, a broader measure of economic activity was needed to account for foreign participation in the equation. Thus, GDP is a superset of GNP that reflects foreign companies as well as domestic companies. The difference was considered nominal. However, as more foreign companies establish complete facilities within the United States and more U.S. companies build capacity outside the country, this distinction becomes increasingly important. Hence, currency traders concentrate more on GDP.

Money Supply and GDP

By the 1980s, currency trading was approximately a decade old. Gold was legalized in the United States in January 1975. The first currency futures were traded in 1972. Prior to 1970, parity fixing limited currency trading and public speculation was nonexistent. This is why fundamental analysis frequently shifted focus. Mike Myers constructed a humorous scene in the movie *Austin Powers* when Dr. Evil is attempting to establish a ransom for his evil inclinations. Lacking a modern frame of reference, he requests a million dollars in the 1990s. He is quickly educated that this isn't a large sum. However, when he returns to the 1960s and requests billions, the amount exceeds the U.S. budget. When the U.S. Federal Reserve became obsessed with combating inflation at the turn of the 1970s, the world experienced an unprecedented interest rate escalation that altered fundamental perspective. Suddenly, GDP components became more important than the whole.

Consumer spending and saving led to a transition from gross numbers to money supply numbers. This is where M1, M2, and M3 took the forefront of fundamental currency analysis. Discretionary spending was linked to inflation. The Phillips Curve principle theorized that high employment begot high discretionary spending, which begot inflation, which begot deteriorating currency parity. Money supply was released at the end of each week. As you might imagine, the ability to lock into a weekly rather than a quarterly number elated currency traders around the world.

Dr. Henry Kaufman, a prominent economist with Solomon Brothers, was affectionately labeled "Dr. Doom" as traders awaited his forecast for money supply and GDP. Unfortunately, the analysis was imprecise and uncorrelated with eventual market direction. The result was a switch away from money supply toward pure interest rates. This move was understandable because currency trading volume resembled the Big Bang. Expansion was global and exponential. The value of currency trading exceeded the value of GDP components. The cart was placed in front of the horse.

The Balance of Trade Model and GDP

As previously mentioned, interest rate spreads translated into forward pricing models. What is the relative yield available between two or more currencies? The interest rate model held through the second half of the 1990s and into the new millennium. Interestingly, as the European Union solidified around the euro, psychology began moving back toward the original balance of trade model. Some may argue that each focal point is simply a component of GDP. Therefore, GDP has always been the primary fundamental focus. This is more coincidence than reality since strategies associated with fundamental correlations are distinctly different.

Net trade was associated with the amount of currency that would be required to accommodate import and export differentials. This association was carried down to the corporate level where imported materials or finished export goods needed to be balanced through currency hedges. For example, Waterford Crystal manufactured in Ireland is priced in Irish pounds that are pegged to the British pound. After calculating materials, capital, labor, and a profit margin, the finished crystal is accordingly priced. Since the United States represents a major export market, pound/dollar parity is critical for maintaining the profit margin. It is easy to understand that a 15 percent margin can be all but wiped out by a 10 percent adverse parity fluctuation. By determining prospective sales, Waterford can sell anticipated dollars forward using an Interbank transaction, futures, or options. This justifies the existence of currency trading and, indeed, represents a good portion of the cash market.

Adding Mercedes, Saab, Porsche, General Motors, Ford, and every other automaker to the same model pales in comparison with the speculative incentive to trade. This means that the net trade equation pales in comparison with arbitrage, interest rate differentials, swaps, and other transaction unrelated to trade. Why, then, is there a continuing fundamental emphasis on the GDP components?

After interviewing dozens of traders in the trenches of daily transactions, the answer seems to be investment. The greatest demand for currency comes from investment rather than imports and exports. In order to determine the best environment for investment, economic health is the paramount consideration. GDP and its components provide insight into a country's investment environment.

If you want to buy German stocks, your account will be settled in euro currency. This holds true for all European member nation investment markets. If you want to invest in the United States, the account is settled in dollars. If the Nikkei appears attractive, yen are required. Since the daily value of international investment markets far exceeds daily imports and exports, it is easy to comprehend why currency trading has grown into the largest combined markets. Simply put, currency trading reflects all trading. It reflects all GDP of all nations.

Private Sector Economic Indicators

This brings us to other fundamental considerations within the overall economic picture reflected by GDP. It would take volumes to explain all fundamental analysis that impacts currency trading. However, certain statistics require special attention. When tracking currency articles in *The New York Times*, *The Wall Street Journal*, *Barron's*, and other print media, there is an inevitable review of the private sector indicators. These include:

- Capacity utilization
- National Association of Purchasing Managers Index
- Consumer Price Index (CPI)
- Commodity Research Bureau Index
- Goldman Sachs Price Index
- Producer Price Index (PPI)
- Consumer Confidence Index (CCI)
- Industrial production
- Inventories
- Durable goods orders
- Factory orders
- Housing and commercial construction

Referencing this chapter title, fundamentals are built on shifting sands. Each listed item reflects economic health. Although the examples are U.S. based, each economy has equivalent measurements. Economic health is grounded in these numbers, yet currency traders interpret changes in seemingly contradictory ways.

Logic dictates that increasing capacity utilization, high industrial productivity, rising durable and factory orders, and rising employment are good. The economy is booming. A booming economy should attract investment. Stock prices should rise. Unfortunately, logic isn't that clear. When the economy booms, central bank intervention is feared. Since inflation control is often a central bank objective, boom means stricter controls as a preemptive strike against rising price indices. Positive numbers warn of pending interest rate adjustment.

This is why the Federal Reserve admits to balancing economic measurements against various price indices. The sand shifted because back-to-back Federal Reserve chairs (Paul Volker and Alan Greenspan) encountered economic impossibilities that structurally altered monetary intervention guidelines. As a result of the energy crisis of the 1970s, President Nixon faced an anomaly of rising prices and falling productivity. The United States was in recession, but prices were spiraling higher. There was no economic theory or principle to explain this new situation. It was a stagnant economy with high inflation. Economists invented the term *stagflation*.

If we think stagflation is unusual, Alan Greenspan witnessed high employment and productivity with virtually no inflation during the 1990s. The term used to describe this anomaly was simply *elation*. Obviously, any currency-trading rules must be flexible when considering that inflation can contradict economic indicators. The nimble traders must identify shifts in relationships and develop effective strategies.

Yes, inflation erodes purchasing parity. This is an absolute. However, the degree of erosion is comparative. It's one nation's inflation rate compared with another's. Equally important, it is one absolute rate of return compared to another. Money flows toward opportunity.

The Effect of Natural Events on Regional Economics

Without being overly esoteric, any examination of fundamental analysis should touch on natural events. This is not to say that a currency trader should dwell on the sunspot cycle or climatic changes such as El Niño and La Niña. However, natural occurrences can profoundly affect regional economics. Droughts, floods, volcanic eruptions, and even sunspots can carry serious consequences. A hard freeze in Brazil can damage their coffee crop and impair their ability to balance trade and repay foreign debt. A drought in Asia can place pressure on North American crops and impact the U.S. and Canadian dollar.

More general disasters such as volcanic eruptions can disrupt global weather patterns and spread climatic uncertainty like a plague. If there is any doubt about the impact of such events, one need only examine the back-to-back adversity that impinged on the world's food supply from 1971 through 1973. As previously discussed, beginning with a virulent U.S. corn leaf blight in 1971 followed by a powerful El Niño, the former Soviet Union lost two primary feed sources: Peruvian anchovy fish meal and U.S. corn. Weather anomalies caused a wheat crop failure that led to the famous Russian Wheat Deal. The United States was forced to sell huge quantities of U.S. grain to Russia at subsidized prices. Although the Arab Oil Embargo was blamed for inflation during the 1970s, the earlier food crisis was probably the catalyst for many of the price spiraling events that followed. All of this is traceable to Mother Nature. The U.S. inflation became so severe that the well-known Hunt brothers from Texas concocted a scheme to realign currency to hard assets. In their case, the monetary link was to silver. The very suggestion that money would return to a precious-metals standard drove these commodities to all-time highs. At the same time, currencies were reeling from lost confidence.

A severe winter impacts oil demand and influences the dollar. A severe summer does the same. In turn, high-energy prices take a toll on Japan's economy while stabilizing Mexico's ability to meet international debt payments. All of the relationships are likely to become increasingly important as the world moves forward toward industrialization and globalization. I urge anyone who is serious about currency trading to keep an eye out for changes in the balance of resources. This holds for temporary effects of weather and structural changes like the development of Kazakhstan's oil fields or the harvesting of Russia's extraordinary forest resources.

In the late 1960s through the 1970s, legitimate forecasts appeared that the world would run out of oil by the turn of the century. A popularized "Report from Iron Mountain" prophesized significant doom and gloom predicated on this natural resource depletion and a pending population explosion. Obviously, the report missed the mark, as did so many environmental disaster forecasts. The reason is simple. In a word, change. The world discovered more oil, China restricted birthrates, U.S. mainstream families were reduced with Generation X, and unfortunate world health problems restricted growth in Africa, India, and several other populous regions.

You may say that this review is getting off track. The link between doom and gloom and currency trading is obscure. The purpose is to train your thoughts toward observing macro changes in environment and resource allocation. Consider that the average U.S. car logged approximately 9 miles to the gallon in the 1960s. By the 1980s, the average more than doubled to 20 miles to the gallon. The 50 percent reduction in gasoline consumption was a contributing factor in avoiding a more pronounced energy crisis. Yes, we have discovered more oil, but conservation is equally important and represents structural change in energy markets. Oil/dollar parity depends on this and future structural change. If auto companies increase efficiency by another 50 percent, many economic models predict a *disinflation* as opposed to a deflation. The term was invented to distinguish between a favorable decline in prices and recession or depression. Which countries are most likely to benefit? Those that are resource-poor or big consumers, such as Japan, the United States, and western Europe? The degree to which each country benefits determines the proportional currency parity influence.

Along other lines, we can trace the impact of particular natural events to understand the potential dynamic. I say potential because the influence in one year may not necessary portend subsequent experiences. In September 1989, Hurricane Hugo attacked the U.S. eastern coast causing more than $7 billion in damage. To cover the cost, insurance companies moved from near-cash assets like U.S. Treasury instruments into cash. The immediate impact was a decline in Treasury values and a rise in interest rates.

As companies moved into cash, eurodollar futures began to slide, as seen in Figure 4.3. By the time storm damage was assessed on September 23, eurodollars gapped lower as indicated by the rule line from the eurodollar chart to the U.S. Dollar Index. Despite a period of easing rates, the storm and its financial consequences moved the market. At the same time, the U.S. Dollar Index responded negatively. Here, the assumption that higher rates would lead to a rising dollar did not hold. Concern over the impact on the U.S. insurance industry took precedence.

While damage was being assessed, currency traders turned their attention to England where Lloyds of London allegedly held considerable reinsurance exposure. The circled area in Figure 4.4 displays a quick exodus from the pound during an already volatile period. It is difficult to construct an exact retrospective causal correlation. Even with 20/20 hindsight, we cannot assess forces exactly associated with insurance claims and

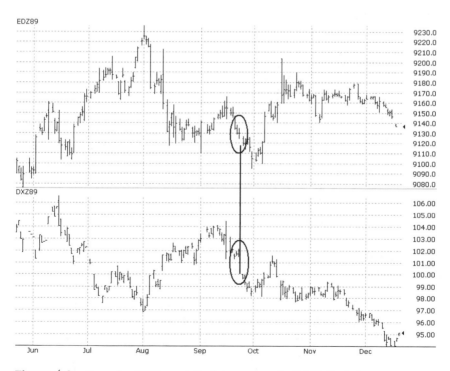

Figure 4.3   December 1989 eurodollar futures versus the U.S. Dollar Index.

Figure 4.4   December 1989 British pound.

those attributed to other events. Still, the chart does reveal a reaction that coincides with the disaster.

Checking the theory further, Hurricane Andrew struck Florida's coast toward the end of August 1992. This was the granddaddy of the century with damages exceeding $25 billion. Pegged as one of the worst disasters in U.S. history, insurance companies were, again, in a cash crunch. It is certainly a credit to the industry that companies were able to weather the storm (no pun intended!). Having experienced Hurricane Hugo 3 years earlier, certain measures were taken to ensure more liquidity during large catastrophes. See Figure 4.5.

Again, the U.S. Dollar Index momentarily moved contrary to the interest rate rule as both the eurodollar and dollar fell with the damage assessment. Reviewing contemporaneous newspaper stories, we see that insurance spokespeople were busy reassuring investors that the extraordinary destruction was well within

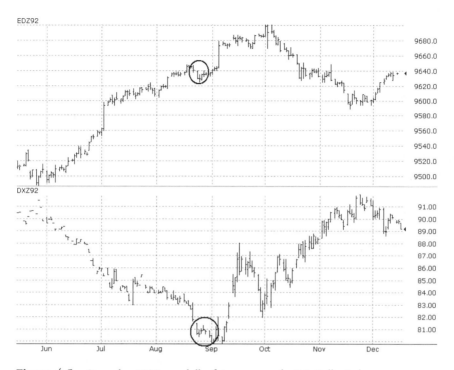

Figure 4.5 December 1992 eurodollar futures versus the U.S. Dollar Index.

their means. Indeed, companies survived and claims were met. The talking up of the market managed to dip rates.

The broad picture suggests that Hugo and Andrew were minor blips in an overall trend. This is true. However, blips on a leveraged basis can be as financially disastrous to the leveraged currency trader as the storm is to life and property. Charts are often deceptive. You may interpret a wiggle as inconsequential until you experience the loss or profit.

If we examine the pound (see Figure 4.6) during the same period, we see that one important influence on the dollar was the precipitous decline in sterling. Again, concern over enormous reinsurance exposure sparked a flight from pounds. To be sure, the pound was not the only western European currency that declined against the dollar. In Figure 4.7, the Swiss franc exhibits a fall against the dollar subsequent to Hurricane Andrew; however, the timing is considerably later and associated with other

BPZ92 MovS=1.5419 MovS=1.5490

Figure 4.6   December 1992 British pound futures .

factors. We know from the news that U.S. claims impacted British insurance carriers and the pound.

In August 1996, Hurricane Fran hit the U.S. shores causing $3.3 billion in damage. This was a sneeze compared with Andrew. However, Figure 4.8 illustrates the same pattern where the U.S. Dollar Index dips in conjunction with rising interest rates (falling eurodollars). This is a contradictory movement when compared with the previous and subsequent trends. Here, we see a clear correlation between rising rates and a higher dollar. However, the instant reaction to Fran exhibits the typical contrary pattern.

Fortunately, storms quickly pass and other market forces appear to take over. What does the fundamental correlation tell currency traders? An analogy to the laws of motion can be made whereby a trend in motion will remain in motion unless acted on by some outside force. The outside force is a temporary cash

Figure 4.7 December 1992 Swiss franc futures.

requirement to meet insurance claims. The charts show that interruptions were not trend disrupters. In fact, they represented potential buying or selling opportunities in the dollar, yen, pound, and U.S. interest rate vehicles.

The Effects of Ecopolitical Events on the Economy

Juxtaposed to natural occurrences are sudden ecopolitical events that were becoming increasingly frequent into the twentieth century. The most blatant were events leading to World War I and II. Imagine—the assassination of the Austrian prince would precipitate a global conflict that could only be ended by the Spanish Flu pandemic that crippled both sides. Thereafter, repeated aggression by Hitler pushed Europe into war, but the Japanese attack on Pearl Harbor represented the single catalyst

Figure 4.8   December 1996 eurodollars futures versus the U.S. Dollar Index.

that brought in the United States and eventually led to the defeat of Axis forces.

Such monumental ecopolitical phenomena shake the very roots of world monetary markets. Enemies simply segregate currency markets. The only intercurrency transactions are underground or black market. As currency traders, the emphasis is on post gold standard and free-floating currency forums (such as Interbank, futures, and options). None were available or needed during the World Wars. The first series of modern currency-influencing events began before Nixon closed the Gold Window with the 1967 Arab-Israeli War. As previously covered, this created the coalition that instituted the Arab Oil Embargo.

Although modern currency markets were not in place, the stage was set for a continuing series of aggression that set up auto-response trading. Vietnam was concurrent with the 1967 Arab-Israeli War. However, it was an ongoing intervention rather than an instantaneous eruption.

Although the Middle East conflict dates back to the formation of Israel in 1948, it became a center of attention when oil was mixed into the picture. With the Middle East representing swing inventory, it became a strategic region for the former Soviet Union and a security interest for western Europe and the United States. Anwar Sadat was incensed by the 1967 defeat and became obsessed with Israel's capitulation and return of captured territories. Hence, the subsequent Yom Kippur War in 1973 was formulated to end the debate with a swift and overwhelming invasion.

Amazingly, Israel prevailed against astounding odds. Since ideological lines were drawn by the United States, Israel's success was a statement of confidence for the dollar. From a low 90, the U.S. Dollar Index achieved a rally just under 110. Thereafter, the energy crisis and general malaise of the 1970s dropped the U.S. Dollar Index to a trading range base of 85.

Rocketing interest rates from 1980 forward propelled the U.S. Dollar Index to record highs of 164 by 1985. It was a 5-year process that would have hardly lent itself to today's short-term techniques.

In April 1982, Argentina decided it would invade the Falkland Islands to reclaim this small chain from British control. Not willing to sacrifice remaining vestiges of its former colonial prowess, the United Kingdom responded with an armada. The victory was swift and the pound achieved a notable reversal of a former downtrend, as seen in Figure 4.9. The initial reaction dipped the pound to a 1.7500 low on April 9. Britain's resolve to keep the islands supported the pound despite the fact that sterling had been in decline right up to the conflict.

Again, unfolding events demonstrate how treacherous currency trade can be if your timing is slightly deficient. Logically, the war would cost Britain needed resources. Logically, the pound's slide should have continued. Why, then, did we see the rally as the invasion progressed? Some analyses of currency transactions showed that certain South American interests were buying the pound and selling Argentinean currency. Additional hedging was conducted in gold, as seen in Figure 4.10. In fact, gold began to rally just before Argentina launched its offensive. Who knew? Argentina's generals knew!

Some market historians view the Falklands as the primary event that severed gold's reactionary link to disaster. As charts reveal, the end of the conflict quickly returned gold and sterling

Figure 4.9   June 1982 British pound futures.

to the trends formerly in progress. The weaning from precious metals was relatively swift compared with the era of asset-backed currency. From the near relinquishment of floating currencies during the 1979–1980 inflationary crises to the 1982 Falklands incident is a flash—just 2 years. This is more evidence of the speed with which economic and monetary perspectives change. The message for all currency traders is be prepared for change and be flexible.

When Islamic fundamentalism demonstrated its cause with the World Trade Center bombing on February 26, 1993, the dollar briefly dipped, as seen in Figure 4.11. No military response occurred from the Clinton Administration and the chart shows the dollar quickly resumed its former trend after a brief consolidation. Nimble currency traders could have taken profits from the wiggle. More likely, the attempt would have whipped the inexperienced trader on both sides for painful losses.

GCM82 MovS=316.3 MovS=326.7

Figure 4.10   June 1982 gold futures.

However, the September 11th attack that brought the Trade Center down and successfully targeted the Pentagon was a different story. We see that the dollar was already in decline; however, the immediate reaction to the devastation was a swift move away from dollars. The Bush Administration's response was equally swift. "We will bring them to justice," became the Bush mantra. Within a week, the dollar reversed its slide and began a progressive rise into 2002. This was particularly surprising because the fundamental premise of a war on terrorism was high expense/low productivity. Furthermore, the war was likely to be significantly prolonged. One might think this prospect would be less than encouraging for dollar parity. The strength of U.S conviction and a rapid initial defeat of the controlling Taliban regime accelerated investor interest in the dollar. The United States was the only superpower. This implied that the dollar was the safest currency. See Figure 4.12.

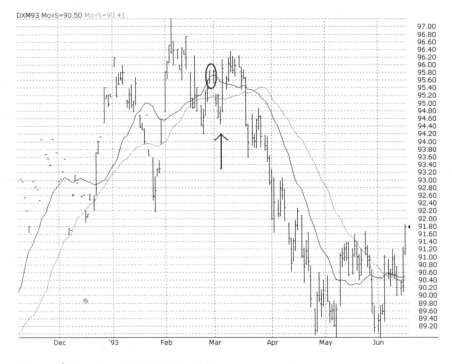

Figure 4.11   June 1993 U.S. Dollar Index.

Almost simultaneously, the euro was placed in circulation in January 2002. This monumental conversion of paper and coin required delicate strategic implementation. Any glitch could have caused a confidence crisis that would have sent the euro reeling. Instead, currencies traded within normal ranges even with unusual circumstances. Dollar traders were interested in retail sales, consumer confidence, and broad measures of U.S. GDP. There was relatively little discussion about formulating trading decisions based on the War on Terrorism.

When comparing incidents, it is important to distinguish between ecopolitical events that can change market sentiment and circumstances that only interrupt sentiment. The critical element always comes down to cash flows. We seek simple answers. Where does the money come from and where does the money go? This brings us to the question of cash flow analysis. Fundamentally, all nations must earn money. Interestingly, this

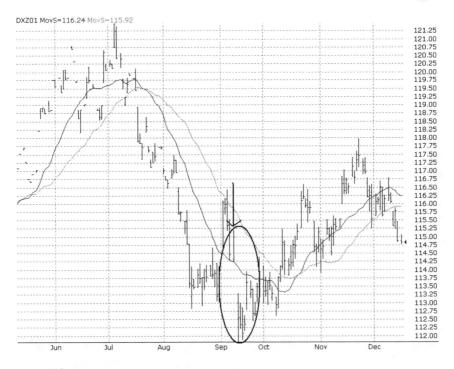

Figure 4.12   December 2001 U.S. Dollar Index.

reality has been depicted in fiction such as the movie *Rollerball* starring James Cann. Nations were reduced to corporations. Well, in many ways this is true. An analogy is associating what a nation produces with what it earns. The corporate performance is reflected by the stock value. In the case of a nation, currency is similar to stock.

Leadership and Politics

We come upon another fundamental concept of leadership and politics. Who is running the store? When good leadership is present, currency tends to hold value. Poor leadership results in weak currency. These rules do not necessarily apply to day-by-day trading. For those interested in minute-by-minute fluctuations, politics can stand down. However, long-term trends can develop from changes in leadership. A shift in the U.S. administration or Congress from Democrat to Republican can sway world opinion about the greenback. A change in Britain's Parliament might imply Labor Party dominance and a public policy alteration. A rift in the European community can unravel the euro.

Everything from a terrorist attack and reprisal must be considered within the big picture. For example, when faced with the daunting task of eliminating or substantially reducing terrorism, the question for the Bush Administration was, "Can U.S. action to curb international terrorism strengthen the world's confidence in the dollar or leave it in isolated limbo?" The answer is inevitably found by examining charts. A move from dollar pricing to euro pricing will alter relative values and change currency parity. Even the possibility of a gold standard is not beyond the realm of possibility.

Instantaneous Influences on Currency Value

Having touched on macro influences and GDP components, we can shift attention to the more instantaneous fundamental influences. This is not to say that a natural disaster won't have an immediate impact on currency values. Nor is there an implication that a sudden political shift won't have a significant influence. However, there is a flow of economic data that generally ripples through currency markets causing more immediate gyrations. This data includes:

- The Beige Book (Fed Open Market Committee Report)
- Jobless claims
- Related labor statistics including productivity
- Farm and nonfarm payroll
- Average hourly earnings
- Consumer Price Index (CPI) and its core rate
- Producer Price Index (PPI)
- Euro Zone inflation indicators
- Euro Zone consumption indicators
- Pacific Rim inflation indicators
- Pacific Rim consumption indicators
- Industrial output

- Industrial capacity utilization
- Business inventories
- Retail sales
- Percentage of factoring
- Savings rate
- Money market net cash flow
- Mutual fund investment net cash flows
- U.S. Treasury auctions (including gold)
- Foreign Central Bank auctions (including gold)
- Foreign investment
- Discount rate and foreign equivalents
- Fed funds rate and foreign equivalents
- Commercial lending rate (prime)
- Commercial occupancy (rent roles)
- Tax revenue (federal and local)
- Purchasing managers' reports
- Consumer confidence

This is by no means a comprehensive list. Furthermore, the list can change with additions and deletions. For example, the price of gold was once a strong economic and sentiment indicator. Well before the Conference Board released its Consumer Confidence Index (CCI), traders looked to gold for a reflection of market consensus. Gold also represented the net cash flow when it was the monetary standard. Gold measured inflation fear, dollar confidence, and cross-parity. Gold was the first cross-commodity arbitrage vehicle for currencies.

Gold lost its luster as an economic indicator in the 1990s and was eventually removed from *The Wall Street Journal* and *The New York Times* as an indicator. The London Fix faded as a number to watch. Hence, gold has been excluded from the previous list. Within a matter of months, gold could easily return to the economic scene with a vengeance. All that would be required would be lost confidence in the paper system, as previously mentioned.

Each listed economic statistic is released on a regular schedule that can be found in any of the published economic calendars. For example, U.S. money supply figures are released every Thursday with the exception of federal holidays that fall on a Thursday. The Fed Open Market Committee Report is also released on a Thursday. Interest rate adjustments are generally released on a Tuesday. Sales statistics usually fall on a Wednesday. Since schedules can change, it is wise to obtain an economic calendar from your broker or consult the Internet. Do not rely on previous statistical calendars found in books or publications. I have purposely excluded such a listing because changes render such listings obsolete and potentially dangerous.

The Beige Book

Some items represent a consolidation of other items. For example, the Beige Book is released eight times a year and contains sections on consumer spending, manufacturing, real estate and construction, agriculture, natural resource industries such as energy and mining, financial services and credit, employment and wages, price levels, and more. The report breaks down economic performance by Federal Reserve District.

This economic overview is used as a standard for more instantaneous snapshots of the same data as released by other government agencies. Thus, the last quarter's employment would be compared to the report and the weekly statistics to discern a pattern or trend. In addition, the Beige Book provides the tone of the Fed that is used to determine probabilities for rising or falling short-term rates.

Jobless Claims

It follows that jobless claims (employment) influence traders' interest rate and inflation perspective. High unemployment has been viewed as positive for lowering interest rates. This is considered *stimulative*. In turn, lower interest rates suggest declining dollar parity unless other nations lower concurrently and to a greater extent. Employment politics are multifaceted and particularly convoluted. As an example, consider President Clinton's first term where he emphasized creating jobs. In all probability, his labor focus was inspired by his predecessor who failed to be reelected because of "The economy, stupid!" However, at the very time President Clinton was giving his State of the Union address that boasted job creation, Fed Chairman Greenspan addressed Congress with the dilemma of rapid job growth. While Clinton was allegedly creating jobs, the Fed was increasing interest rates to reduce jobs. Who was in control?

Political rhetoric frequently contradicts reality. The wise currency trader would likely place more credence in Greenspan than Clinton because Greenspan's initiatives could be more rapidly implemented and more definitively measured. "Who's in charge here?" is an important question to ask because appearances are not necessarily reality. When former President George Bush said, "Read my lips, no new taxes," a Democrat majority in Congress overrode him. Congress creates the tax laws and the President signs them.

Neither Congress nor the President set monetary policy. The Fed is independent to the extent that it is not beholden to the political entity that put it in place. Once in the job, the position of Fed Chairman is reasonably secure. The entire efficacy of monetary policy depends on freedom from political influence. Of course, we do witness Fed interventions during election years that are designed to improve circumstances for incumbents. For the most part, the Fed has attempted to direct policy in accordance with practical and economically healthful goals.

Related Labor Statistics and Farm and Nonfarm Payroll

Related labor statistics such as productivity tend to be less enthusiastically received by currency traders because this is a measurement that influences a longer-term policy. As the workforce becomes more productive, inflation abates as long as there are no other influences. We produce more goods for the same price. Supply increases while demand is presumed to remain static. Average hourly earnings are associated with efficiency. The obvious question is whether productivity has increased with a boost in wages. If so, there was a price. These labor statistics seem to rotate around one another much like a moon around a planet. Labor rarely hikes its productivity without eventually asking for compensation. The issue is which comes first.

Farm and nonfarm payroll is an extension of jobless claims and is viewed in tandem. A rise in farm payroll does have implications for agriculture. Increasing farm jobs suggests greater supply and may be in response to growing demand. In the United States, that demand is frequently attributed to exports.

Inflation

Inflation numbers play a big role in Fed action and do generate strong reactions among currency traders. The problem with this fundamental focus is its metamorphosis from negative to positive—and possibly back again. As previously mentioned, an inflating currency loses purchasing power within the country of origin. This is a loss of purchasing parity. The natural conclusion is that cross-currency parity will deteriorate against more stable currencies. However, inflation is treated with doses of higher interest rates. This generates a positive interest rate spread that drives the weaker currency in a contradictory direction.

CPI and PPI

Although it may seem helpful to list components of the CPI and PPI, I refrain from doing so because both of these cornerstones of inflation measurement are subject to change. Although not implemented during the Reagan, Bush (41st), Clinton, or Bush (43rd) Administrations, loud grumbling was heard about changing the CPI to be more reflective of modern price level measurements. The CPI was threatened with complete makeovers that were illusive, at best—remove the old grocery basket while adding a services component. The objective during the late 1980s through the first half of the 1990s was to curb inflation by simply denying it. Since so many contracts are linked to the CPI as an inflation index, altering the number alters the contracts. Thus, any wage indexed to the CPI would be frozen or even diminished. So would most real-estate rent rolls. Price of living indices on everything from insurance contracts to medical care would be affected. Therefore, the CPI is a tool that can be used to manipulate the entire economy.

Whenever serious talk about changing the CPI comes into play, rest assured an underlying inflation is present. As of this writing, Uncle Sam has not messed with the original index. Therefore, I have no basis to relate what the reaction will be. It is fair to say that most who rely on the index to keep up with inflation will experience a serious case of CPI indigestion if an adverse alteration is made. To be fair, we have experienced a shift in the basket of goods and we do rely more heavily on services that impact our lifestyles and pocketbooks. There may be powerful and realistic incentives to alter the CPI. These include the potential decline in domestic tobacco consumption and a change in overall diet. Consideration might be given to cable television, Internet expenses, and communications. The possible introduction of diversified education selection and a national school voucher system might significantly change education expenses. All of this may become reality and should be objectively evaluated in conjunction with impacts on interest rates and currency value.

Euro Zone and Pacific Rim Indicators

Since I live as a U.S. citizen, my view tends to be U.S. oriented. Admittedly, I cannot read the *International Herald Tribune* or *The Financial Times of London* to the same extent that I peruse *The Wall Street Journal, Barron's, Forbes, Fortune, Business Week, Investors' Business Daily*, and a host of other "required reading." This personal deficiency should not reflect on would-be currency traders. The Euro Zone produces parallel statistics covering labor, inflation, productivity, inventories, exports, GDP, and so on. So do Pacific Rim countries. This is the comparative data that enables us to formulate possible parity trends.

Industrial Capacity and Output

Broad economic measurements have already been touched on. Industrial capacity and output present efficiency ratios. High capacity suggests more goods and lower prices. High utilization lowers such prospects. Economists attempt to mix and match industrial output with capacity to determine if the economy is accelerating or slowing down. High business inventories point to sluggish movement and are associated with recession. Retail sales reflect consumer spending—the driving force behind American and European economies.

Savings Rate, Money Market, and Mutual Fund Indicators

Savings rates are another moving target that has changed configuration. The line between savings and investments is blurred. When we buy stock in our 401(k), IRA, Keogh, Defined Benefit Plan, Defined Contribution Plan, and myriad other savings vehicles, are we saving or investing? The distinction is important because savings were once thought of as time deposits within the control of banks and savings and loans. Recall that the Fed regulates banks that set reserve requirements. In turn, the reserve requirement defines the monetary multiplier or loan-to-deposit ratio. However, if a saver uses the stock market, no such multiplier exists. To the minor extent that stock is held in "Street Name" to be loaned and margined, some capital base expansion occurs. However, this is limited to equities or bonds and commercial paper.

This is why rules change. Money placed in mutual funds is not spent on consumerism. It is hoped to be deferred spending, but does little to boost immediate consumption. With change comes new terms of art. Although we do not see invested money enter the mainstream of Main Street or mall shopping, the Fed has identified the wealth effect that states people will allocate more income as disposable if their investments provide the perception of greater wealth. If I have $1 million in the stock market, I may feel more comfortable taking on a $500,000 mortgage because I feel wealthy. So even investing creates transaction velocity.

Consumer Confidence and Purchasing Managers' Reports

I categorize some statistics as smoky. For lack of a better descriptor, compilations like consumer confidence and purchasing managers' reports are not solid. The methodology used to collect and evaluate these numbers seems overly flexible. Too often, consumer confidence registers a gain when all other numbers show a miserable state of affairs. What is consumer confidence?

This is also the case for questions of purchasing managers' intentions. I recall going to Merrill Lynch to sell them a comprehensive interest-rate-forecasting package over the now reorganized Telerate Information System. The purchasing manager was ready to sign, but the directors put a freeze on all new contracts. Thus, the purchasing manager's sentiment was not reduced to a purchase.

Currency Reactivity

A great deal of study has gone into measuring currency reactivity with each government statistic. My review of these studies shows too much inconsistency from period to period. There are general rules that do seem to correlate. If the Fed hikes U.S. rates to slow economic growth during a low inflation/high productivity period, it's a good bet the dollar will strengthen as long as it is not a move in response to Europe or the Pacific nations.

A surprise in any statistic (more than 10 percent variation from expectation) will jerk prices. Technical considerations take precedence under such circumstances to determine if a trend has been broken or strengthened. As a trader, you must determine if you are seeking to participate in the knee-jerk reactions or the longer prevailing trends. This decision ultimately defines your strategy and the markets within which you participate.

Currency is an integration of public and private economic interaction. This means that public funding (fiscal policy) influences private investing and spending. This is why local, state, and federal tax revenues are important. These are leading indicators for everything from the economy to interest rates. When tax receipts are down, governments have a few choices. Raise taxes, stimulate, borrow, or all of the above.

Raising taxes drains money from the private sector, but the public sector finds ways to reintroduce tax money through less productive and unproductive projects. When the Treasury borrows, it initially drains cash from circulation. This lowers the price level assumption formula of $P = M \times V$ as previously explained.

Fundamental considerations are vast and require far more study than the presentation within these pages. Each category has enough analysis to fill its own volume. Some can fill several volumes. The objective is to become familiar with those fundamental developments and statistics that influence currency relationships. This leads us to another fundamental development that is worthy of its own particular examination. As we will see, manipulation has become a fundamental aspect of currency trading. What is it and what are appropriate strategies for dealing with the many forms of manipulation?

Chapter 5

INTERVENTIONS, SCAMS, ROUGES, AND MANIPULATIONS

Some of the most spectacular currency opportunities have been born out of market manipulations. Some, such as interventions, are considered legitimate. Groups of the major currency nations meet to contrive ways of changing parities. The most common involve the former Group of 5 (G5) that expanded to the Group of 7 (G7). This could become the Group of 10 or Group of 20. Alternatively, the consolidation of western Europe's currencies in the euro could reduce the group to four or less. As of 2002, G7 included finance ministers and central bank governors of:

- Canada
- France
- Germany
- Italy
- Japan
- The United Kingdom
- The United States

Russia was invited to attend with the finance ministers in 1998, despite the fact that no formal entry into the official group was given. The G8 represented foreign ministers as opposed to

G7's finance ministers. We can see that the westernization of Europe/Asia is likely to expand participation unless or until additional currency consolidations occur like the euro.

Interventions and Manipulations

Whatever the group, intervention is another word for manipulation. Governments agree to buy or sell currencies within the group to alter parity. Such intervention is frequently a surprise. However, any unscheduled group meeting is forewarning that some action is pending. This does not suggest that scheduled meetings cannot result in intervention efforts. However, emergency meetings such as those held during the 1980s generally signaled some form of joint effort to adjust currency parities.

Most discussions covering intervention deal with primary world currencies like the U.S. dollar, pound, euro, and yen. However, important and significant manipulations occur in the Canadian dollar, the Mexican peso, the Brazilian real, and even the Russian ruble, to name a select few. Traders who are inclined to seek out intervention opportunities should carefully observe the actions of major debt holders relative to nondominant currencies. Yes, the Fed helps those in need as does the World Bank. The key phrase is *strategic interests*.

Collective and Unilateral Interventions

Several forms of intervention are available; however, all fall into two categories: collective and unilateral. Collective efforts are more effective for driving currency parity because the risk and expense is spread over several treasuries and central banks. Collective interventions usually involve G7 gatherings during which finance ministers and bank governors formulate specific intervention strategies and objectives. Sometimes the intent is obvious. Other times the maneuvers are clandestine.

When the Fed dramatically moved against inflation during the early 1980s, ancillary effects included a powerfully rising dollar at the expense of trading partners. This is illustrated in Figure 5.1. This chart shows a decline in dollar parity from

Figure 5.1 December 1985 pound futures.

1.2800 in November 1984 to 1.0185 in February 1985. The dollar was viewed as too high against Europe and Japan. A concerted effort did reverse the dollar's ascent; however, it was not merely an intervention. In fact, intervention episodes specifically failed. In September 1985, the G5 announced a surprise intervention to put the brakes on the dollar's fall. The immediate impact was a spectacular decline in the pound. However, the secular trend recovered within a short time, as apparent in Figure 5.2.

Unilateral interventions isolate currency trading to a specific central bank such as the Fed or the Bank of Japan. These interventions are attempts to fine-tune parity or influence relative interest rates. This type of intervention involves the purchase or sale of foreign assets by the central bank. The goal is to pressure the sold asset while bolstering the purchased asset. However, it also decreases reserve assets and monetary aggregates (money supply). To counter the domestic impact, a central bank engages

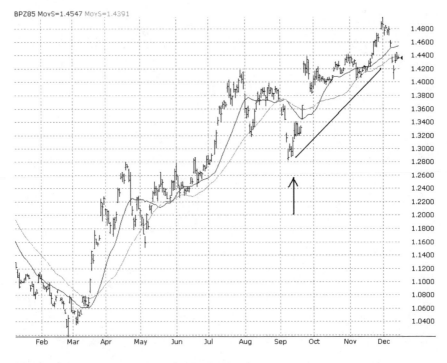

Figure 5.2   December 1985 recovery of pound futures.

in open market adjustments. For example, the Fed might accumulate or distribute U.S. reserve assets to create or absorb liquidity. This has been labeled a *sterilizing* intervention.

The Impact and Success of Interventions

Hundreds of correlative studies attempt to measure the impact and success of interventions. For the most part, data reveals that the interventions are simply too little and, usually, too late. As shown in Figure 5.2, the spike was short lived.

Intervention creates huge profit potentials because market forces are dislocated. Central bank members gather to decide that certain parity relationships are too high or low. When currency speculation was gaining velocity during the 1980s, governments were disgruntled by traders' ability to move currencies outside of target ranges. Lacking faith in the market, central banks considered intervention a cure for the dislodged target.

Traders quickly discovered that intervention generally had very short-term effects on parity. Once digested, the few millions or billions allocated toward altering the trend would fade and the market-generated direction would return. Central banks refer to this action as *defending the currency*. However, the only real solution for deteriorating parity is a fundamental economic shift. Those forces that are driving the currency up or down must be reversed.

Therefore, an intervention provides opportunity if we assume the market will recover from the attempt. If the United States sells dollars and buys yen as a defense against a rising dollar and falling yen, contrary strategy is probably a good bet. Absent some manipulation of actual trade of a concerted effort to alter interest rate spreads, not enough liquidity can be responsibly dedicated to intervention relative to daily volumes generated by import/export trade and currency speculation.

Conspiracy theorists argue that the Fed and its equivalents in other countries are engaged in massive collusion to manipulate parity and collect huge gains. Although these alleged profits have not appeared on any publicly available balance sheets, a strong contingent of traders are sure the Fed speculates on its own form of inside information. Yes, profits and losses do reflect the purchase and sale of foreign assets (currencies); however, the central bank is not considered a for-profit organization.

Believe it or not, a lawsuit was filed against the Fed and Alan Greenspan that alleged conspiracy to depress gold prices. I found the arguments humorous because Greenspan was always a proponent of gold!

In a 1999 paper entitled "Is Sterilized Foreign Exchange Intervention Effective After All?—An Event Study Approach" by Michael Hutchison and Rasmus Fatum (Department of Economics, University of California), an empirical analysis reveals a poor correlation between Fed intervention and successful parity adjustment. Data for the yen and mark was analyzed from October 1982 through August 1993.

Picking from the historical tabulation, the Fed intervened against the dollar and in favor of the yen from April 28, 1989 through October 12, 1989 for a total commitment of $10.5

billion. It was the largest and most extended effort from 1982 through 1993. As Figure 5.3 reveals, the effort was unnoticed by the market. In fact, traders were saying "thank you" as the dollar continued to climb. (Note: Figure 5.3 represents the cash as opposed to the futures market. The parity is yen to dollars, whereas futures market is quoted as dollars to yen.)

According to Hutchison and Fatum's study, interventions against the dollar have poor success rates, while those in favor of the dollar appeared to correlate with a change in trend. This suggests that the dollar was dominant for the period selected and exhibited a favorable (upward) bias. Of course, *trend* can be an amorphous term because we must define a period. Figure 5.4 shows a brief opposite intervention favoring the dollar over the yen in 1993 from May 27 through June 8. The chart shows a complete contradiction; however, the dollar spiked shortly after the effort. The implication is that the excessive and artificial force

Figure 5.3   Yen-to-dollar cash cross.

FXUSJYMUL O:133.38 H:133.38 L:132.38 132.67 -0.71 MovS=107.88 MovS=107.77

Figure 5.4 Yen-to-dollar cash cross.

absorbed by the market caused an oversold dollar. Once the Fed stepped away, a temporary liquidity void occurred.

These illustrations serve to warn traders that interventions are not always what they seem. The natural tendency to go with the intervention's intended direction can be disastrous since the probabilities of success are mixed. Still, interventions can have a spiking influence in either direction that will require defensive action regardless of your position. Even if the spike is favorable, it is usually wise to move stops close or simply take profits. Historically, spikes rapidly retrace.

Interventions, by definition, are attempts to influence market direction or strength. Although some argue that stability rather than trend manipulation is the ultimate goal, charts paint a different picture. This is logical since stable parity does not require intervention. By the time we recognize the need for intervention, a trend is already in place. An intervention in favor of an existing trend is rare or, alternatively, not publicized. Usually, a trend that is favored by the central bank receives positive or supportive rhetoric. The Fed may announce that it is satisfied with the dollar's performance. That is often enough to maintain status quo.

Regardless of efficacy, intervention sends an important message. Whether unilateral or collective, intervention is designed to impact currency parity. This means that the controlling powers want to affect change. The trader's goal is to determine why change is required and how change can be accomplished if not by intervention. Think of any intervention as an announcement that things are not in balance. When finance ministers talk about altering currency parity, they usually have a goal.

During the 1980s, Japan was keen on keeping the yen/dollar parity low to favor Japanese exports to the United States. Toward the end of that decade, Japanese dollar accumulation was forced into circulation and the yen began to climb. The yen's strength ultimately led to a shopping spree that snatched up everything from shopping centers to major U.S. office buildings. Japan needed to spend its dollars.

Scams

U.S. songwriter/actor Kris Kristofferson starred in the movie *Rollover*, which conjured up a crisis based on a Middle East manipulation. The movie lacked credibility because it was factually flawed. However, it highlighted the potential for a powerful financial group such as OPEC to conspire against a currency. Most traders believe that currency manipulation is beyond the reach of mortals. This is to say that few individuals have the financial capacity to move major currencies. After all, central banks have intervened and failed.

This reality has not prevented some from trying. Most notable is the world-renowned George Soros, whose Quantum Fund NV boasted a phenomenal 25-year record based on highly courageous trades. In an interview on ABC's *Nightline*, Ted Koppel suggested that Soros' massive British pound trades were harmful to England's economy. Soros replied that the trades were good for England and simply bad for the bank on the opposite side of his position. Many believe Soros manipulated currency markets. More likely, he observed that interventions generally fail. By opposing central bank trades, Soros was able to reap extraordinary profits exceeding several billion dollars. When discussing strategy, he frequently points out that the market is larger than the bank. Thus, go with the market and not the bank.

Soros maintained a verifiable trading record. His skills and those of his money managers were generally restricted to extremely high net worth individuals. Therefore, his hedge funds were out of reach for the average investor. Further, Mr. Soros was not without setback. Toward the end of the 1990s, the Quantum Fund stumbled and received considerable press about "losing the touch." A stumble for Soros could bankrupt a small country!

The intrigue of Soros and other legendary currency traders has titillated the public. Unfortunately, the intrigue of pocketing hundreds and even thousands of percent from currencies leaves the public vulnerable to scams. There is a saying: "If it sounds too good to be true, it probably is!" Despite this pragmatic warning, hundreds and even thousands of individuals place money in currency scams. For many investors, currency trading is a daunting task, requiring constant attention and a well-developed plan. As you will discover, there are dozens, if not hundreds, of ways to participate in several different forums. Currency markets have a language and style all their own. A layperson generally won't walk into a medical lecture and understand the techno-speak. Hopefully, currency terminology will not appear as complex or intimidating as medical terminology! Perhaps that is why currencies are so appealing to doctors.

The allure of extraordinary returns coupled with the complexity of formulating a plan has led many investors to professional managers, currency pools, partnerships, and futures treading accounts. Unquestionably, professional assistance can achieve desired results—huge profits. Using a professional permits participation without the time commitment. However, it may also take some of the fun and excitement out of the process. Every individual has a unique personality that will dictate whether he or she manages an account or uses professional help.

This raises an extremely important question: What constitutes a professional? Since currency trading became popular during the 1970s, it remained unregulated. Even now, regulation is limited. Although supervision and registration requirements are being developed and implemented, only the futures markets had the oversight of the Commodity Futures Trading Commission and National Futures Association (NFA). Unfortunately, even with the assumed protection of these regulatory organizations, thousands of investors fall victim to Ponzi schemes, frauds, and swindles.

Individual investors should not feel alone. The appeal of currency trading is so powerful and intoxicating, some of the most venerable institutions have succumbed to frauds perpetrated by unscrupulous individuals. Even worse, well-meaning traders have buried themselves and their firms by overextending in these dangerous markets. As the saying goes, "The road to hell is paved with good intentions."

The Kohli Fraud

One such financial fiasco was perpetrated by Charles Kohli (aka "Chuckles") from Princeton, New Jersey. Kohli engaged in limited currency trading with impressive success. Based on his initial experience and a series of formulas he derived from market observation, he embarked on a management venture. According to the case record, Kohli began managing funds for third parties. Again, he had success. He was trading through Prudential Securities, Inc. around 1989. According to Kohli, he stimulated the interest of Prudential representatives who encouraged him to expand the scope of his operations. Eventually, he formed a number of investment entities named Sigma, Inc., Geronimo, Inc., Vol Partners, L.P., and Savid Group. Kohli convinced approximately 400 investors to place more than $60 million under his management from 1989 through part of 1995.

As previously mentioned, correlations that guided investors during the 1980s changed in the 1990s. Perhaps Kohli's approach no longer applied or he simply became overexposed after experiencing a setback. There is a propensity to go into gambling mode by doubling up when times get rough. Whatever the reason, Kohli attempted to recover his losses by raising new money. He paid old investors with new deposits. The eventual result was a Ponzi pyramid. In the process, Kohli hired salespeople and established extremely attractive offices that projected an image of legitimacy and success. Visitors would come into his trading room and hear the banter of currency terminology. They were shown fictitious account statements that were essentially irresistible. Even a professional currency trader was lured into investing substantial sums!

All the while, Kohli was never registered with the Commodity Futures Trading Commission, despite the fact that he traded on the U.S. futures exchanges. He was not an NFA member. Apparently, none of the investors investigated his credentials or registration status. More shockingly, he traded with some of the most reputable and well-known brokerage houses on the street including Dean Witter Reynolds, Inc., ING Securities Futures & Options, Smith Barney, Merrill Lynch, Pierce, Fenner & Smith, Inc., First Options of Chicago, Inc., Saul Stone & Company, LLC, Prudential, and others. All combined, these brokerage firms made millions in commissions as Kohli desperately struggled to earn back losses.

In the end, investors lost more than $40 million. Kohli was indicted and convicted of criminal fraud. He went to prison, but the investors never recovered a dime.

Although we may be quick to blame investors for not fully investigating Kohli, the rules of the NFA state under bylaw 1101 that members may not conduct business with nonmembers. The natural conclusion is that none of the firms should have allowed Kohli to trade since he was not an NFA member. Indeed, investors brought a class action against the brokerage firms that had so handsomely profited from Kohli's endeavors. Alas, the courts did not rule in favor of the investors. Even an attempt to bring the question before the U.S. Supreme Court was turned down.

So the lesson is, "Investors beware! Caveat Emptor." When reviewing the record of a potential manager/trader, ask for his or her NFA registration number. Call the NFA's toll-free information number and find out about any complaints, membership status, or pending disciplinary actions. Check with the Commodity Futures Trading Commission, too. It is your money; do not be timid about asking questions and fully checking out the individual. Certainly minor infractions can have explanations. Even the most honest and successful managers can accidentally break some rules. It is still your responsibility to weigh any negatives.

As an extra precaution, ask to see trading confirmations with the name of the clearing brokerage firm. This is true for futures and cash trading houses. Call the trading house and ask to verify that the trades were, in fact, placed. This may seem extreme, but false track records can be presented in many ways. Your investigation can be made simpler by looking up the activity in historical data or on charts provided by quote vendors. Take your time. Remember that the markets will always be around, but your money may not be if you get involved in a scam.

Rouge Traders

In addition to operators like Kohli, other significant frauds have been instituted by would-be genius currency traders. Such incidents were frequent enough to popularize the term *rouge trader*. These individuals have literally destroyed entire financial institutions. In some cases, governments have come perilously close to disaster. Unlike Ponzi operators, rouge traders wield huge amounts of money and can impact markets. More importantly, a rouge trader can wreck the firm where customer accounts reside. Thus, a review of rouge traders is important.

Barings Bank

For more than 200 years, Barings Bank of England was a pillar among British financial institutions. From July 1992 through February 1995, a single currency trader named Nick Leeson managed to lose approximately £850 million in a long series of trades that included cash, futures, and options transactions. Despite customary internal controls, Leeson skillfully disguised his trading by suppressing the account listings and negotiating lines of credit on Barings' behalf. Although Leeson's trading appeared to have no effect on currency markets, it did throw a major scare into London's financial community.

Figure 5.5 shows that the dollar fell against the pound immediately following the Barings failure. This was contrary to expectations that such a large and prestigious bank failure would

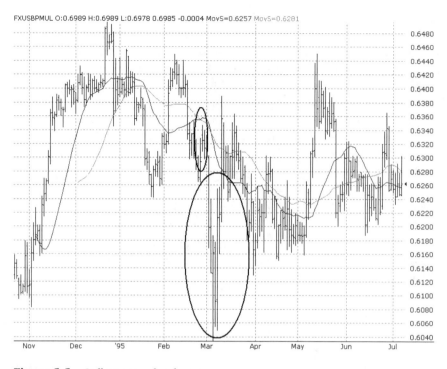

FXUSBPMUL O:0.6989 H:0.6989 L:0.6978 0.6985 -0.0004 MovS=0.6257 MovS=0.6281

Figure 5.5   Dollar-to-pound cash cross.

weaken the British currency and raise questions about other possible banking problems. Whether the pound was intentionally supported or the rise was merely coincidence, we see that seemingly logical assumptions about the impact of financial disasters do not always hold. This is why it is best to avoid heavy positions when you cannot be comfortable about the potential results. As Leeson and Barings Bank found out, currency trading can be hazardous to your wealth!

Allfirst Bank

One might believe that the demise of Barings would leave an indelible mark on internal controls that would prevent such rouge activity from reoccurring. Not so! In 2000, John Rusnak, a currency trader for Allfirst Bank in Baltimore (a U.S. subsidiary of Allied Irish Bank), came onto the scene. Like Kohli, Rusnak believed he had a formula for success and accumulated huge exposure in yen/dollar positions. However, the yen was in far deeper trouble than Rusnak could have imagined. Through 2000, the dollar continued strengthening against the yen until Rusnak had racked up $690 million in losses.

As shown in Figure 5.6, the dollar/yen parity took a wild ride through 2000. The series of sharp and erratic swings coupled with interday volatility became unmanageable for Rusnak. Indeed, the chart reveals a pattern that would have been extremely treacherous for any trader, skilled or not. Again, we cannot extrapolate how much influence Rusnak's activities may have had on the yen. It is sufficient to say that whatever it may have been, it certainly was not as Rusnak had intended.

Figure 5.6   Dollar-to-yen cash cross in 2000.

Princeton Economics, Orange County, and More

As if this was not enough, a brash investment advisor named Martin Armstrong defrauded sophisticated Japanese investors out of hundreds of millions of dollars through bogus and simply bad currency transactions. Under the name Princeton Economics International, Ltd., Armstrong managed to strong-arm the Republic National Bank into clearing transactions on behalf of his customers. Like Kohli, the NFA and Commodity Futures Trading Commission did not oversee Armstrong's activities until after investors were bilked out of their cash.

Frauds extend beyond private institutions. California's Orange County went bankrupt trading derivatives. The huge German conglomerate Metallgesellschaft lost more than $1 billion in energy futures. Sumitomo of Japan lost an equally impressive amount at the hands of a rouge copper trader. The lesson should be apparent. Currency trading along with all leveraged trading vehicles represents a very high-risk game. Even the most prominent institutions are vulnerable to fraud and stupidity. More importantly, the appearance of legitimacy and success is not always reality. This is why so many investors would rather trade themselves.

A major concern has been raised that speculation in derivatives will result in the complete destruction of our financial institutions and monetary systems. Consider that even Alan Greenspan has warned that central banks are not immune to fraud and rouge activities. Consider that trading can bankrupt a county government. If this activity climbs the ladder to the state or federal level, we could see financial chaos. This is why it is particularly wise to keep market fraud in the back of your mind. However, the question of legitimacy should always be at the forefront of your mind when considering a currency fund, pool, or trading manager. Given the relative ease with which we can check registration status, credentials, and backgrounds, there are few excuses for getting involved in a trading scam. The fact that major firms have been deceived shows how dangerous the greed button becomes when unchecked.

Chapter 6

UNDERSTANDING THE MARKETS OF CASH, FUTURES, AND OPTIONS

Perhaps the most important currency trading issue investors face is choosing the right marketplace. Generally, foreign exchange (FOREX) occurs using three distinct vehicles: Interbank, futures, and options.

The Interbank

The Interbank is a network of international banks that creates a market in all currencies. This is called the *cash market* because settlements are made in cash. It is likened to primary dealer markets in government debt. Until the turn of the millennium, the Interbank was almost exclusively the domain of exceptionally large traders, corporations, central banks, commercial banks, and dealers (brokers). Small investors could not afford to trade in the large cash blocks transacted among Interbank participants. Early on, the Interbank was primarily a communications network and process. As FOREX progressed, computerization changed the dealing and matching mechanism to the point where several dealers were able to subdivide large cash blocks into smaller pieces that could be automatically matched and tracked.

Eventually, banks became comfortable offering transactions under $1 million and opened cash trading to a far wider range of investors, speculators, and hedgers. Interestingly, access became broad enough that some touring companies used the Interbank to convert customers' money in advance of trips at more favorable rates than offered at the typical airport exchange window. In the process, the touring companies could pick up a few pips. As previously mentioned, a *pip* is the unit of trading defined for the cash market.

Increasing confidence in automation created a submarket for Interbank trading that included margined transactions. Unlike futures and related options, margined cash transactions require funding. For example, as of this writing, REFCO, Inc. formed a subsidary, REFCO FOREX Limited, that offers a cash currency program for individual investors with opening balances as low as $10,000. For some reason, cash trading has become particularly appealing and popular because of the lower entry requirements, increasing ease of use, and exceptionally wide diversification. Virtually all currencies are available through cash transactions. All that is required is a creditworthy counter party willing to take the opposite side.

The cash market has major FOREX centers that are identified by volume. Approximately two-thirds of all transactions are conducted through New York and London. Tokyo maintained the third position with 10 percent. Germany, France, Switzerland, and Hong Kong each shared approximately 5 percent, whereas Singapore acted as a hub for Pacific Rim players with approximately 9 percent. To be sure, speculative and commercial transactions are directed through the Cayman Islands, Bahamas, Antilles, Liechtenstein, and other investment havens. However, the large volumes as well as transactions from these participants usually pass through a trading center.

The International Organization of Standardization (ISO) developed abbreviations for each foreign currency to establish a common language among banks and traders and to provide more efficiency over using each currency's name. Therefore, the U.S. dollar is referred to as USD, and the Australian dollar is the AUD. The euro is EUR, whereas the Japanese yen is JPY. The British pound is GPB, but is also referenced as the sterling and cable. These names are leftovers from the time when the pound was based on silver and transactions were conducted via cable-gram or telex. Although it is now a distant memory, sterling was once the preferred reserve currency. A complete listing of currencies and related ISO codes can be found in Appendix A.

A strong word of caution is necessary before moving onto the other currency markets. Although ISO codes are universally used in the cash market, they are not the standard for futures and options on futures. In fact, ISO codes are not even universally used by quote vendors for the cash market. This means that traders must be fully versed in all abbreviations to avoid making mistakes. This is more the case when arbitraging between markets.

Spot and Forward Markets

The cash market has several types of transactions that fall within two categories: spot and forward. The spot market is for immediate transactions that must be closed within 2 days from the time the trade is matched. Anything beyond 2 days is considered the forward market. Forward transactions can be days, weeks, or even months. Obviously, the longer the time, the greater the risk of an adverse fluctuation.

Spot and forward markets use specific terminology that helps narrow the trading process down to easily communicated and understood words and phrases. In a market that can change values in seconds, brevity is an asset and verbosity is a liability. Some terms are common to other markets such as the *bid* (a request for a price by a buyer) and the *offer* (the price presented by a seller). More often than not, the bid and offer will not exactly match. The difference is called the *spread* and is expressed as pips. As described earlier, a pip is the last significant decimal of the exchange rate. For new traders, a pip can be confusing because the decimal place is not the same for all currencies. Assume the dollar is trading over the yen (¥). When quoted to the dollar, the yen is expressed as perhaps 131.57. This means there are 131.57 yen to the dollar. Figure 6.1 is a chart of the dollar in yen. It answers the question of how many yen it will take to buy $1.

This is the usual manner used in expressing currencies to the dollar. However, it is possible to express the relationship as dollars to yen. This answers the question of how many dollars it will

FXUSJYMUL O:131.75 H:131.88 L:131.13 131.57 -0.18 MovS=131.80 MovS=132.10

Figure 6.1   Dollars-to-yen cash cross.

take to buy ¥1. This relationship is illustrated in Figure 6.2. As
the charts reveal, each is a reciprocal of the other. Futures and
related options that are traded through the U.S. exchanges are
always expressed as dollars to the foreign currency—in other
words, dollar parity.

It is very important to take a moment or two to ponder these
relationships and representations. The most common beginners'
errors I have witnessed (including my own many years ago) have
been caused by confusing parity direction. In both Figure 6.1 and
Figure 6.2, the yen is declining against the dollar. When
expressed in the spot and forward markets, the bid and ask is
expressed as 131.57/67. This means the buyer is willing to pay
131.57 and the seller wants 131.67. The spread is 10 pips. It is
also called *10 wide.*

Not all spot quotes are expressed to the dollar. For example,
the pound is quoted as dollars to pounds. This is true for the euro
as well. So extreme caution is required to avoid mistakes. Once
accustomed to these relationships, quoting generally becomes

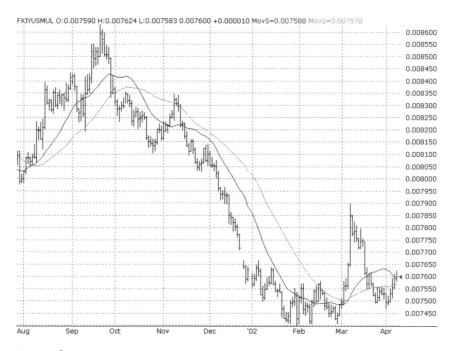

FXJYUSMUL O:0.007590 H:0.007624 L:0.007583 0.007600 +0.000010 MovS=0.007588 MovS=0.007570

Figure 6.2   Yen-to-dollars cash cross from 2001 to 2002.

second nature. Still, even seasoned currency traders have been known to glance at a chart and get it wrong.

Cross-Rates Table

One of the most useful tools for determining parity direction in cash markets is a cross-rates table. This is tabulation of currencies along the horizontal and vertical axes. Since currency parities are constantly changing, these tables are extremely dynamic. Traders establish cross rates on their quotation equipment by simply establishing a currency matrix. Examples of cross-rate tables are available in *The Wall Street Journal, The Financial Times of London,* and several other dailies. Standardized cross-rate tables area available on certain services such as Reuters, Telerate, and Bloomberg. Table 6.1 lists currency cross rates.

Figure 6.3 illustrates the cross of sterling against Swiss francs. As we can see, the market had a range from approximately 2.5500 Swiss francs to the pound down to about 2.2700.

Table 6.1

Currency Cross Rates

			Late New York Trading Monday, April 22, 2002				
	DOLLAR	**EURO**	**POUND**	**SFRANC**	**PESO**	**YEN**	**CDNDLR**
Canada	1.5707	1.3973	2.2785	0.9514	0.16961	0.01209	. . .
Japan	129.93	115.59	188.48	78.698	14.031	. . .	82.721
Mexico	9.2605	8.2381	13.433	5.609	. . .	0.07127	5.8958
Switzerland	1.651	1.4687	2.3949	. . .	0.17828	0.01271	1.0511
U.K.	0.6894	0.6133	. . .	0.4175	0.07444	0.00531	0.43889
Euro	1.1241	. . .	1.6306	0.68086	0.12139	0.00865	0.71567
U.S.	. . .	0.8896	1.4506	0.60569	0.10799	0.0077	0.63666

Figure 6.3   Sterling-to-Swiss-franc cross from 2001 to 2002.

If you purchased £1,000,00 using Swiss francs, it would cost 2,227,000 Swiss francs. It's simple multiplication. As you hold the pound to a rate of 2.4400, the same £1,000,000 buys you 2,440,000 Swiss francs for a profit (in Swiss francs) of 213,000 Swiss francs. The sterling appreciated 12 percent against the Swiss franc.

This would be a forward transaction since it required more than 2 days to accomplish this parity change. In the spot market, differentials would be much smaller. The movement might be less than 10 pips. On 1 million sterling, you multiply 0.0010 for a 1,000 Swiss franc differential. These moves represent fractions of a percent; however, transactions can be £100,000,000 for a 100,000 Swiss franc differential. If you can conduct the transaction with only 10 percent margin, the profit becomes extraordinary.

Consider the dollar versus the euro. On September 24, 2001, the spot euro opened at .9076 dollars to the euro and declined by 1.92¢ to .8884 by the close. This is illustrated in Figure 6.4. Here, parity is expressed in dollars. For 1 million euros, the selling price would be $907,600.00. By the end of the day, you could buy back 1 million euros for $888,400.00 or a $19,200 profit in a single trading session. This represents a 2.12 percent profit for a day's work—if you were on the correct side! If you had bought $1 million on the open, you would have paid 1,101,806.96 euros. By the close, it would have cost you 1,125,619.09 or 23,812.13 more euros to buy back the $1 million.

Figure 6.4   Euro expressed in dollars from 2001 to 2002.

1,000,000EUR @ .9076USD = 907,600USD
1,000,000EUR @ .8884USD = <u>888,400USD</u>
                          19,200USD

1,000,000USD @ 1.101806EUR = 1,101,806EUR
1,000,000USD @ 1.125619EUR = <u>1,125,619EUR</u>
                             23,812EUR

Note conversion is the reciprocal. 1/.9076 EUR to USD
1/.8884 EUR to USD.

Cash Trading Screens

Virtually 24 hours a day, currency market makers are available. Some have as many as four or five screens packed with bids and offers from dozens of sources. Quote vendors use contributors who post their bids and ask for particular cross rates. The entire process is extremely dynamic and requires the concentration of an air traffic controller.

Table 6.2 provides an example of a typical cash trading screen. From left to right, we see the currency symbol, the contributing party (market maker), the bid, ask, last, change for the session, time, and a brief description just to make sure. A blank line separates each cross. Within each grouping, the first line represents spot followed by spreads going out 1 month to a year. The illustration in Figure 6.5 is limited to a few quotes. The trading room will likely have hundreds of listings.

The contributor provides bids and offers it has available. These are the primary bank participants who quote to the traders. Names in the contributor column constantly change depending on which institution is making the market. The change simply reflects the difference from a previous session. Traders observe the time of the information and, as mentioned, the specific market is described in the last column as an additional reference.

The example is actually a proprietary Microsoft® Excel spreadsheet that is dynamically linked to the quotation platform and a trading system. The trading screen is not illustrated since it shows actual transactions. However, it is interesting to note that the spreadsheet is actually programmed to seek out arbitrage and spread opportunities. When it is detected, the transaction is

Table 6.2

Cash Currency Trading Screen (Calculated)

		0.105	0.099	0.103	0.102	0.102	-0.001	
6 Month	Barclays LON							08:23 AM
12 Month	Barclays LON							04:09 AM
Swiss/Dollar	CMS NYC	1.6652	1.6656	1.6785	1.6643	1.6654	-0.0104	05:37 PM
1 Month	Tullet LON	0.0004	0.0004	0.0005	0.0003	0.0004	0	04:46 PM
2 Month	U B S W LON	0.0011	0.0008	0.0011	0.0006	0.0009	-0.0001	01:58 PM
3 Month	U B S W LON	0.0017	0.0013	0.0017	0.0009	0.0015	-0.0001	05:00 PM
4 Month	Tullet LON	0.0024	0.0023	0.0025	0.0023	0.0023	-0.0001	10:43 AM
12 Month	U B S W LON	0.0117	0.0107	0.0127	0.0109	0.0112	-0.0011	05:34 PM
Aussie/Dollar	Calculated			1.8959	1.8873	1.8914	-0.0037	05:34 PM
Aussie/Dollar	Barclays LON	2.2195	2.2205	2.2387	2.219	2.22	-0.0161	05:36 PM
1 Month	R.B.C. TOR	0.0003	0.0003	0.0005	0.0001	0.0003	0.0002	04:31 PM
2 Month	R.B.C. TOR	0.0006	0.0006	0.0006	0.0001	0.0006	0.0005	04:31 PM
3 Month	R.B.C. TOR	0.0081	0.0082	0.0082	0.0081	0.0081	-1E-04	04:31 PM
6 Month	U B S W LON	0.002	0.002	0.002	0.0005	0.002	0	05:34 PM
9 Month	U B S W LON	0.0005	0.0005	0.0005	0.0002	0.0005	0.0003	10:25 AM
12 Month	U B S W LON	0.0002	0.0002	0.0005	0.0002	0.0002	0	05:34 PM
Mark/Dollar	U B S W LON	0.0003	0.0003	0.0005	0.0003	0.0003	0	03:10 PM
1 Month	U B S W LON	0.0004	0.0004	0.0005	0.0003	0.0004	0	03:10 PM
4 Month	U B S W LON	0.0004	0.0004	0.0005	0.0001	0.0004	0.0003	03:10 PM
5 Month	U B S W LON	0.0002	0.0001	0.0005	0.0001	0.0001	-0.0001	05:34 PM
10 Month	U B S W LON	0.0005	0.0005	0.0005	0.0005	0.0005	0	03:10 PM
Euro Currency		0.8801		0.8801	0.876	0.8801	0.0061	02:48 PM

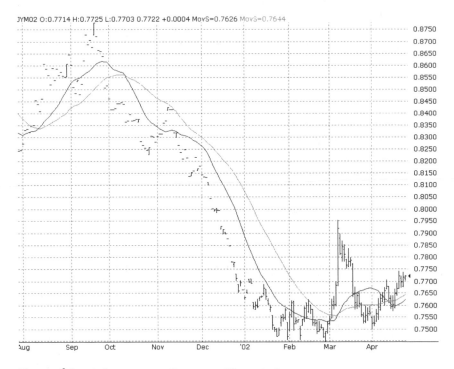

JYM02 O:0.7714 H:0.7725 L:0.7703 0.7722 +0.0004 MovS=0.7626 MovS=0.7644

Figure 6.5   Cash currency trading screen (illustration).

automatically compiled and sent for execution. Such a system may generate hundreds of daily trades for just a few pips each. At the day's end, the result can be very impressive since trading amounts are in the millions.

CHIPS and SWIFT

It is fair to say that mechanisms clearing these transactions have become extremely sophisticated. It is not necessary for the average investor to understand all the relationships; however, you might hear about CHIPS and SWIFT. CHIPS is an acronym for Clearing House Interbank Payment System. Several large banks primarily based in New York City own the system. The system interfaces with more than 100 depository institutions that clear dollar currency transactions. After the September 11th attack on the World Trade Center, there were discussions about decentralizing clearing operations. Although CHIPS ownership originated among New York institutions, changes in banking regulations made most of these institutions national and even international.

SWIFT stands for Society of Worldwide Interbank Financial Telecommunications. As currency trading expanded toward the late 1970s, traditional use of telex became cumbersome. Remember that the pound is still referred to as cable—left over from the days when transactions were consummated via cablegram. SWIFT standardized telecommunication to expedited order transmissions and other Interbank transactions. This brings up an interesting question. What is the Interbank?

What Is the Interbank?

Many people operate under the misconception that the Interbank is a big bank housed in a building. The practice of capitalizing the name lends to this misunderstanding. The Interbank is actually the network of banks and dealers that make up the cash currency marketplace. Thus, multiple systems like CHIPS and various methods and channels for clearing cash currency transactions are available. Recall that FOREX is largely unregulated.

It is not likely that the average investor will find him- or herself in front of a primary trading or dealing screen or in a dealing room. Therefore, trading terms used in the FOREX dealing rooms are not a requirement for investor participation. For example, when a bid is matched, you might hear or see the word "yours." Offers are made with the phrase "I sell at" or "Selling at." As electronics dominate, language is replaced by blinking bids and asks, whereas matched trades may only change colors. See Figures 6.6 through 6.11.

Prior to computing convenience, traders limited their view to a few currencies and were exhausted by the process of seeking these little profit opportunities. The study of market theory inevitably reveals the concept of efficiency. The Efficient Market Theory states that as more participants seek out profit potentials, the spreads become increasingly narrow until opportunities disappear. This implies that the illustrated spreadsheet has a limited

Figure 6.6 REFCO FOREX order entry system screen 1 (REFCO, F/X Associates, LLC.).

Dir	EUR.USD		USD.JPY		USD.CHF		GBP.USD		EUR
	I Sell EUR	I Buy EUR	I Sell USD	I Buy USD	I Sell USD	I Buy USD	I Sell GBP	I Buy GBP	I Sell EUR
SPOT	0.8684	0.8689	133.81	133.87	1.6947	1.6954	1.4175	1.4182	116.22
TOM (OR)	0.34	0.37	0.65	0.68	0.13	0.18	0.90	0.95	1.02
TN (SWAP)	-0.37	-0.34	-0.68	-0.65	-0.18	-0.13	-0.95	-0.90	-1.09
1D (OR)	-0.37	-0.34	-0.68	-0.65	-0.19	-0.14	-0.91	-0.84	-1.09
SN (SWAP)	-0.37	-0.34	-0.68	-0.65	-0.19	-0.14	-0.91	-0.84	-1.09
1W	-2.60	-2.52	-4.65	-4.55	-0.90	-0.70	-6.00	-5.90	-7.52
2W	-5.25	-5.10	-9.30	-9.15	-1.80	-1.40	-11.85	-11.65	-15.10
3W	-7.75	-7.60	-14.00	-13.80	-2.80	-2.40	-17.65	-17.35	-22.52
1M	-10.25	-10.10	-18.70	-18.50	-3.20	-2.80	-23.40	-23.20	-29.94
2M	-21.70	-21.40	-40.75	-40.25	-7.50	-6.50	-49.75	-49.40	-64.34
3M	-31.70	-31.40	-60.30	-59.80	-10.00	-9.00	-72.90	-72.50	-94.59
4M	-41.80	-41.30	-82.50	-81.50	-14.00	-12.50	-97.50	-96.50	-127.23
5M	-51.50	-50.75	-105.50	-104.50	-19.00	-17.00	-121.64	-120.64	-159.99
6M	-59.75	-59.00	-128.75	-127.75	-23.50	-21.50	-145.00	-144.00	-190.99
7M	-68.25	-67.25	-155.70	-154.20	-31.00	-28.00	-169.39	-168.12	-225.47
8M	-75.00	-74.00	-180.50	-178.50	-37.00	-34.00	-190.09	-188.59	-255.75

Figure 6.7 REFCO FOREX order entry system screen 2 (REFCO, F/X Associates, LLC.).

useful life. According to the Efficient Market Theory, when everyone is using the same technique, the game will be over.

If markets were efficient, arbitrage would have disappeared decades ago. The fact is that there are too many levels of market participation. Theoretically, there might be a point where spreads or arbitrage is no longer worthwhile. We have not seen it yet.

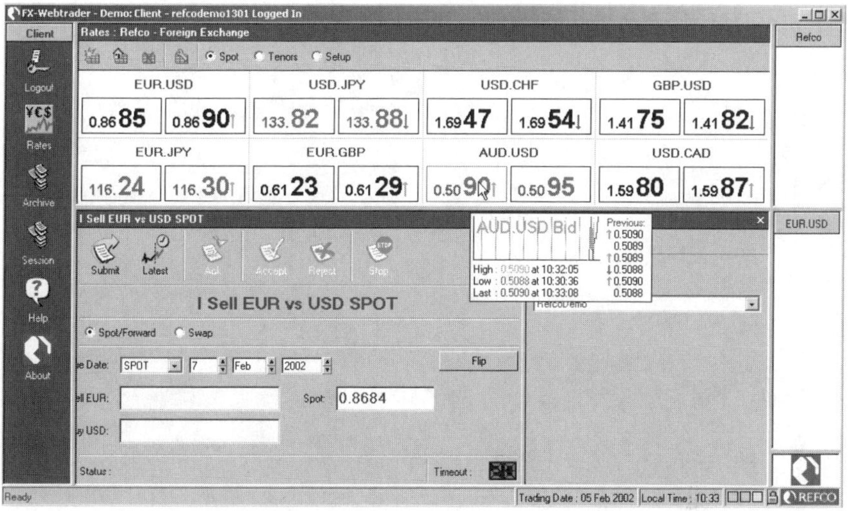

Figure 6.8 REFCO FOREX order entry system screen 3 (REFCO, F/X Associates, LLC.).

Figure 6.9 REFCO autotrader trading ticket screen.

Risk Components of Spots and Forwards

When trading spots and forwards, any given transaction has several risk components. These fall into basic categories:

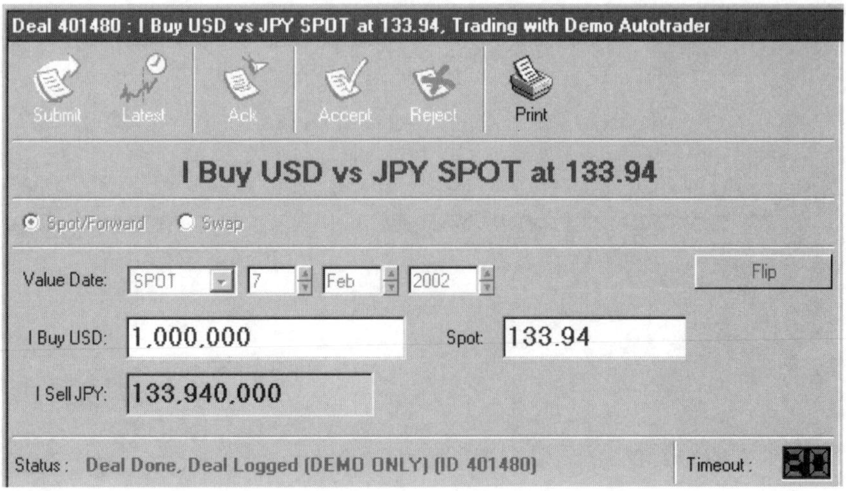

Figure 6.10   Trading ticket screen.

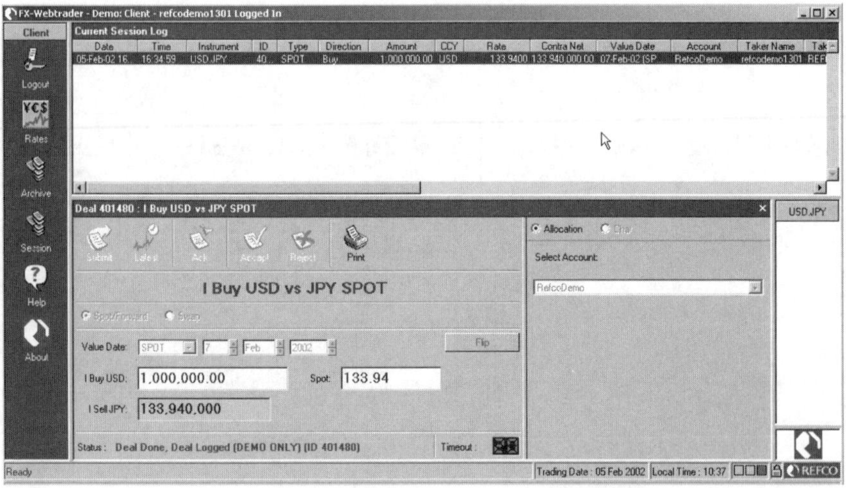

Figure 6.11   REFCO autotrader currency session trading log screen with pending ticket.

- Volatility
- Exchange rate risk (time)
- Credit risk (counter party)
- Monetary risk

- Interest rate risk
- Intervention

Volatility

As previously mentioned, each component is related to the extent that one flows from another. Volatility is a function of market participation and uncertainty. However, volatility is generated by changes in interest rates, monetary aggregates (reflected by government statistics), possible intervention, potential defaults, and relative exchange rates. In turn, volatility can create credit risk if it weakens a counter party to the point of default that circles back to volatility. It should be noted that risk components mentioned previously generally pertain to nonspeculative interests. Consider the trading participants:

- Corporations
- Banks
- Brokers
- Speculators
- Governments

Visualize the broker as the entity sitting between banks, corporations, speculators, and even governments. For the broker, risk is only inherent in the time he or she has unmatched transactions. Most brokers avoid taking on *naked* positions. This means they match trades for a small piece—a few pips.

Corporations may deal in a variety of currencies. If they manufacture in several countries, wages and raw materials may be paid for in domestic money. Finished goods might be sold in various countries, too. This means revenue is realized in several different currencies unless a demand is made for the currency of origin—the home currency. At any given moment, a multinational company can have considerable exchange rate risk among several different currencies. Consider a simple example of Waterford Crystal made in Ireland. A significant amount of their product is sold in the United States. The Irish pound is linked to the sterling. If $10 million worth of crystal is shipped to the United States, a lag occurs between the time it reaches the store and the time it is invoiced and paid. If the dollar appreciates against the sterling, all is well and good. However, if the dollar parity deteriorates, the amount received back and converted to Irish pounds will be less than at the time of shipment. With today's volatility, the difference can be significant.

As a solution, Waterford might hedge the value of the shipment in the forward cash market by selling dollars for delivery at the time the invoice will be collected. The comptroller or treasurer must carefully analyze cash flow to determine the appropriate amount and timing of the hedge to avoid being over or under the hedged. When the hedge is placed, the company faces a new credit risk associated with the invoiced amount. If the buyer fails to pay, the hedge was against an amorphous receivable. The hedge must be based on historical observations, such as the ratio of bad debt over time.

On the other side of the transaction is the store or distributor that intends to sell the crystal. They would worry that the sterling might appreciate against the dollar before they pay their invoice, thus making the product more expensive in dollars. Their hedge would be to buy sterling. Why don't they simply buy with sterling and pay with sterling? Indeed, some companies do request payment in their domestic currency to avoid exchange rate risk. However, no matter how the payment is made, one party is always at risk when currency conversion is required as part of the transaction.

The same transactional logic that applies to Irish pounds and U.S. dollars is used in crosses with nondollar currencies. The most common are European currencies against the yen, or Canadian or Australian dollars. There are combinations and permutations for all currencies that are not linked like the Irish pound is to the sterling. As reviewed earlier, multiple cross-parity provides arbitrage opportunities. Frequently, a spread exists between multiple currencies against the euro, U.S. dollar, or yen. By rapidly buying the undervalued leg while simultaneously selling the overvalued leg, an automatic profit is achieved equal to the difference.

Exchange Rate Risk

By far, exchange rate risk is the cornerstone of FOREX. Without such risk, there would be no need to trade currencies and no profit opportunity. For this reason, many currency traders talk about exchange rate exposure rather than risk. Forces that impact exchange rates are called *other risk factors*.

Although it is rare, monetary collapse is possible. For example, in 2002, Argentina's monetary problems accelerated, causing a confidence crisis and a cascade in the Argentinean austral. Argentineans rushed to convert to dollars, euros, and even gold. The move did boost demand for these currencies, with the dollar receiving the greatest immediate benefit. Gold reached its highest level of enthusiasm in more than 2 years. However, the rise above \$300 per ounce was not exclusively the result of Argentina's flight to quality. Middle East tension was escalating with Iraq's call for a 1970s' type of oil embargo against the United States.

Counter Party Risk

Having touched on the debacles of Barings Bank, Allfirst, and other institutions, it is easy to comprehend how a counter party can represent risk. Up through the beginning of the new millennium, the market was extremely fortunate. Near failures such as the Continental Bank of Illinois or the collapse of prestigious firms such as E.F. Hutton and Drexel represented minor wrinkles in the fabric of Wall Street. Currency trading departments were quickly taken over and counter party defaults were minimized. This is not to say that insolvency was not a problem. It simply suggests that the system was able to absorb such misfortunes without being substantially impacted. This is easy to say as long as you are not on the receiving end of a sour transaction. When dealing with large Interbank players, counter party risk is believed to be minimal. As Interbank opens to wider and more diversified investors, this is bound to change. Although default levels may increase, there is a positive side—more participants indicate more liquidity. Liquidity usually smoothes market volatility by providing narrower and more competitive bids and asks.

Interest Rate Risk

Interest rate risk primarily pertains to forward trading because changing rates affect the theoretical returns of cross-currency spreads. When quoting a forward position, the interest rate plays a critical role in determining the differential based on disproportionate rates between the two (or more) currencies. The basic relationship was expressed earlier. Few developments are more devastating than an adverse interest rate change when holding an unhedged forward position. Entire strategies have been trashed by sudden interest rate adjustments.

This has created a pattern of fluctuating liquidity whereby markets lose participation just prior to any interest rate announcement. After the announcement, markets go into a feeding frenzy as traders attempt to adjust positions to match the perceived impact of the adjustment. Frequently, the direction prompted by the rate change is temporary. This requires nimble trading and the discipline to exit if profits are threatened by reversal. This will be covered in the technical forecasting subject matter.

Intervention

Intervention poses particular problems since it is frequently sprung on markets without prior warning. Such was the case when the former Group of 5 (G5) attempted to regulate the dollar relative to Europe's currencies. A sudden move by a central bank can send parity soaring or crashing. Even if the effect is temporary, the power of related moves can be sufficient to bust an investor broke! There are few protections against intervention. However, even if suddenly announced, it is almost always the case that the objective is known in advance. Officials talk about a "need to adjust" cross rates in advance of intervention. If the market does not take the hint, intervention follows.

Hedge Funds

The fundamental reason for FOREX is to facilitate trade between nations. Since every economy marches to its own drummer, parity fluctuates to create exchange rate risk. Even with the apparent need to offset exchange rate risk, FOREX volume is enormous in comparison with the total amount of trade conducted among all countries combined. That being the case, there is more than hedging and trade facilitation. We identified this as speculative participation and government regulation. By far, speculation has become the largest component. Some may argue that currency trading is not speculation because it is used to off-set certain financial transactions. Since the birth of currency trading, these financial transactions have been a disguise for prof-iting through risk. One of the more amusing misnomers of the twentieth century was *hedge funds*. Practices of these funds had little to do with hedging. The strategies were (and are) to forecast market direction and potential and speculate in unhedged posi-tions. Hedge funds imply offsetting risk when, in fact, they profit from risk. Hedge funds have become enamored with currency trading because the profit potentials are so tremendous. FOREX is one of the few places where exceptional returns are regularly available to satisfy the charter of these high-flying funds. Perhaps as important, cash currency trading has remained unregulated.

Futures

To say cash currency markets are changing is an incredible understatement. Everything from clearing methods to the play-ers is changing. This is why a broad perspective serves better than details. Although people may be curious about the CHIPS members or specific dealing room techno-speak, we find that environments, participants, and rules change too rapidly and fre-quently to learn with any consistency. This is also true for infor-mation and information sources. In 2000, Bridge Information Systems was a major information vendor that included the for-mer Dow Jones Telerate. By February 2001, Bridge was bankrupt and in liquidation. By 2002, Reuters had assumed most of Bridge with the exception of Telerate and Commodity Research Bureau (CRB). Within that same period, the New York Board of Trade (NYBOT) dropped the CRB Index as a futures contract. This index had been used by traders as a heads up on raw commodity price direction—hence, inflation potential. Although some switched to the Goldman Sachs Index (GSI), as of this writing, there was too little volume and open interest for the GSI to be used for hedging.

Chase Bank assumes Chemical Bank. United Jersey Bank becomes Summit. Summit becomes Fleet. First Union becomes

Wachovia. Quote vendors go in and out of business. Michael Bloomberg becomes Mayor of New York City. Western Europe unites its markets. The euro currency replaces individual European currencies. Change is inevitable.

Among the most significant changes and developments in currency markets was the creation of futures. For those unfamiliar with futures (formerly *commodities* or *commodity futures*), they are negotiable contracts to make or take delivery of a specific commodity at a fixed price at a fixed future date. Unlike the forward market, futures are traded on regulated commodity exchanges through clearing members who guarantee transactions. As such, futures have little (if any) counter party risk.

Futures were developed centuries ago as a way to protect producers and consumers against adverse price movements by transferring risk to speculators. This process is called *hedging*. Although futures are not the only means for hedging, they are the most widely used instruments. Futures represent everything from agricultural products to energy. As mentioned in the Introduction, currency futures made their appearance in 1972. These were the first financial futures. Since that time, other financial contracts include U.S. Treasury instruments, derivative interest rate vehicles, and stock indices.

The popularity of futures is substantially derived from the extremely high leverage routinely available. It is not unusual for margins to be as low as 1 percent of the total contract value. In general, initial margin ranges from 1 to 10 percent. During particularly volatile times, exchanges may raise margin as high as 25 percent or even 100 percent. In 2001, the New York Mercantile Exchange (NYMEX) increased the palladium margin above 100 percent to prevent a possible price manipulation as prices soared over $1,000 per ounce. For a brief moment, palladium became the most valuable precious metal traded on any commodity exchange.

Futures Margins

Margin for futures contracts is not the same as margin for stocks or other investments. In fact, three types of futures margins exist: the initial margin, maintenance margin, and variation margin. Initial margin is actually a good faith deposit that binds the futures contract as a legal instrument. Lawyers and most business people are familiar with the concept of consideration. In order to validate a contract, there must be consideration by all parties. The most common form of consideration is monetary, although it can be an action. With futures, buyers and sellers post margin with their brokers to, in effect, prove the existence of the agreement—the futures contract. Thus, no interest is charged on the leveraged portion of the contract since margin is not a loan as it is with stocks.

As a first line of protection against default, the broker will add or subtract the amount of money associated with each session's price fluctuation—for example, from the open to the close of one trading day. Assume that you are a buyer of one euro currency contract. The amount of the contract is 125,000 euros. As of January 2002, the initial margin was approximately $2,500. I say approximately because brokerage firms have the option of charging in excess of minimum exchange margin that is established by the exchange—in this instance, the International Monetary Market division of the Chicago Mercantile Exchange. As we can calculate, initial margin is about 2 percent.

Each 1-point fluctuation has a value of $12.50. If the price rises by 10 points, you would gain $125.00. Unlike stocks, this is not a paper gain. It is an actual transfer of $125.00 into your account. The change in contract value is called variation margin because it relates to the contract's variation in value. However, if the value declined by 10 points, $125.00 would be subtracted from your account and transferred to a trader who was short— someone who had sold the contract to you.

If the position goes against you by a certain amount, it reaches the maintenance margin level. As with other margined investments, when this level is reached, you are asked to remargin your position to its initial margin. If your account has funds in excess of margin, you will not receive a margin call. The brokerage firm simply margins up from your spare cash. If your total account balance is deficient, you will be requested to send more money.

This margin process is one of the most significant distinctions between futures and stocks. Futures markets do not have paper gains or losses. All differences between your initial position and the close of business is marked to the market and charged or credited to your account. Thus, all gains and losses are actual. For example, if you were long (a buyer) December euro currency and the market moved up from your entry price, your brokerage firm would deposit the difference into your account. You could use that money to buy new positions or even request a check. The money is immediately yours. As most of us are aware, a gain in stock value is only a paper gain unless and until the position is liquidated. Although you may be able to borrow money based on your stock's face value, the amount is always a percentage of face value and the money must be returned with interest.

As we have painfully learned from the Great Depression and a string of bear markets since, stock values can become overinflated. This means that the paper gains are excessive compared with the average liquidations. As more individuals seek to liquidate, there are no buyers to take their place and values collapse. Although this same process can occur in futures markets, the degree of the implosion is limited by the amount in the market. As we know, for every position, there is an initial margin and the daily exchange of cash. Panics are rare. To further regulate orderly markets, exchanges impose a maximum amount certain contracts can move in any single session. From experience, we know that stampedes are often stopped once we have had a time to back away and examine the situation.

Long and Short Positions in the Futures Market

Futures can take advantage of price moves in either direction with equal facility. This is true for all currency forums. Many investors have difficulty grasping the process of selling short in the futures markets because it is, once again, not the same as selling stocks short. In the stock market, a short seller actually borrows the shares from the house or broker to sell. As some stage, the short seller of stock must purchase shares to return to the one who lent to them. With futures, you simply sell a contract that is a promise to deliver the underlying instrument (in our case, currencies) upon expiration. Nothing is borrowed. Most people ask, "How can I sell something I don't have?" This query comes from a lack of separation between the actual commodity and the futures contract to deliver the commodity.

A good analogy is a building contractor who enters into an agreement to build a house for a particular price. A smart contractor figures the basic labor and materials, interest on work in progress if applicable, and some margin for price fluctuations to derive a price. When he signs the contract to build the house, he has sold something he doesn't have. It is like selling short one house. Following the transaction further, the contractor stands to make more money than anticipated if the price of labor and materials declines while he is building. Alternatively, he could make less or actually lose money if the prices rise before completion. This is exactly the case in futures markets.

Order Types and Their Rules

A new purchase establishes a *long* position. A new sale creates a *short* position. The liquidation of a long position is called *closing long*. The liquidation of a short position is called *covering short*. As we can see, the language is easy. Techno-speak is minimized. Like other investment vehicles, futures have various order types, such as stop orders, limit orders, one-cancels-other (OCO) orders, good-'til-canceled orders (GTC), market-on-open orders (MOO), and market-on-close orders (MOC). Some orders such as MOC are not accepted by all exchanges. In addition, some electronic markets do not accept open stops. Rules on order types and placements change. Therefore, it is wise to consult your broker about the latest rules and orders available for those markets you intend to trade.

As of 2002, U.S.-based currency futures were primarily traded on the International Monetary Market (IMM) with the exception of the U.S. Dollar Index traded on the FINEX division of the New York Board of Trade (NYBOT). In addition, the Chicago Mercantile Exchange established GLOBEX2 electronic trading as a side-by-side market in the spring of 2001. The GLOBEX2 sessions run from 4:00 A.M. to 4:00 P.M. Monday through Thursday and terminate Fridays. Sessions resume for weekend hours to provide nearly round-the-clock access throughout the entire week. The implementation of side-by-side trading demonstrates the incredible dynamics of these exciting markets. As we know, the world operates 24×7, meaning all day, everyday. In particular, currencies represent a continuous market that is being traded in every time zone.

Rules for trading are different between GLOBEX2 and the regular session. The most significant difference is that GLOBEX2 only accepts limit stop orders. You cannot use market-if-touched (MIT), market-on-close (MOC), or market-on-open (MOO) orders. The electronic contracts also have price-banding limits that prevent someone from entering buy or sell orders in excess of predetermined amounts. This shadows the open outcry session conducted in the traditional manner on the exchange floor.

It is important to note that rules, regulations, and trading mechanisms can change. Therefore, listing the price bands or even the specific contracts that are available might be rendered obsolete. I hesitated to even provide trading hours and expiration schedules for fear that they could be altered after readers acquired this text. It is extremely important to continuously check with your broker or the exchange Web sites to confirm trading specifications. For example, after the September 11th terrorist attacks on the World Trade Center, trading was halted in New York markets and temporary facilities had to be activated. When the NYBOT and NYMEX reopened, trading hours were shortened. Even the commodity exchanges where you intend to trade can change or consolidate. The NYMEX merged with the Commodity Exchange (COMEX) to bring together all the precious and base metals under one entity. It is also essential to know that currency futures are also traded on foreign futures exchanges.

The Popularity of Futures

Futures and related options have become increasingly popular among individual traders because they are considered easier to use. Since their inception in 1972, currency futures have always been accessible to the general public, whereas Interbank trading required substantial capital and creditworthiness. Thus, futures and their options have emerged as the common man's popular trading vehicle. This does not mean large sophisticated traders do not use futures. To the contrary, futures are a valuable and extraordinary adjunct to cash trading. As touched on earlier, whenever the same commodity or currency is traded in different market forums, an arbitrage opportunity arises. Indeed, some traders in the FINEX U.S. Dollar Index contract actually construct the index using the basket of currencies to make a market. This presents them with an arbitrage while simultaneously adding liquidity to the market.

Unlike cash markets, U.S. currency futures are all priced in dollars. This eliminates some of the confusion over inverting values. However, converting futures into cash pricing is relatively easy. As we know, it is simply the reciprocal. Even when the currency is priced to the dollar, the contract value is always derived in dollars. For example, Figure 6.5 illustrates the yen for June 2002 expiration. The closing price on April 22, 2002 for the contract was 0.7722 dollars to yen. The cash market equivalent is 1/0.7722 or 1.29500 yen to dollars.

However, currency futures traded on non-U.S. exchanges are priced in the foreign currency of the local exchange. All profits or losses are posted in the currency of origin. This requires special attention to detail if you decide to trade in these forums. In particular, a U.S. investor must monitor the transaction profit or loss while simultaneously watching dollar parity for the local currency. Remember that any time you are trading in a foreign currency, you have exchange rate risk against your own currency. Thus, trades marked to the sterling may appear profitable. However, should the sterling decline against the dollar, the profit realized on a cross of sterling and euros could evaporate against dollars.

In reality, futures markets offer the simplest approach for most investors. They are easily accessible, have the broadest brokerage house participation (as of this writing), are highly regulated, and are protected by multiple guarantees. There is rarely confusion over the price direction since all contracts are expressed in dollars. Of course, this is a dollar-centric view under the assumption most readers are participating in the U.S. markets.

A clear disadvantage of futures is their narrow scope. Don't expect to speculate in wild gyrations of the Bangladesh taka. You cannot trade the Angola kwanza or Chinese yuan as of this writing. Even the venerable western European currencies like the deutsche mark, Swiss franc, and French franc have consolidated into the euro. This limits the trading scope to relatively few but active currencies. Despite this limitation, the frequency of large parity shifts should be more than sufficient for the most enthusiastic participant.

Futures versus Spot and Forward Markets

Consider the combinations and permutations of the few actively traded futures relative to cash spot and forward markets. As a matrix of bids and asks are displayed in the spot and forward markets, futures offer a simultaneous quote. Any difference between these markets can represent instant profit for the skilled and nimble. Most currency futures expire on the quarters: March, June, September, and December. Delivery as cash takes place on the third Wednesday for each of these months. This schedule can remain consistent because no federal holidays fall within this timeframe. Exceptions include the Mexican peso, the Brazilian real, and the South African rand, which all trade in consecutive months with the same expiration schedule. Keep in mind that contract specifications can be changed by the exchanges. It is important to check with your broker or the exchange to make sure your information is up to date. The expirations described provide approximate 90- and 30-day spacing for arbitraging against the forward cash quotes. For example, you may see a 10-pip spread between the 3-month forward sterling and futures. Depending on transaction costs, this could be sufficient for an arbitrage.

You may notice that the spot euro is unusually low relative to futures 60 days out. After a quick calculation, you find that the interest cost is less than the differential. You quickly buy spot euros and sell futures to lock in the spread. Naturally, your credit is impeccable so you borrow to pay for your euros. When the contract expires, you deliver the spot euros and collect the spread that is less than the interest you paid to borrow the money. Paying back the loan completes the transaction. The intricacies of the delivery process are available from the exchange. As with the cash market, delivery is posted through the SWIFT system and the foreign agent bank transfers funds to the buyer's account. In essence, futures become cash on delivery.

This euro/dollar strategy works because futures are highly leveraged. Remember, you do not pay interest on the full futures contract value. Margin is a good faith deposit that binds the contract. Things become more exciting when dealing on margined cash positions. If you only borrow a portion of the cash requirement, your profit potential expands. Professional traders are continuously seeking differentials to lock in profits. In fact, computer programs scan for these opportunities and automatically execute trades when the calculations reveal an opportunity.

Calulating Spread in Futures

Although I implied futures do not have appreciable technospeak, you may encounter words such as *basis, contango,* and *backwardation.* Basis refers to the difference between the futures and spot prices. In the case of currencies, there is also a basis between futures and forward cash. The difference between futures contracts, for example, March and June, is the spread. For currencies, the spread is progressively positive to reflect a positive cost of money (interest rate) associated with the time between contract expirations when the contract is quoted in dollar parity. When I was young, this was called a *normal market.* Unfortunately, the term normal market was just too normal, so traders decided to label a progressively positive spread a *contango market.* If it sounds like a dance, sometimes it is!

The opposite condition would be a progressively negative spread. This would mean March would be higher than June, which would be higher than September. Again, this condition used to be called an *inverted market* because the normal condition of progressively higher months was, indeed, inverted. This wasn't a sophisticated enough description. Traders decided to call such circumstances a *backwardation.* Frankly, I preferred the old terms since they were readily understandable. Then again, I remember when *like* meant "similar to" or "to be fond of." My children and their friends believe *like* is the universal descriptor—"like, ya' know?"

To illustrate the relationship, consider the following spreads in yen:

(Note: The decimal point has been removed for convenience.)

June @ 7718
September @ 7759
December @ 7810

September − June = 7759 − 7718 = 41
41/7718 = 90-day interest rate spread = .005312257
.005312257/90 days × 365 days =
.021544 implied annualized interest = 2.15%

December − June = 7810 − 7759 = 51
51/7759 = 90-day interest rate spread = .006573011
.006573011/90 days × 365 =
.026657 implied annualized interest = 2.67%

Please understand that this is a simplified example that assumes an exact 90-day interval between the expirations. As mentioned previously, contracts expire on the third Wednesday of the month. Therefore, you must count the exact number of days between expirations to use as the divisor. The formula expression would be:

E = Expiration date
P = Price
I = Annualized interest
D = Days (between expirations)

Subscripts denote near and far contracts and related prices:

$$E_2 - E_1 = D$$
$$(P_2 - P_1/P_1)/D \times 365 = I.$$

Checking the London Interbank Offering Rate (LIBOR), we see that these rates are likely to be derived from this interest rate benchmark. Other standards are Fed funds and the eurodollar rate. We discover that the efficacy of any spread transaction is highly dependent on the rate available to the trader. Is it pegged to LIBOR, T-Bills, eurodollars, or Fed funds? A point in yen futures equals $12.50. If transaction costs are $20.00, a 2-point profit is required to cover costs. Unless the transaction is very large, the amounts may seem unremarkable. When a high degree of confidence exists and the amounts are large, spreads make dollars and sense.

Keep in mind that the variable for days can be used to calculate the implied interest spread between cash and futures. As with the cash formula, the relative interest rate of the foreign currency should also be considered. In futures, each position of a spread is referred to as a *leg*. The difference between the futures formula and cash is the fact that you are always dealing from the dollar side. The pound, however, is quoted as pounds to dollars as is the euro. Since the contract is still priced in dollars (in other words, your profit and loss is marked to dollars), you only need to be aware of the interest rate translation.

The concept of trading against an implied interest rate is neither new nor unique to currencies. The strategy was formulated for precious metals before interest rate contracts existed. To clarify the logic, consider a physical commodity such as gold. Gold futures are the same as currency futures. Unlike agricultural futures, gold is not seasonally related to a crop year. This means that spreads are a function of carrying costs. Holding gold implies several costs that include insurance, storage, assay, and the opportunity rate of return. Discounting storage, assay, and insurance, the bulk of the spread between contracts is interest. If August gold climbed in excess of the costs implied between the August and June expirations, you could buy June, take delivery, pay the storage, insurance, and assay, and collect the difference. In other words, you would earn the implied interest. The objective would be to have an implied interest that exceeds your actual cost of funds for the carrying period. If you left the gold in the approved depository, you would have no assay fee, further reducing your expenses.

Market Access and Open Interest in Futures

Currency futures have distinct symbols that differentiate them from the ISO abbreviations used in cash markets. Electronic markets have distinct symbols, too. However, the electronic market is fully fungible with open outcry positions. This means that a trade in GLOBEX2 euros can be offset in open outcry, and vice versa. They are truly side-by-side forums.

Market access has been a significant issue for FOREX trading. The advent of electronic trading has brought new systems for order entry and execution. However, a trader must be a member of the exchange to obtain a GLOBEX2 workstation or handheld trading device. Secondary interfaces to GLOBEX2 are available that permit a *straight pipe*. This suggests that a trader can gain access to the workstation itself. The exchange is not interested in diluting its dominance or membership value. Thus, it behooves the exchange to construct an advantageous layer of market access for seat holders. Still, opportunities for the general public abound. Workstations are allocated to product pools or groups of member traders who are making markets in the product. Where there is more than one market maker, there is more than one bid and ask.

We often hear the paranoid cry, "They picked off my stop!" This ethereal "they" is a subject of great debate. It conjures up an image of conspiracy whereby market makers dealing in hundreds, if not thousands, of transactions are focused on individual one-lot or two-lot trades. If you witness the frenzy of primary trading and market making, it is unlikely you will be able to identify a concerted effort to pick off stops by "they." In short, "they" do not exist.

However, "they" are aware that many speculators use popular moving averages to establish support or resistance objectives for protective stop placement. Under such circumstances, powerful interests can seek to drive prices toward known stop levels, for example, a 20- or 10-day moving average. However, even "they" cannot drive a market very far. If the average were more than a few pips away from the current bid/ask, it would be mighty expensive and risky to attempt a manipulation.

A common term used among traders and regulators is *market transparency*. This refers to the ability to clearly see how the markets operate from one end of the transaction to the other. For example, a nonmember without a GLOBEX2 workstation is unable to directly see that level of the trading process. Although the bid/ask is posted, membership has clear advantages. Transparency also refers to market scope. We hear about market breadth that generally describes participation. For stocks, breadth is measured by volume. Unfortunately, volume does not tell a transparent story because we do not know who is buying or selling. Although public companies do report insider trading, they do not report large block trading that may have technical or fundamental market implications. Also, the issued number of stock shares remains constant (absent new issuance or splits). Logically, for every share sold, one must be bought—it is a *zero sum*.

Futures and related options have the unique characteristic of having *open interest* in addition to price and volume. Open interest represents the total number of contracts existing between buyers and sellers. On the very first trading day, open interest always begins at zero. When a seller, John, and a buyer, Henry, come into the market and consummate a single transaction, the volume is one and the open interest is one. (See Figure 6.12.) Obviously, these are the first participants. It always requires two parties to trade. If they transacted two contracts, the volume would be two and the open interest would be two. Things get slightly confusing for those unfamiliar with futures when a third participant enters the arena.

Suppose Mary decides she wants to buy and Henry wants to sell the contract he bought from John? Mary puts in her bid while Henry makes his offer. If they match, Henry sells his contract to Mary. What is the volume? As with stocks, the volume is two: one trade between John and Henry, and a second between Henry and Mary. What is the open interest? A frequent mistake is to assume the open interest is also two. However, the same contract existing between John and Henry now exists between John and Mary. Thus, the open interest remains one. See Figure 6.13.

As we will see, this variability in open interest provides additional insight into accumulation and distribution patterns. When trading stocks and bonds, an accumulation means ownership is moving from weaker hands to stronger hands on increasing volume and price. It is always an assumption that the weak

John •———————————————➤ Henry

Figure 6.12   Single transaction.

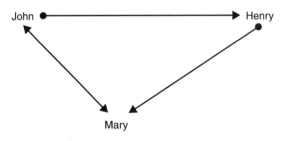

Figure 6.13   Three participants.

are feeding the strong, but this is not always the case. A distribution takes place when the strong sell to the weak on declining prices and increasing volume. Again, we really have no way to identify the sellers and buyers until after the fact. In all cases, the same amount of stock is available at all times. Even short selling is offset by borrowed stock.

In contrast, an accumulation in futures or related options can take place when prices are rising or falling as can a distribution. For example, the September Mexican peso contract may accumulate a 2,000 open interest on increasing volume and rising prices. This would be identified as a long-side accumulation because the actual number of positions is rising. Recall that every futures position must post initial margin on both sides: buyer and seller. As open interest increases, the amount of margin that accumulates in the September peso also increases. However, if the price is rising and the open interest is declining, we are seeing a distribution because the initial margin, plus or minus any variation margin, is distributed back to buyers and sellers.

By the same token, prices could be falling while open interest and volume are rising. Here, there is a *short-side accumulation*. Margin is accumulating, while sellers initiate new commitments at decreasing prices. Again, should the open interest decline as prices fall, a distribution of margin would be sent back to the participants. This plays heavily in technical analysis where open interest variation actually defines the amount of money deposited with the brokerage firms for the specific futures contract. Open interest adds to technical transparency because it enables analysts/traders to measure true accumulation and distribution. Regardless of how many times a potential manipulator wants to push the market, you always see the net cash accumulation or distribution. This is not the case in cash markets. Estimates for a daily transaction value that is likened to open interest are available, but it is not as precise.

As cash and futures become more progressively integrated, open interest changes will reflect sentiment among all market participants. This is a statistical phenomenon associated with sampling. Futures represent a fraction of daily currency transaction value much the way sampling 1 piece from a 10,000-piece batch is a very small percentage. However, the representation is sufficient to provide a statistically accurate view of the overall market just as the 1 in 10,000 sample may suffice for quality control. Most of us are familiar with this process during election coverage when television commentators use exit polls to determine prospective winners in each state. No statistical measurement is without its flaws as we saw during the Bush/Gore presidential contest. It is fair to say that statistical estimates usually work.

Options

Now that we have covered cash spot, cash forwards, and futures, we can examine options. Approximately 5 to 7 percent of all currency trading is transacted in cash and futures options. An option is the right, but not the obligation to make or take delivery of a specific currency at a designated price on or before expiration. As such, options have four components:

- **Premium**   The price paid for the option
- **Strike price** The price at which the option may be exercised
- **Expiration** The date when the option right expires
- **Instrument** The underlying futures contract or cash position on which the option is based

The significant difference between options and underlying futures is the premium associated with the right to buy or sell. Two option types are available. The right to buy is a *call*. The right to sell is a *put*. Most investors are familiar with these terms even if they do not fully understand how options operate.

A futures contract is a contractual obligation to make or take delivery of the commodity—in our case, currency. When the futures expire, the buyer must pay the execution price and the seller must accept that price. If the contract declined to zero, the buyer would lose 100 percent of the total contract value. In the case of currencies, the contracts can be valued in $125,000 and $100,000 increments. The yen is 12.5 million and the pound is 62,500. Each contract represents a fixed currency amount that varies relative to the dollar on U.S. exchanges. The same holds true for foreign currency futures. Depending on the execution price, the exposure can be significant when considering that the margins may be less than $2,000 per position. If the price doubled, a short seller could lose the same. A decline to zero or a doubling is not likely to take place within the life of a contract, but these are theoretical exposures. Options have fixed premiums upon execution. Although the premium value varies in accordance with the underlying futures or cash price, a buyer can only lose to the extent of his or her premium and no more. Thus, a buyer's exposure is limited to the premium. If the option expires without the futures or cash reaching the strike price, it becomes worthless and all premium is lost plus the transaction cost.

A seller gives the right to buy or sell at the strike. Thus, a call seller has unlimited exposure should the futures or cash exceed the strike while a put seller suffers the same fate up to the full contract value if futures plunge below the strike. However, the seller collects the premium from the buyer. If the strike is not achieved on or before expiration, the seller pockets the premium. Selling options is also called *writing* options. The terms are interchangeable. A typical trade might be to sell a June 2002 yen 810 call at 20. This translates to the following: selling the right to buy the June 2002 Japanese yen futures at .8100 for a .0020 premium. For simplicity I will refer to options on futures.

In futures, each point is called a *tick* as it is in many investment vehicles. Efficiency dictates dropping the decimal point and dealing as though there were whole numbers. Be careful. This does not apply to all futures. For example, Treasury instruments are quoted in 32nds, 64ths, and 128ths. There are even one-halves of the fraction. Fortunately, currency futures remain base 10.

Since the yen contract is 12.5 million, every tick has a variation value of $12.50. Thus, the 810 call has a premium of $12.50 —20 or $250.00. The missing number is the futures price on which the premium is based. In this example, the price was .7795 at the time the .0020 premium was offered. This means that the buyer of the option must see the price exceed .8120 before a profit can accrue at expiration. The key phrase is "at expiration." Option premium is derived from four variables: the underlying futures price, the proximity of the strike, the time remaining before expiration, and the volatility of the futures. All of these components represent probability parameters. The seller prices the option in accordance with the chance that the strike will be reached before expiration. The buyer is making the same assessment. This adds a level of complexity since pricing tends to be indirect.

The Structure of Options

Before moving forward, it is wise to take a step back and fully investigate structural differences between options and futures or, for that matter, cash. You are very likely to hear the claim that options have limited risk. This selling point is bantered about with little consideration for the true meaning. It is complete and utter bunk! As explained previously, option buyers can only lose the amount of their premium and no more. This does not limit risk. It simply fixes the exposure. For clarification, suppose the probability of success is zero. If there is no chance the option will ever reach the strike, risk is 100 percent. This means you are positively sure to lose your entire premium when the option expires. Risk is a function of probability, whereas exposure is a function of amount.

Another illustration would be betting on the flip of a fair coin. We are all aware that the chance of heads versus tails is 50/50. Over a sufficient number of flips, we expect to break even. On any given flip, I might offer to bet you a dime. Would you take the bet? For the sake of a good time, your answer might be yes. Suppose I were to increase the bet to $1 million. Would you still take the bet? A prudent man or woman would probably walk away. However, the chance of winning or losing, that is, the risk, is exactly the same for the 10¢ bet as it is for the $1 million. The only difference is the exposure. The same is true with options.

This concept is extremely important because options are frequently pitched as great opportunities with limited risk. Often, the concept sounds good. You are being asked to buy an option. Since the majority of investors are accustomed to buying investments, the more popular sales are call options—the right to buy. The farther the option strike is away from the market, the cheaper the option. This is because the probability of achieving such an objective diminishes as the distance from the current price increases. When a strike price is very far away from the current price, it is called *deep out of the money* (DOMO). When a strike is achieved, it is said to be *in the money*. Of course, if the strike is substantially exceeded, your option is deep in the money.

Most options expire worthless. This is to say that the strike is not achieved by the time the options expire. However, those options that have a high probability of success are usually priced to account for this possibility. On less frequent occasions, a DOMO option makes its strike. However, this is only part of the battle. To be reasonably profitable, the option must exceed the strike by more than the premium on an expiration basis.

Risk Aversion with Options

The key to profiting is often a hit-and-run strategy if you are an option buyer. This means that you take profits before the option expires. For example, you may have a euro call expiring in December that calls for a .9200 strike when the current price in August is .8766. If the price moves to .9050, your call will appreciate because the probability of achieving .9200 is enhanced. Since option prices are based on the current price, time to expiration, and volatility, you can gain value as long as the price appreciation offsets any loss in the time value.

This suggests that risk is a function of these components (that is, time, volatility, and strike price). It is foolish to buy DOMOs because the risk is very high while the exposure is low. No matter how little you lose, you still lose! The concept brings up another element of risk that is almost always ignored. Each individual has a particular risk aversion profile that is somewhat unique to his or her personality. This is best explained with the example of two people who are invited to go parachute jumping. To one person, the thrill of free falling is worth the risk that the parachute may not open. For the other, the thrill is inconsequential compared to the consequence of death should the parachute fail. Each has a different risk aversion profile. The same is true for investing. For some, the thrill of reeling in a huge profit by risking a small fortune is the challenge and enjoyment. For others, the purpose is to avoid the thrill in favor of steady and reasonably assured returns.

However, we should not be fooled by the risk aversion concept or the seemingly logical explanation of risk versus exposure. Human emotions are far from linear and rational. This is illustrated by the rapid increase in lottery ticket sales as the jackpot climbs. Statistics dictate that the same combination of numbers exists at all times. The Big Game exhibits 1 to 76 million odds. Thus, the combination of numbers is fixed. However, the exposure to profit changes to breach the threshold of buyer resistance. Would you buy a lottery ticket for $1 if the jackpot were $100? Most say no. But at $100 million, most say yes. Thus, risk aversion works both ways.

For options, would you risk $200 to make $5,000 when your odds are 100 to 1? It is a paramount question because too many salespeople leave out the most important transaction characteristic—the odds. All we tend to hear, and therefore evaluate, is whether you would risk $200 to make $5,000. As we can see, an affirmative response is more easily cajoled from unwary investors when odds are conspicuously missing.

Option Pricing Using the Black-Scholes Model

The dynamic between time, volatility, and proximity is more clearly depicted in Figure 6.14, which plots the June 2002 euro against the related .9200 call option. It is immediately apparent that as the futures price was rising, the call value was sinking. This is because the probability of reaching .9200 from the February lows below .8550 decreased with time. Notice the futures price has a shallow slope that reduces the chance of the needed gain within the required period. Only after the price slope

CECM029200

ECM02 O:0.89860 H:0.89870 L:0.89800 0.89800 -0.00100

Figure 6.14   June 2002 euro .9200 call versus euro futures.

dramatically increases do we see a commensurate rise in the option value. This relationship between changes in futures prices relative to the option is called *delta* and is signified by the Greek character Δ. Delta is a volatility measurement that also provides insight into the most anticipated price movement. Extreme futures price volatility translates into a higher chance the strike can be achieved. This shows up in the change in option premium.

Relationships between option premiums and the components of time, proximity, and volatility are usually logical. This is to say that we can deduce the potential rise in premium value based on observing the futures price movements. In the early 1970s, Fischer Black and Myron Scholes derived the famous Black-Scholes model for option pricing. The model is based on relationships between stocks and their options and established the foundation for modern hedge fund strategy. In their model, delta measures the reactivity an option has to small changes in share value. Black-Scholes presents a rather complex and tedious explanation for option pricing that is based on several assumptions that are not necessarily true for futures and, in particular, currencies. Recall that we mentioned Efficient Market Theory. This is one of the many assumptions used in creating Black-Scholes.

The actual formulas are not as important to the average investor as the principles. For example, *gamma* is a derivative of delta and measures the sensitivity of delta to changes in share price. *Theta* is used to determine the premium's sensitivity to proximity. *Vega* calculates the premium's sensitivity to changes in volatility. All of these combine into a total option pricing mechanism. Premium is assumed to have a maximum value, intrinsic value, speculative value, and actual value reflected by the price.

Any application of Black-Scholes to futures must take into consideration that the model is based on stocks that are assumed to be held long—bought. The initial purpose was to derive a riskless portfolio by selling calls against underlying stock to the degree where the stock's potential downward movement would be matched by the premium deterioration. For currency traders, options go considerably beyond formulating riskless positions. Since futures can be bought and sold with equal alacrity, options can be written against calls and puts with the same ease. This presents combinations of futures, calls, and puts that can be exceptionally complex and intriguing. For example, consider the pound in Figure 6.15 where the price ranged between 1.4100 and 1.4600 from November 2001 through April 2002. With 20/20 hindsight, we know that a potential strategy would have been to sell the 1.410 puts and 1.460 calls. Pound options drop the last digit because they are traded in even 100-point increments. Figure 6.16 plots the June 1.480 pound option that expired in May 2002. In January and February, this option yielded approximately 62 points. The premium deteriorated with time and the decline in futures. However, before expiration, June futures reached toward the 1.480 strike.

One characteristic of options is that they tend to move less than the underlying instrument. This is to say the delta as a ratio is less than one until the option goes into the money. Once beyond the strike, the option is worth the same as the underlying instrument because it can be exercised for a point-to-point value. Of course, the time and volatility components are diminished. Figure 6.16 shows the June pound 1.480 call option,

BPY O:1.4642 H:1.4683 L:1.4642 1.4677 +0.0055 MovS=1.4480 MovS=1.4371

Figure 6.15   British pound cash from 2001 to 2002.

whereas Figure 6.17 graphs the June pound 1.410 put option with an approximate 75-point premium in April 2002. Under the assumption June futures would remain within that 1.410 to 1.460 trading band, a speculator might have sold the 1.480 call and 1.4100 put for a combined 130 points, giving some margin for slippage. One thing is certain. Only one of the options can expire in the money, while the other must expire worthless. This transaction is called a *short strangle* because you are boxing, or strangling, the assumed range.

Buying and Selling Options

Speculators are predominantly option buyers—they are long. Professional traders tend to sell options and collect premiums. It has been said that options only achieve the strike price about 20

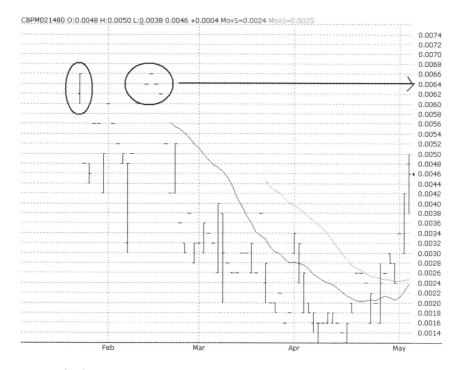

CBPM021480 O:0.0048 H:0.0050 L:0.0038 0.0046 +0.0004 MovS=0.0024 MovS=0.0025

Figure 6.16 June 2002 British pound 1.480 call.

percent of the time. Thus, 8 out of 10 options expire worthless. These statistics suggest that we would all be wise to sell rather than buy. However, selling options carry that extra risk of unlimited exposure.

Options offer a variety of strategic advantages because they can be combined with futures and cash markets to develop extremely creative profit potentials. As mentioned, proximity determines a portion of the premium value. The closer an option strike is to the current price, the more premium it commands. This means a trader can sell near options while buying far options for a credit and hopefully a profit. Depending on the strikes, the trade can be relatively risk free because the amount of premium collected exceeds the exposure between the near and far strikes. The far strike covers the near strike if it goes into the money. These are *combination trades* that represent extremely interesting and profitable approaches if you identify opportunities in time.

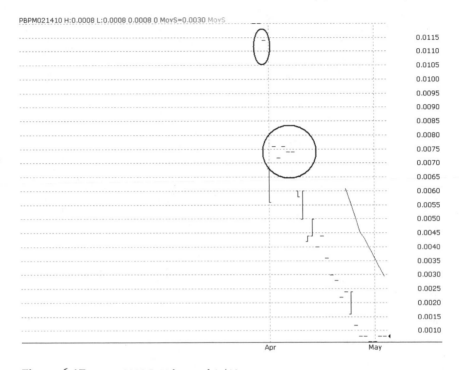

PBPM021410 H:0.0008 L:0.0008 0.0008 0 MovS=0.0030 MovS

0.0115
0.0110
0.0105
0.0100
0.0095
0.0090
0.0085
0.0080
0.0075
0.0070
0.0065
0.0060
0.0055
0.0050
0.0045
0.0040
0.0035
0.0030
0.0025
0.0020
0.0015
0.0010

Apr   May

Figure 6.17   June 2002 British pound 1.410 put.

Understand that the combination can work for puts as well as calls. This expands the combinations that can be placed to achieve credit trades. Assuming the underlying currency does not move beyond the first strike or strikes, the credit becomes a realized profit. To make transactions more complex, you can add futures and sell covered combinations. This involves selling a near call against a long position while buying a far call as a way to reestablish a long position if there is a breakout. Obviously, a similar strategy works for puts.

You are likely to hear the terms *synthetic long* or *synthetic short*. These expressions refer to put and call combinations that favor the long or short side. In effect, the position creates a long position without actually being long in the futures or cash markets. Synthetic options are also available that rely on futures positions that cancel exposure when certain objectives are reached. These objectives are similar in function to an option strike.

Many books and articles have been written about trading options that go beyond the basic descriptions in this text. The important consideration is to become familiar with the different methods of participating in currency trends through different markets. Each trading forum has advantages and disadvantages. Each individual investor must decide which markets and strategies are right for his or her available time, money, and profit objectives. As we know, trendsetting news materializes in an instant. Successful currency trading requires time and careful monitoring. It can be a hobby, but you had better be a serious hobbyist!

By 2000, markets were expanding at a geometric rate. This is to say that certain market geometry was growing while other lines and angles were not. Overall, the complexion dramatically changed with the introduction of the euro and the consolidation of western European markets. This daunting transition was accomplished without a hitch. Despite new global unrest and political uncertainty, populations of western Europe were able to accept their new currency without major incident.

These monumental monetary alterations are not unique and should be expected from time to time. Such was the case when the world abandoned the gold standard. Such would be the case if the standard were readopted. Electronic trading in Interbank cash and forwards was not accessible to small traders. Today, amounts as low as $5,000 can participate. The world is opening up to the average individual and the profit potentials have grown enormously. The critical component is simply being prepared.

Chapter 7

PRACTICAL TRADING STRATEGIES

All trading strategies consist of three components:

- A forecast
- A decision
- Money management

Often, we hear that strategies are either technical or fundamental. However, this only refers to the method for predicting market direction and perhaps magnitude. Whether you employ technical timing or fundamental analysis, the objective is to forecast the market's most likely direction. As mentioned in the previous chapter, an option seller might also want to predict a market's lack of direction within a particular timeframe.

Three infamous phrases are heard in the currency markets and, for that matter, all investment markets. "I should have. I would have. I could have." The implication of these three remarks is that the speaker had previous knowledge of what was going to occur, but failed to act. For example, one day Harry came into the bar boasting that he had guessed the winning lottery number. Joe asked, "So how much did ya win?" Harry replied, "Nothing! I forgot to buy a ticket."

Even the best forecasting algorithm is useless without a set of effective and consistent decision rules. In other words:

Based on forecast X, take action Y.

I bring this up because of its simplicity and lack of application. Too often, we spend enormous time trying to perfect a forecasting technique. If it is technical, we are likely to use historical data and computer programs to back test the forecast and perfect its accuracy. What we fail to do is spend the same effort on developing consistent decision rules. Many are familiar with the simple moving average. It is a method of smoothing a series of numbers by adding an interval and dividing by the interval value. A 10-day simple moving average would add 10 consecutive closing prices and divide by 10. The average moves forward because you are always adding the current day while dropping the previous tenth day.

The Moving Average Forecasting Tool

We may observe that the Japanese yen tends to continue in the direction of a 10-day moving average crossing. This means that when the closing price breaks out above the 10-day moving average of closing prices, the prices move higher. When the price busts below the average, it continues lower. This can become a simple technical forecasting tool. Alone, it accomplishes nothing. By adding the decision to buy on a breakout and sell on a bust, we have a decision rule. We have satisfied two criteria of a trading strategy. The remaining question deals with exposure and risk.

Three statistical performance measurements are available for any methodology. All too often, we ignore these very important criteria. In countless presentations at investment shows and financial planning sessions, we hear about recent performance and projections without consideration for accuracy, efficiency, and consistency. In fact, we all know about accurate predictions, but few of us ask about the efficiency of capturing profits. We may touch on both and neglect to ask how consistently accurate and efficient an approach has been over a reasonable period and through diverse circumstances. This is one reason why so many investors lost so much after the Nasdaq high-tech bubble burst in 2000. In the entire history of the stock market, no bull market lasts forever. In particular, events such as the wealth evaporation that took place as the new millennium began are well documented as speculative crescendos. In currency markets, this is vitally important.

Accuracy and Efficiency

When we have a forecasting method like our 10-day moving average example, we need to know its accuracy. How many times after the average is crossed by the closing price does the price pursue the same direction? This becomes a tricky question because mathematicians will argue that it occurs 100 percent of the time. This suggests that if the average is crossed, by definition the price moves in the same direction. To solve this dilemma, we also measure the efficiency of the method by tracking how far the market moves after the average is violated to either side. The degree to which we are able to identify and capture a profit, therefore, is an efficiency measurement. Anyone with market experience understands that markets trend or trade within ranges. When a market is trending, a fundamental force is causing value realignment. When a market is relatively stable, supply and demand are in equilibrium. This is true for currencies as for other commodities and financial instruments. A simple moving average often acts as a filter that simply follows a trend up or down with a certain efficiency. In a powerful trend with few corrections, a short moving average will be effective because it will closely follow the rising price and capture a significant amount of the move. If the market is trending but volatile, a longer moving average will be more effective because it will provide sufficient distance to accommodate interim corrections while following the market to an inevitable top or bottom.

Figure 7.1 illustrates the moving average process. As we can see, the average mimics the price while lagging behind. If the distance of the trend is sufficient relative to the moving average, a profit can be realized. The lag between the top of the price trend and the point where the moving average is violated represents

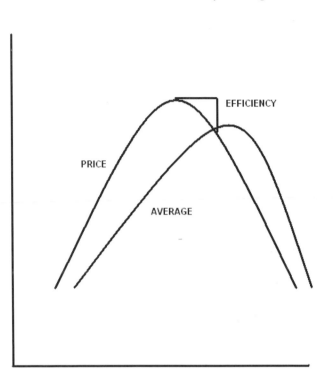

Figure 7.1   Moving average efficiency.

the efficiency and is sometimes referred to as *slippage*. Unfortunately, slippage has several meanings among traders. Therefore,
the term should be used with care. The distance a market moves
from an objective is also called slippage as well as the variation
in execution price received during a trade.

Understandably, a shallow or brief trend may not provide a
profit opportunity because the slippage is too great. Figure 7.2
illustrates a moving average that breaks even because the entry
is the same as the exit. This is either the result of an average that
is too close or a trend that is too shallow. Over time, the basic
moving average filter can provide a reasonable accuracy and efficiency. The key is to balance these two components to avoid
drawing down investment capital to the point of being financially incapacitated. Today's increasingly powerful computers
are able to derive more accurate forecasting tools and efficient
decision rules. This presents the final question: How consistent

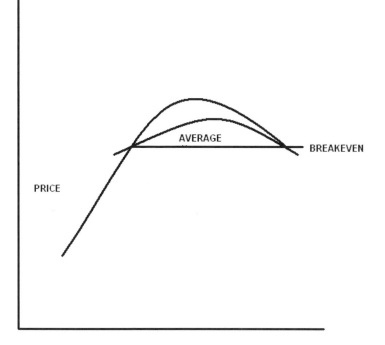

Figure 7.2 Moving average yielding breakeven.

are these two performance criteria? For example, currencies can enter periods of relative stability where parity fluctuations are minimal. If a forecasting method loses its accuracy during such periods or the decision process lacks efficiency, the approach is only effective in particular markets. Thus, the performance will be inconsistent.

Consistency

Consistency is, perhaps, the most important performance measurement because you may never know when a set of forecasting and decision rules is about to fail. However, even a system with a less-than-optimal forecasting ability and lower-than-desirable efficiency can produce comfortable gains if it is highly consistent. Consistency permits traders to plan for known contingencies such as capital drawdowns and potential profit build-ups. I often relate consistency to a life insurance actuary. The objective is to determine the probability that a nonsmoking 40-year-old male will die over the course of a life insurance policy. Can the cash build up sufficiently from all premium contributions to accommodate the entire domain of insured individuals? The question is answered by observing death rates that are translated into probability tables. However, we know that the survival rate has been increasing over the past several decades. Thus, the consistency of actuarial tables has been altered or skewed toward a longer life expectancy.

This analogy serves us well since numerous trading techniques are available that will have specific accuracy, efficiency, and consistency profiles. Each set of parameters implies a different implementation and profitability. Too frequently, we become obsessed with discovering the Holy Grail while incredibly profit-prone trends pass us by. At some stage, commitment is required to realize gains. That is what strategy is all about.

Forecasting Strategies in Up, Down, and Sideways Markets

Having generally reviewed strategic concepts, a more detailed examination breaks down components into more useful tools. This process requires a simplified framework on which more sophisticated applications can stand. For example, only three forecasts are possible—up, down, and sideways. Regardless of how one arrives at such forecasts, decision rules are a permutation of these three potentials in conjunction with available trading vehicles. Thus, a forecast for rising prices may provide the following decisions:

- Buy cash.
- Buy futures.
- Sell puts.
- Buy calls.

These are the obvious actions. Depending on the assumed strength of the move, combinations may be applicable:

- Buy calls and sell puts.
- Buy futures and sell puts.
- Buy futures and use long puts as protection.

Single Trade Strategies

Each strategy carries different expense, risk, and exposure. Buying cash requires cash unless you are dealing with a firm that facilitates margin transactions. Without margin, the strategy relies on the ability to pay for the purchase. Buying futures is, by nature, a leveraged transaction. However, volatility and funding are still considerations. As previously explained, any change in value reflects the full contract size regardless of how small the initial margin may be. Prudent futures trading usually requires stop protection or the use of an option to ensure against an adverse price swing. When trading futures, exposure must be aligned with total account capital to avoid the risk of total equity depletion on the trade.

When you sell puts, you have unlimited exposure if the market climbs above your strike. From a practical standpoint, this exposure is limited because we know prices will never approach infinity. We are not concerned with such extremes. The price can break out above our financial tolerance and wipe out our speculative capital. The put option also requires margin. This transaction has an expense. By the same token, we could buy a call option. Here, our exposure is limited, but the risk that our strike will never be reached is unlimited. A deep out of the money (DOMO) option is very likely to expire worthless. We need to know how frequently such an expiration is likely to take place so that we can extrapolate the amount of capital this approach will require over the long haul to be profitable. You may see the greatest system in the world demonstrated. But for affordability, we would all trade that system!

Combination Trade Strategies

The combination trades that buy a futures contract and a put have a balancing problem. The expense of the put (premium) will impinge on the profit of the futures position. As prices rise, the put premium deteriorates. This means that you must balance the premium expense against the potential futures profit. If the futures fall, you have 1:1 losses in the contract, but fractional profits in the option. Recall that delta is the degree to which the option price responds to futures movement. Delta is less than one until the strike is exceeded. Your protection is partial up until the strike is hit.

If delta is reasonably measured, it is possible to construct a delta-neutral position by using different ratios of futures and options. The problem with delta-neutral strategies is the fact that delta is a moving target. Increasing volatility increases delta, whereas low activity diminishes this reactivity, as we will see in a moment.

There is always the good old futures position with a stop. Here, exposure is the difference between execution (entry) and the stop (exit). It is possible to fix exposure to the extent that volatility remains modest. An extreme bust could plow through the sell stop and cause losses well in excess of expectation. Although the frequency of such price spikes is very low, Murphy's Law dictates that it will happen to you! This is why moderation is so critical. Given the profit potential, it really is not necessary to overexpose your trading capital.

If you are certain the trend is higher, you can buy a combination of futures and call options while selling puts. Many traders question the efficacy of combinations because they believe you go for the highest leverage when there is certainty. As we know, there is no such thing as a sure thing. That axiom aside, combinations make sense when the price of the option is extremely low or the time on the option gives additional staying power. When puts are sold in conjunction with purchasing calls or futures, the premium collected on the puts pays for a portion, if not all of the call.

If the initial futures margin is $2,000 per contract, the maximum number of positions you can place with a $20,000 account is 10. I would not recommend such a leveraged transaction since a very modest move can have an extremely immodest impact on your account balance. Still, such a position would be possible. However, if call premiums were only $200 each, you could purchase 100 calls with the same $20,000. Thus, you have increased your potential participation 10-fold. At the same time, your exposure is limited to the premium, as previously mentioned. The financial aspects of any particular transaction can dictate the strategy that is most effective. Keep in mind that the zero margin only pertains to buying options. This is because exposure is limited. If you decide to sell options, you must post margin. However, the premium you collect adds to the value of your account.

Rolling Positions Up and Down

As primal as it may seem, it is critical to grasp basic transactional relationships. What seems obvious can often be obscure. Anecdotally, I was dealing with a trader who was selling puts on a rising market while enjoying appreciation in long call positions. As the market was rising, he would sell higher put strikes to finance additional calls. I tried to impress on him that he should cover his DOMO puts to reduce exposure, but he did not want to pay the transaction fees. As Murphy's Law implores, prices began to decline. The puts rapidly appreciated while his calls deteriorated. A once profitable strategy turned terribly wrong from a lack of common sense and an understanding of how the positions would respond under changing circumstances.

This brings up the strategy of rolling positions up and down. Unquestionably, a rising market will alter option values. This means that you can construct a window or spread of option strikes that moves up and down with the futures or cash price. Using the rising market example, consider the cash euro in Figure 7.3. From November 2000 through May 2002, the euro fluctuated in a wide trading range between approximately .8400 and .9300. This wide band provided substantial opportunities to sell puts while buying calls and reversing. Monthly expirations gave sufficient diversification over time to limit exposure associated with holding beyond the turning points. Of course, this chart provides 20/20 hindsight. Thus, it serves as an illustration of what might have been achieved. The reality is sometimes sobering. Unless you were able to pick turning points and sustain interim variations, the hypothetical performance implied by the picture is nothing more than looking at desserts behind a

ECY O:0.93160 H:0.93580 L:0.93130 0.93580 +0.00680 MovS=0.88797 MovS=0.89347

Figure 7.3   Euro currency cash from 2000 to 2001.

locked glass display case. To bring the point home, examine
Figure 7.4, which depicts the same contract on a daily basis.

Here, the euro moves up from its .8580 February 2002 base
until encountering .8840 resistance. Rolling up the sale of puts
would have worked, but the call purchases hit a wall until the
eventual breakout. This action translates into an obvious graphic
illustrated in Figure 7.5, which displays the .8950 June 2000 call
(on top) against the .8600 put. At the time the curves take effect,
this was a logical combination for a long-side strategy. The put
fetched approximately .0060, while the call cost fetched 0.00500.
Assuming such an ideal situation, you actually had a credit—the
put sale yielded more premium than the call purchase. Did
Figure 7.4 reveal this likelihood?

Regardless of one's clairvoyance, we see how the dynamic
plays. For the moment, we are simply concerned with the strat-

ECY O:0.93160 H:0.93580 L:0.93130 0.93580 +0.00680 MovS=0.91578 MovS=0.90161

Figure 7.4   Euro currency cash daily prices from 2001 to 2002.

egy under known circumstances. It should be clear that the very dynamic that works in a rising market holds true using opposite positions in a falling market. The U.S. Dollar Index approximates a reciprocal of the euro during the same period. Understand that the U.S. Dollar Index comprises the euro and other currencies including the yen. Although the euro is a heavy component, there can be a variation if the yen chooses a counter-euro trend. Nonetheless, Figure 7.6 shows the June Dollar Index 119 call against the 117 put. Compare the beginning of the curve in June to the actual price chart in Figure 7.7. Notice how the price remained within a 1.1900 to 1.1750 band. Since the options are traded in even strikes, the 119 call and 117 put represent the logical choice. When the price fell below 1.1750, a technical bust would have signaled a definitive strategic move into the long put/short call position.

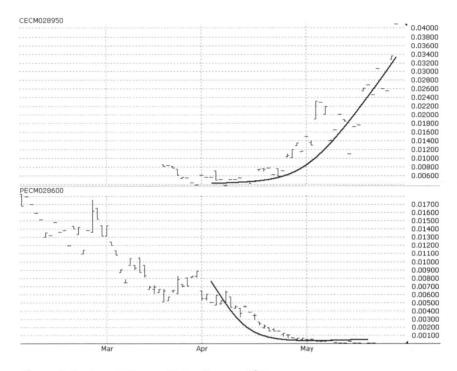

Figure 7.5   June 2000 euro .8950 call versus .8600 put.

Synthetic Transactions

You may encounter the terms *synthetic short* or *synthetic long*. These refer to the use of options to synthesize a net long or short futures position, as described previously. When you buy a call and sell a put, you are essentially long the market. As the call appreciates and the put deteriorates, you defray the cost of the position, but lose the limited exposure represented by simply buying the call. As with an outright futures position, a drop in the price will obliterate the call value while enhancing the put. Your exposure is up to the full amount of the decline beyond the put strike. A pure synthetic buys and sells the same strike. For example, you might buy the U.S. Dollar Index 119 call and sell the 119 put. This makes you long at 119 and a loser below 119.

The purpose of using this strategy as opposed to futures can be twofold. First, you are fixing the cost at your net premium

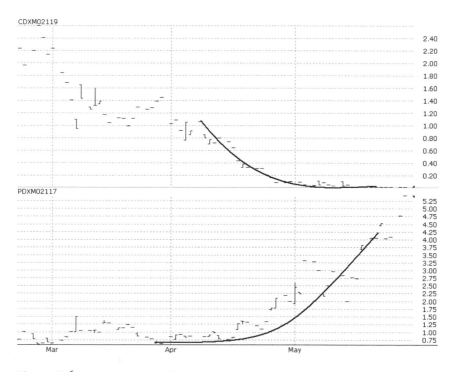

Figure 7.6   June 2002 U.S. Dollar Index 119 call versus 117 put.

plus any commission and margin. If the price is at the strike, your net should be close to or at zero. The call and put premiums should be equal. However, if you forecast a rising price and you sell an *in-the-money* put while buying an *out-of-the-money* call, you should receive a credit. The put will yield more than the call. Prior to 1988, synthetics offered a way to trade for free. By balancing put and call premiums, you could establish enormous positions with a net zero premium. However, the industry realized this posed enormous risk commensurate with the positions. The solution was a valuation method called Standard Portfolio Analysis of Risk (SPAN). SPAN was implemented by the Chicago Mercantile Exchange to approximate relative position exposure and set a margin for net and credit synthetics. The design uses a moving history of volatility to estimate the largest loss exposure for any net position from day to day. The margin is elevated to a quasi-performance bond that protects the clearing member from excessive exposure.

DXM02 MovS=113.76 MovS=115.42

Figure 7.7   June 2002 U.S. Dollar Index futures.

SPAN has removed much of the fun from synthetic positions. Since the formula represents a variable, every synthetic transaction requires prepricing before you can determine the efficacy of the synthetic over simply buying the futures. When considering a pure synthetic, the choice is likely to favor futures because your premiums are net zero and margin will probably be the same or more than an outright futures position. More detailed analysis of options transactions is available in texts dedicated to the specific subject. However, it is important to become familiar with the basics so that any trading strategy you develop or adopt is derived from an appropriate knowledge base.

Short Strangle

Referencing the Australian dollar in Figure 7.8, we see a period from November 2001 through March 2002 where the price held

ADY O:0.5643 H:0.5657 L:0.5640 0.5640 +0.0001 MovS=0.5500 MovS=0.5430

Figure 7.8   Australian dollar cash.

between 0.5040 and 0.5250. Assuming you were convinced the range would remain between these prices, you could sell the 505 put and 525 call for a combined premium. This strategy is called a *short strangle* as though you had a short hand and long hand around the neck of the 210 point range. Your desire is that the range continues until option expiration and you collect both premiums. Each side of this transaction, that is, the call and the put, is called a *leg*. Obviously, only one leg can be in the money upon expiration or at any time. Thus, the usual margin for this position is for a single futures position. The broker also holds your premium, but it counts as equity in your account. Before a strangle loses money on an expiration basis, the futures or cash price must exceed the strike by more than both premiums. Therefore, even if the underlying currency moves beyond either strike, there is still a margin of safety represented by the collected premium.

Suppose you were able to realize 30 points on the call and put for a combined 60 in premium. This means that the price would need to exceed 0.5250 by 60 points or decline below 0.5050 by the same amount before you would be a loser on an expiration basis. Your effective profit range would be between 0.4990 and 0.5310. Both levels are within the market range. The question is whether a breakout or bust would occur before option expiration. Strangles make sense in trading ranges or when there is significant volatility for a short period that is close to the option expiration. Volatility fattens premiums and calm flattens them. In many cases, premiums can offer a wide safety margin above the call and below the put. Understand that exposure can be quite nasty if the market breaks out or busts. When choosing this strategy, you must balance your forecast accuracy against the time you will be exposed and the potential amount you may sacrifice. Referencing Figure 7.8, consider holding a short June 2002 525 call after April. The breakout resulted in a $4,000 move by June 1. The premium would have been well under $1,000, yielding a net loss of approximately $3,000.

This exemplifies why a general retail bias exists toward buying options rather than selling. When buying a put or call, the exposure is always limited to the amount of premium. This loss limitation presents a more positive sales pitch. However, most options expire worthless. More significantly, most options are DOMOs that have very little chance of reaching the strike before expiration. This separates the typical retail trader from the professionals. Pros *sell* options, while average investors *buy.* In Chapter 6, we covered the difference between risk and exposure. This concept becomes increasingly important when formulating strategy. If your chance of reaching the strike is slim, you are better off selling rather than buying.

The potential $3,000 loss in Australian dollars assumes that no protective action was taken. Stops are as useful in limiting exposure in options as with futures. Therefore, the $3,000 is a theoretical loss based on history. Currency volatility generally increased through the 1980s and 1990s. Once unthinkable, 1 and 2 percent daily swings became far more common as the game expanded in scope and volume. Just as the Berlin Wall came down and the Cold War abated, uncertainty was ignited by the Radical Muslim Movement. The rule is to be prepared. The European recession during the latter part of the 1990s and Japanese economic woes excited interest in the dollar to the point where it climbed 50 percent against the euro's initial high just after it was released. The subsequent decline in 2001 to 2002 was equally impressive. This volatility became a main attraction for investors seeking to escape lack-luster stock market performance and microscopic interest rates on money markets and short-term debt instruments.

Trading Range Strategies in Trendless Markets

We can always encounter a comparatively stable currency environment. In fact, central banks have repeatedly stated that the overall objective is to stabilize world currency parities. If this is, indeed, the ultimate goal, how can one make money if the market is not trending? Trendless markets actually offer a wide variety of strategies. In many cases, a trading range can be more profitable than an interim trend. Available strategies include:

- Neutral stance (no positions).
- Sell options.
- Buy the envelope
- Sell the envelope.
- Trade the envelope.

The term *envelope* may be interchanged with *range*. These strategies can use cash, options, or futures. Using the trading range illustrated in Figure 7.8, consider the following transactions:

- Sell 525 call—Sell 505 put.
- Buy 505 put—Sell 525 call and then reverse buy 525 call—Sell 505 put.
- Sell futures at 0.5240 buying 530 call for protection—Buy futures at 0.5040 buying 500 put.
- Sell futures at 0.5240 with 0.5280 buy stop—Buy futures at 0.5040 with 0.5000 sell stop.

The first strategy of selling the call and put is the strangle option sale as previously discussed. As long as the price stays within the envelope or range, the options expire worthless and both premiums are pocketed. Buying the 505 put and selling the 525 call represents the synthetic short; however, the objective is to reverse this position when 0.5050 support is achieved. In other words, you take advantage of the range established within the envelope. In the case of Figure 7.8, there are three tops and two bottoms that represent five potential trades using the synthetic short. Of course, this is an illustration since it would be difficult to know, in advance, that these swings would take place. On each swing, the purchased options appreciate, while the sold option deteriorates.

Perhaps more realistic is the sale of futures at 0.5240 using a 530 call for protection against a breakout above the range. When the price declines to 0.5040 support, you buy the futures using a 500 put for protection against a bust below this support. This strategy requires you to buy a call and put. If you buy near each strike, the premiums will be high. Thus, placing your protection when the price is in the middle of the range provides a cheaper entry. Still cheaper would be to buy the call when the price is at support while buying the put when prices reach resistance. Wouldn't that be nice? So would a crystal ball.

From an efficiency standpoint, profits on gross price swings must exceed premiums paid for protection. If not, the proposition is a loss. This brings us to the alternative of using a stop-loss order for protection on either leg. As prices reach 0.5240 resistance, you would sell futures placing a stop above the range for protection—at 0.5280, for example. Once prices declined to 0.5040 support, you would reverse your position by covering the short sale and buying long. At the same time, you would place your stop below 0.5040 support, that is, at 0.5000. As prices bounced back and forth within the range, you would cancel and replace your stop to avoid automatic or accidental execution on your stop order.

The Element of Time

Time is an essential element of any of the preceding strategies. Since time affects premium values, any decision about using futures, options, cash, or a combination will depend on the amount of time associated with the transaction. Unlike the buy-

and-hold philosophy adopted by long-term stock investing, currency trading tends to have a short life span. Futures and related options have specific expirations. Even cash transactions assume a delivery in spot or forward. Thus, the efficiency of any strategy will depend on the vehicles used and timing.

Returning to Figure 7.8, notice how each swing lasts approximately 20 days and bisects each month. This means that timing could coincide with this cycle. We know when options expire. Using that as the basis for timing, we can select when it is most advantageous to buy or sell options. The cycle has less to do with futures since your concern is with the final expiration and the swings between support and resistance. There is no premium to consider. With options, we can conceivably optimize our strategy with effective timing.

Straddles

If we know approximately when the price will reach a halfway mark between support and resistance, we might choose to sell *straddles* during the cycle. A straddle is a strangle that has the same call and put strikes. A straddle placed at the money tries to collect the maximum combined put and call premium while seeking expiration at or near the strike. Notice that strike is singular since they are the same. If the futures or cash were to expire exactly at the strike, both options would be worthless for all practical purposes. It would not make sense to exercise an *at-the-money* option.

Assuming one or the other option was slightly in the money, you simply cover the exercised option with a futures or cash transaction. You still collect the bulk of premium that was based on volatility and time. Like strangles that are rolled up and down, straddles can be laddered to take advantage of near-term volatility. If expectations are for a calming market (after a storm), you might sell straddles as prices are rising and falling around the range median. As time moves toward expiration and volatility calms, you lift outside straddles, working your way toward the middle. The objective should be obvious. You are maximizing premium on the sale while anticipating low premiums close to expiration.

Delta Analysis

This returns us to the concept of delta. Recall that delta is the ratio of movement between the option and its underlying vehicle. The underlying vehicle always has a value of one, while the option delta is a percentage of one. If the euro increases by 10 points and the call advances by 5 points, delta is 50 percent, or .5. Once an option moves beyond the strike and into the money, its delta may equal the underlying vehicle. At that point, it is as if you were long with a call or short with a put from the strike. Do not confuse delta with the total value. Although an in-the-money option will fluctuate in step with its cash or futures counterpart, it can have a higher value because you still have your initial premium investment inherent in the option value. This is the intrinsic value. In fact, time value deterioration tends to hold delta below 1:1 even after the strike is violated.

Delta analysis can add additional combinations to our previous futures and options strategies or forwards and options. Using the Canadian dollar, assume March futures are trading at 7200 (72¢ U.S. dollar). According to your analysis, you believe the Canadian dollar will fall against the U.S dollar. However, you are concerned about certain political developments in Canada that could impact your prediction. One approach to your uncertainty might be a delta-neutral option strategy that buys the underlying vehicle, that is, Canadian dollar, while also buying Canadian puts on a ratio that equals a gross delta of one. Thus, if the 7000 puts exhibited a .33 delta, you would buy 3 March Canadian puts in conjunction with your long March futures. Here, futures act as your counterbalance or protection. If something goes wrong, your puts are balanced by the futures contract with an approximate one delta. However, if your forecast is correct, your options should appreciate more substantially than the losses on your single futures position once your 7000 strike is surpassed. At that point, you would be making three points for every one point lost on your futures position.

Drawbacks to trading delta-neutral positions include transaction fees, margin, premium costs, and the variation in delta. Delta is a moving target. An increase in volatility will probably increase delta. A calming market will decrease delta. The farther away the price is from the strike, the faster your premium may deteriorate. Thus, the assumption that the futures will balance your options is not entirely correct. The closer you are to expiration, the lower the time value. This means that you can buy options cheaper if you believe your forecast will come to fruition within the time you have left on your options.

Forecasting Multidimensional Strategies

Having reviewed one-dimensional transactions available during up, down, and sideways markets, we can proceed to multidimensional strategies under similar circumstances. Recall that the euro represents a reciprocal of the dollar when priced in dollars. Revisiting parity, all currency values are relative to alternative values. The dollar cannot rise in a vacuum. There must be a declining currency against which the rise takes place. A forecast for rising dollar values is inevitably a forecast for another currency's falling value. A buy in the U.S. Dollar Index may offer a sale of the euro, yen, Canadian dollar, Australian dollar, sterling, and so on.

Using the yen as an example, let's assume we forecast that the yen will rise against the dollar. Certainly, the one-dimensional transaction is to buy the yen as futures, cash, or options. However, the alternative could be to sell the dollar as futures, cash, or options. The dollar is not traded as a futures contract since the reciprocals are already available. To buy the dollar against the sterling is simply to sell sterling. Hence, the futures is, as mentioned, an index of weighted currency values.

However, cash options and forwards permit mirror strategies such as buying yen calls while selling dollar puts. A lengthy discussion of the various combinations should not be necessary since the logic is the same as one-dimensional transactions. However, the combinations are augmented by the addition of the second currency leg.

Where multidimensional transactions become interesting is when several currencies decide to pursue different directions relative to each other. Is the yen rising against the dollar while falling against the sterling? If so, the sterling must be rising proportionately more against the dollar. Strategically, it makes sense to seek the more dramatic parity change. However, different rates of relative change can provide opportunities to buy or sell options at more advantageous premiums between the three currencies. It is not an absolute rule that the most aggressive parity change will equal the most effective trade. Considerations include capital constraints, exposure, and transaction costs. As we know, some of the option premium is based on volatility. The more powerful the change in the exchange rate, the greater the option premiums.

Having previously covered arbitrage and cross-parity trading, we can consider adding options into the mix. This becomes particularly effective if we are also considering government debt instruments. From a simplistic determination of whether to buy long or sell short, we can emerge with strategies for yield enhancement, parity protection (hedging), arbitrage, and intra-commodity spreads using oil, coffee, copper, gold, silver, platinum, palladium, and other internationally traded goods that have more than one market forum. Assuming euro bonds have a higher yield than U.S. notes, an investor can buy the German bonds and hedge against adverse parity with a euro put or a dollar call. The put or call would be set at a value equal to some minimum acceptable rate of return on the German bonds.

Caution is required because the interest rate differential can work against the hedge. Remember that higher interest rates attract investing and can push the denominating currency higher. Since this is the normal reaction, you might expect the euro to climb if euro rates rise relative to the dollar. This is not an absolute correlation. Markets are becoming increasingly reactive to forces outside of the interest rate equation. The key to locking in the higher euro bond return remains protecting against an adverse parity swing before the euro bonds are converted to dollars. The opposite objective would be true for a European Community (EC) investor when considering purchasing U.S. debt if his or her yields were more attractive.

The equation does not pertain exclusively to government issues. Corporate paper is just as easily hedged and has the same criteria when considering fixed income choices. If Phillips has a $6^1/_4$ percent yield relative to a Ford Motor Company U.S.A., which has a $6^7/_8$ percent yield, the $^5/_8$ difference could be sufficient to justify diversifying into Phillips' debt. A logical next step is to examine different stock market potential. If the German,

French, or Italian markets appear more valuable, any investment can be protected against adverse currency fluctuation by hedging in the appropriate currency, that is, the euro.

Deciding to Trade or Not to Trade Currencies

An intriguing question that is conspicuously absent from most how-to books on investing is deciding whether you should trade currencies. It is appropriate to pause before tackling more specific trading methodologies to ponder one of the most important strategic challenges—to trade or not to trade currencies. The assumption is that readers have an interest in trading currencies. If not, why spend the money and time to read this text? After all, the introduction is filled with the possibilities of making extraordinary returns in these fast-moving and diversified markets. Still, one strategy that is almost never considered is abstinence.

Abstinence

When you don't invest in stocks, you are employing a strategy. Your decision is that stocks do not offer appropriate appreciation relative to the risks. Perhaps you do not have the funds to commit to equities. By the same token, currency trading requires considerable skill, knowledge, intestinal fortitude, time, and (of course) money. In order to arrive at an appropriate decision on whether to trade currencies, everyone needs enough background to make the right choice. Further, it is impossible to decide whether to trade currencies if you are unaware of the various vehicles available such as cash, futures, cash options, and options on futures. Hopefully, the previous pages have established sufficient understanding to approach the ultimate question. Are currencies right for you?

Investment and Speculative Capital

The overwhelming deciding factor boils down to investment capital. Although this is not a book on overall portfolio design or financial planning, each individual determines his or her overall investment objectives. Not to be supercilious, but the average investor should not give up his or her day job in favor of becoming full-time currency traders. Yes, total commitment to currency trading can be a career; however, the education required for such a transition goes well beyond the scope of these pages. Today's currency markets offer average investors opportunities to participate in exceptional interim and secular trends. How can you determine if these markets are right for you?

Although offers are available to become involved in currency options with as little as $1,000.00, the caveat is, "Buyer beware." Any offer to purchase an inexpensive option can be an offer to sacrifice hard-earned investment capital. As mentioned, most options expire worthless. Options become less expensive as the strike moves farther away for a reason—the chance for success diminishes. If you commit as little as $1,000, the decision should be based on sound analysis rather than a sales pitch from someone over the telephone.

Trading currencies is right for you if you have speculative capital that you can afford to risk without having it substantially impact your lifestyle. This may sound like a financial planner's cliché. After all, any loss affects your lifestyle to some degree. Therefore, any commitment is a matter of percentages. Few can afford to risk their entire retirement accounts on a speculative currency trading venture. This is not to say that you should not invest a reasonable portion of a retirement account in currency trading once you have mastered essential skills. Unfortunately, all endeavors usually require some practice. When practicing currency trading, the experience can be more expensive than the venture can yield. This is particularly the case if you exhaust your account before happening upon the Holy Grail of currency trading.

Money Management

As a general rule, acquiring the skills of order entry, analysis, and money management takes at least 6 months or approximately 50 trades. The time and number of transactions are not mutually exclusive. It can be a combination. For example, your first experience may fortunately yield immediate profits. This means that you will not need to learn from your mistakes since success implies there were no mistakes. If your first attempts are unprofitable, you may decide to go back to the drawing board. It is helpful to draw a distinction between mistakes versus success or failure. You can just as easily make a profit by mistake as you can experience a loss. An incorrect order entry that yields a positive result remains a mistake. Of course, if you must err, it is more enjoyable to err in the right direction!

Paper Trading

There is no substitute for experience. If you are totally new to currency trading, it makes sense to establish a paper-trading account that mimics real trading. This enables you to practice without encountering real losses. From personal experience, the problem with most paper trading is that it does not provide a realistic emotional setting against which one can truly test trading aptitude. There is an extremely strong tendency to cheat. After all, cheating has no consequence when trades are fictitious. Paper trading has no sting when you experience a loss. You also do not develop those tiny beads of sweat when entering a real order and risking real money. You cannot truly empathize with the gut-wrenching feeling as those tiny beads of sweat turn into a torrent as losses mount and panic sets in. However, you can become overly enthusiastic and confident if your paper trading appears successful.

The allure of trending markets is difficult to resist when it seems a methodology is working. One successful trade, then another, and then another. The excitement frequently becomes unbearable. It may seem like taking candy from a baby. When your willpower weakens, you jump in. For some reason, markets are not so kind when real money is at stake. Alas, you find yourself in losing trades with no paper experience to guide you. You have not seen how bad it can get if you fail to use proper money management. In short, it is vitally important to *test before you invest*. Any test must have sufficient time and market diversification to be reasonably sound. Just as medical research requires double-blind studies, so should testing currency trading aptitude.

When setting up a paper-trading program, start with realistic numbers. Concentrate on determining the actual amount you can afford to risk. Beginning capital defines your ability to survive a string of consecutive losses. It provides a backdrop for setting realistic stop-loss parameters for each trade. If you are using a mechanical system, it may be necessary to filter out trades that have excessive exposure or costs relative to your probabilities for success and failure. Simply put, a $10,000 account can only survive 10 consecutive $1,000 losses in a row. The math is easy. The experience is not.

Risk and exposure parameters are frequently integrated into a particular approach. Returning to the moving average example, there will be a historical record of successes and failures over time. Profits and losses are associated with every trade. Eventually, you have a basis for determining a statistical profile for your moving average paper trading. What are the average losses versus profits? How many consecutive losses did the moving average experience? How many consecutive profits? What was the maximum capital depletion during the string of losses? This is often called *capital drawdown*. The critical question is whether you could have survived the drawdown. If the answer is yes, you're okay. If not, it's back to the tweaking process.

Three Distinct Bookkeeping Records for Paper Trading

After decades of trading, I have found that actual and paper trading distills down into three distinct records. The first acts like a check ledger and tracks your account balances on a monthly basis. I call this the Personal Information Sheet or Account Balance Ledger. Since I deal with several trading accounts, each ledger identifies the account by name, number, and brokerage house. Individual investors do not usually trade with more than one brokerage firm at a time. Some information may not be necessary. See Table 7.1.

Enter a date when the account (real or hypothetical) is opened. Although the first column says Month End Date, the reference is for an ongoing basis when booking your monthly trading performance. Obviously, you can add or withdraw funds at any time during the month. Your first entry should record the initial deposit, for example, $10,000.00, as listed previously. At

Table 7.1

Personal Information Sheet/Account Balance Ledger

Personal Information Sheet

Account name:_____

Account number:_____

Broker:_____

Order phone:_____

Month End Date	Total Equity	Deposits	Withdrawals	Commissions	Net Monthly Profit and Loss
01/03/2003	10,000.00	10,000.00			

each month's end, you would record the net account balance. Any deposits or withdrawals are posted in the appropriate column and brought down to the next line when calculating total equity. Each month, you record your net gain or loss for quick reference in the sixth column.

As the name implies, the Daily Trading Log is a record of each day's prospective and retrospective activity. Before each trading session, log your daily orders to this form so that you can efficiently enter and track trades. This form carries an account identifier (usually the account number) and trading date. The log can be divided into two sections: one for new orders and one for stops. If using options for protection, the option can be logged to the stop section. See Table 7.2.

Any new positions or trades that close existing positions would be posted under the New Orders and Offsets section. The usual sequence is to note whether the order is a purchase or sale, the quantity (as in amount of cash currency or number of futures or option contracts), the month of expiration (if not cash), the particular currency or commodity (for cross-parity trades), the @ sign designates the type of order (as in market, limit, or stop), and whether the order is for a new position or an offset. The columns marked Fill Price, In, and Log are used after the trade is placed in the market. Once your order has been entered, place a checkmark in the In column to indicate that the trade has been placed. As trivial as this may seem, it is a system of checks and balances that prevents double order entry.

Table 7.2

Daily Trading Log

Daily Trading Log

Account identifier:_____

Trading date:_____

New Orders and Offsets

Fill Price	Buy Sell	Quantity	Month	Currency Commodity	@	Order/Type Marketplace	New Offset	In	Log
9263	Buy	2	Dec	Euro	@	MKT	New	✔	✔
7737	Sell	1	Dec	Yen	@	7737 Stop	Offset	✔	✔
	Buy	3	March	Aussie	@	MOC	Offset	✔	

Trading can become a frenzied activity. This is more the case if you are engaged in other activities that can be distracting or if markets are extremely active. The objective is to avoid mistakes you have made in the past. Did you enter that trade? Although it is easy enough to check with your broker, you will find that most are very busy people during the open session and even the night session. You may not receive the cooperation you need when you need it. A simple checkmark to note the trade was entered saves time, effort, and money.

When a trade is executed or filled, you mark the price in the first column. At the end of the day, any blanks immediately alert you to a potential problem. Why was this order not filled? If all is correct, the last column is used as a cross-check against a Historical Trading Record. Once you log your daily activity to the historical ledger and place a check in the Log column, the process is complete. Stops are separated from the New Orders and Offsets section because you do not necessarily expect to be stopped out. In addition, an automated or mechanical trading method such as a moving average may calculate a stop that is out of the market range. These can be labeled OOR under the Type column for "out of range." For convenience, you can separate the stop section from the New Orders and Offsets section with a colored marker. In all other respects, the two sections are identical.

Another advantage to this type of bookkeeping is the ease with which you can transfer your stops from one daily log to another. You simply scan down the unfilled stop column and you know which trades need protection for the following session. As a word of caution, always remember to cancel or draw lines through stops on positions that have been offset. If your offset is different from your stop protection, the offset can be reached and the stop will no longer be covering an open position. As mentioned in the section covering orders, a stop can be good for the session or open until cancelled. You are responsible for keeping track of your stops and open orders.

This brings us to the Historical Trading Record, which tracks your overall trading activity. Again, the form is headed with the account name and identifier. This form is usually closed out each month with open entries carried over to a new monthly sheet. See Table 7.3.

From left to right, the quantity references the amount bought or number of contract positions. Currency/Commodity references what you have traded. Long or Short is self-explanatory as are most of the remaining columns. The Profit and Loss columns are calculated by subtracting the close price from the open price when long or subtracting the open price from the close price when short. This difference must be multiplied by the appropriate point value for futures and options to determine the gross profit or loss. From this number, you must subtract transaction costs that would be the spread in cash (in pips) or the commission and fees for futures and options. Some traders prefer to post the net profit or loss after deducting costs. Remember to add costs to losses and subtract from profits.

When trading regulated futures and options, you will receive confirmations that operate in the same manner as your Daily

Table 7.3

Historical Trading Record

Historical Trading Record

Name:_____

Account Identifier:_____

Month/Year_____

Amount	Currency/ Commodity	Long or Short	Open Date	Close Date	Open Price	Close Price	Profit	Loss	Cost	✔

Trading Log with the exception that the trades are marked to
market like the Historical Trading Record. Warning! Brokerage
firms can and do make mistakes. It is your responsibility to
check your statements and promptly correct any errors. An
unchecked error can end up costing you money. Many firms have
a policy of holding you to *their error* if you fail to tell them in a
timely manner so that they can eliminate any exposure. Hence,
the last check column is used to verify that your record corresponds to the brokerage statement. Once this final check is complete, your bookkeeping activity is reconciled.

Some traders like to keep track of additional columns for
margin and intratrade drawdowns. In futures, you may design a
portfolio of currencies that becomes too expensive for the
amount of capital you have available. Keeping an eye on margin
protects against an unexpected margin call. The Historical
Trading Record is sometimes referenced as a *one-write method*
because every trade is only written once for both the entry and
exit. One advantage to this is the ability to immediately identify
open positions by empty Close cells. This provides a way to scan
for necessary stops. If you see an open Close box, you know an
open position exists that needs protection—unless you are one of
the courageous traders who does not use stops.

You may wonder why all this paperwork is necessary if your
broker provides confirmations and monthly account summaries.
As mentioned, it is your system of checks and balances. Equally
important, you cannot paper trade without such a system. These
records will help you conduct that test before you invest.
Admittedly, this paper system is a throwback to days before electronic order entry and PC programs that automatically track
trades. If you have trading software that facilitates this type of
bookkeeping, you may dispense with the manual method. Still,
it remains helpful to go through the trading process using these
forms as a guide.

Optimization Trading Strategy

Assume you are paper trading a method over a 6-month period.
During that time, you notice that all trades dipping below $600
per position never recover. This may be difficult to quantify in
the cash market. However, you can calculate a similar level

using a percentage rather than an absolute. Thus, any trade losing more than 2 percent never recovers. These trades either close out with a loss of $600 or more or are stopped with similar results. Based on this observation, you might spike your trading at a $600 automatic exposure. Why risk more? If the stop derived from your method is less than $600, then the lesser amount applies since the position would no longer be valid after the stop was violated.

As we can see, the history helps us perfect a trading strategy based on a particular method. This process is sometimes called *optimization*. Others simply label the exercise *money management*. The observation over 6 months assumes there is a reasonable consistency for the $600 or 2 percent rule. In other words, this is assumed to be the case for more than the 6-month test. Clearly, it is a broad assumption since we know market conditions can change dramatically from day to day, week to week, month to month, and even year to year. We want to know how closely our method tracks price movements over time. Here, we enter the realm of more complex statistical measurement. Unfortunately, 6 months is too brief a time to obtain a statistically valid data sampling. However, computer programs are available that will enable you to back test your method using historical data. Thus, you can trek back through years or even decades of data. Although some programs and databases may be expensive, they are not as costly as trading an untried method in real markets if the method is flawed.

Once sufficient data is gathered, it is possible to measure how consistent the $600 or 2 percent observation is over time. This is accomplished by compiling the number of observations we see during discrete periods, for example, from year to year. If data is tracked from 1995 through 2005, we want to compare the frequency of our data even from 1995 to 1996 and from 1996 to 2001. The more discrete periods we compare, the more sure we are that the rule is consistent. This process is not only applicable to these observations, but it is also applicable for all observations including profitability. The Chi-Squared Goodness of Fit test is an efficient formula for measuring consistency over time. The test uses histograms or historical observations to calculate consistency. Anyone interested in learning more about using statistical measurements should review an introductory statistics text. Statistical programs are also available for the PC and Apple.

If we find that the $600 rule is consistent and therefore reliable, it leads us to an approximation of our survival. With $10,000 in starting capital, we can afford 16.66 losing trades before our balance is zeroed out. The actual amount is less since we must account for transaction costs and margin. Still, we have a basis for extrapolating our survival. Since we can measure the frequency of a 16-time losing streak, we know the probability of a straight plunge into oblivion. More likely than not, the chance is slim, but not impossible. We are more concerned with smaller losing streaks dispersed among insufficient winning streaks. It's similar to the saying "two steps forward, three steps back." If the method carries such a 2:3 ratio and the losses exceed the profits, we know the end result. It is a slow demise rather than a straight ride to the poorhouse.

A 2:3 ratio can be profitable as long as the three are small and the two are large. Hence, we hear the expression, "Cut your losses short and let your profits ride." This saying is based on an assumption that one's approach is not designed to take instantaneous bites out of price movements like a day-trading system or arbitrage. Our ultimate objective, under the circumstances described previously, is to balance the losing streaks against profits to ensure a climb to pinnacles of profit ecstasy.

Principles for paper trading and constructing a survival tree are not exclusive to trend-following systems. Suppose you develop a spreadsheet that is dynamically linked to live price data in cash forwards and futures options. When the spreadsheet identifies a discrepancy between the two markets, it constructs a trade. You quickly execute this strategy of arbitrage between forwards and futures. Depending on how long the spread exists and your execution speed, you will successfully profit or miss your opportunity. Thus, even this methodology has accuracy, efficiency, and consistency measurements. You can use the same record-keeping constructs as we have covered to test your arbitrage skills. However, arbitrage has two or more legs. This means that your entries must take into consideration both the long and short leg as a single trade.

When dealing with arbitrage strategy, you can double your columns on the Daily Trading Log and Historical Trading Record to record both legs as a single transaction. If you are looking at the March futures expiration against 2-month forwards in late

January or early February, you might find that the futures were selling at a premium to the forward offered by the Royal Bank of Canada. You buy from the Royal Bank while simultaneously selling March futures to lock in the differential. The transaction is the same regardless of the currency you are trading. You may discover that the Royal Bank of Canada is offering 3-month forwards at a discount to Citibank. You immediately buy from the Royal Bank and sell to Citibank. As long as the difference is sufficient to cover all transaction costs including the cost of money, you can achieve a profit. Such situations are fleeting. Rest assured that trading banks are just as interested in arbitrage as you. Spreads in the cash market are not easy to find. Spreads between futures and cash or the options are more likely to be available since there are more individual speculative participants randomly entering or exiting to influence spreads.

Investment and Trading Philosophies

The final element of strategy involves your investment or trading philosophy. This has become an increasingly important point because markets and investment strategies are evolutionary as opposed to simply revolutionary. This is to say that new trading and investment products are being created from which new strategies eventually evolve. The revolutionary aspects of currency trading revolve back to old standards that may be applied in new ways. It would be revolutionary to return to a gold standard. It was evolutionary to move into a completely floating world monetary system.

Floating currencies came first, then currency futures, and then options. The Interbank has been computerized to the point where adjunct systems can parse multimillion dollar, yen, sterling, or euro transactions in blocks worth $5,000. All of these monetary alterations and trading vehicles dictate new strategies and, equally important, investment philosophies. As you explore various market approaches you will need to decide whether you want to tackle day trading, short-term trading, trend following, arbitrage, or other philosophies. Each involves the same forecasting, decision making, and money-management components. However, applications are different.

The easiest distinction between philosophies is usually the time available for currency trading. Day trading requires you to monitor the markets all day (and often all night) in search of your entry and exit points. Short-term trading carries a similar time-consuming burden. Arbitrage is, perhaps, the most intense pursuit with the alleged exception of automated arbitrage systems. This leaves trend following as an endeavor that may provide less time constraint and more freedom to branch out into other activities.

Philosophy does not only pertain to you as the investor. Should you decide to hire the skills of a professional, he or she will usually adopt one of the four mentioned philosophies. Although some professional currency traders may claim expertise in all philosophies, a multitalented trader who can pursue all philosophies with equal zeal and success is rare—exceptionally rare. Such a blessed individual is more likely to use trading skills to build a personal fortune rather than altruistically offer their golden goose to Joe Public as management services. Having expressed that bit of reality, it is time to examine market behavior so that we may further develop profitable trading strategies.

Chapter 8

MARKET BEHAVIOR

To forecast market behavior, you must understand market behavior. For some, this exercise is the most daunting and intimidating process. Individuals with advanced degrees in economics and mathematics spend decades attempting to understand market behavior, only to be frustrated by a series of unsuccessful hypotheses. Given such experiences of the highly educated, it may seem presumptuous to tackle market behavior in a chapter. However, some individuals seem to possess a sixth sense about market behavior and have an uncanny ability to analyze causal correlations and foresee changes in price direction. Unfortunately, it is impossible to bestow a sixth sense on every reader. However, we can try to peer into the dynamics that enable a sixth sense to become operative. Who knows, you may be one of the gifted.

Alternatively, a review of certain market patterns can instill enough understanding to begin building or selecting a quantitative methodology. Rather than being intimidated by the failures of those who have gone before, you should be challenged by the possibilities that lie ahead. In reality, all market behavior is derived from five behaviors:

- Random events
- Sequential events
- Seasonal influences
- Cyclical patterns
- Secular trends

Random and Sequential Events

Each behavior lends itself to certain trading philosophies as covered in the previous chapter. Traditional texts list these behaviors in reverse. In the old days, random events were called *noise* because they were considered unpredictable as suggested by the word *random*. Sequential events such as the release of market or economic statistics were considered public knowledge because the information allegedly became available to all investors (traders) simultaneously. The assumption that such instantaneous and universal knowledge would lead to a perfect price became known as the *efficient market*.

Seasonal Influences

Seasonal influences include fiscal periods, holiday seasons, accumulation seasons, political transitions, tax seasons, and other specific events that are associated with particular times of every year. Traditionalists lighten up on the efficient market argument to confess that seasonal influences can be predictable within some narrow parameters. The belief remains that everyone is capable of empiric study to the extent that we all try to capture seasonal patterns in the same way and at the same time. This brings up the question of a self-fulfilling prophecy. If everyone acts in concert, the action will cause a market reaction. This logic can get us caught up in an endless tautology. It is sufficient to say that old-line thinkers were (and remain) skeptical about any market predictability including seasonality.

Still, seasonal patterns show certain regularity that can be statistically measured for frequency, consistency, and strength. For example, most government economic statistics are seasonally adjusted. This means that the actual numbers are altered to statistically smooth out measurable seasonal patterns. Thus, employment is seasonally adjusted because summer jobs reflect the availability of an expanded cheap youth market. Employment tends to increase in the United States from Thanksgiving through the first 2 weeks in January. Temporary hiring by retailers during the busy holiday shopping season causes this employment blip. If we did not adjust for known seasonal irregularities, we could not tell whether employment is truly rising or falling.

Interestingly, the statistical method for smoothing economic data is often a moving average. Using a 12-month summation of data divided by 12, we can discern an up- or downtrend. A moving average not only displays more regularity in a price chart, but it also calms economic numbers to reveal true direction. Other smoothing methods develop monthly adjustment indices or factors that are multiplied by the actual numbers to provide a weighted value. Although we briefly touched on using a moving average as a predictive tool, I have yet to read anything in a statistical text that alludes to using moving averages to forecast price direction. Although smoother data can extract a price bias, the books do not say a moving average that is violated by its components (such as price) will move in the direction of the breakout or bust. However, the moving average breakout system has become one of the most popular technical approaches practiced today. It permeates everything from day trading to long-term trend following. From a 5-minute intraday average to the well-known 100-day stock moving average, the application appears to have technical relevance beyond an accusation that moving averages are self-fulfilling prophesies. As we will see, moving averages continue to serve their traditional role of identifying regularity where none appears to exist.

Cyclical Patterns

A transition occurs from the normal cycles associated with seasonal changes and longer cycles associated with business, politics, weather, and demographics. These four areas are not exclusive. During the course of study as market technicians, many readers have probably encountered theories about sunspots, planetary cycles, and even the Earth's perturbation on its axis. Although these are interesting intellectual exercises, currencies are more likely to be immediately influenced by more down-to-earth cyclical tendencies.

Business Cycles

Foremost in the minds of currency specialists is the pertinent business cycle. This is the aspect of any cycle that influences currency valuation. Thus, several subcycles justify attention within the business cycle; two that quickly come to mind are booms/busts and recoveries/recessions. For a brief moment during the 1990s, economists were beginning to wonder if the business cycles associated with inventory fluctuations were finally overcome by as-needed inventory and manufacturing controls. Empirical evidence supported the contention that capital accumulation was associated with the demand for inventory and/or goods and services. A consequence of building capital to meet demand is an overshoot resulting in overcapacity. In turn, too much inventory causes a glut and prices fall. A recession begins and capital is allowed to recede until capacity falls short of demand. This series of events repeats because business is never able to accurately gauge demand.

The advent of computerized inventory and manufacturing controls decreased the time required to order and receive goods as well as process and manufacture orders. This efficiency seemed to cure the inventory cycle as the United States enjoyed one of the longest booms of the twentieth century. The unusual lack of inflation coupled with high-capacity utilization and full employment suggested a pyridine change. Had we seen the last of the traditional business cycle? Was Karl Marx wrong when he insisted that this cycle was a natural consequence of capitalism and the rift between labor and capital ownership? In truth, the computer has altered the business cycle and capitalism has become more efficient and less susceptible to former boom/bust swings. As-needed ordering and manufacturing reduces shelf time, inventory financing, storage costs, spoilage, and even pilfering to the extent that inventory is more consistently on the move.

However, these efficiencies only address a portion of the overall cycle. Also, the shuffle between boom and bust has been identified as an irregular cycle lasting between 8 and 12 years. Beyond these swings are more significant shifts that were originally identified by the Russian economist Kondratieff as an approximate 60-year cycle from peak boom to devastating bust. This *Grand Cycle* is supposed to be the culmination of all the intermediate business gyrations. Since expressing his theory, other empirics have investigated economic ups and downs to hone in on a more precise series of 11-year peaks and troughs. For the astronomers among us, it is true that the sunspot cycle coincides with an observed 11-year business cycle. However, the influence of solar storms has not been identified yet.

In truth, economists are still sorting out the business cycle. From a currency-trading standpoint, it is sufficient to know that such a cycle exists and varies from region to region. A boom in Japan does not necessarily correspond with good times in western Europe. Some nations that practice or have practiced forms of communism, socialism, and quasi-dictatorship are not as vulnerable to business swings. By the same token, they do not enjoy the same per-capita prosperity of the capitalistic regimes that also benefit from democratic government processes.

The Grand Cycle, however, is supposed to encompass the global economy because it is the cumulative effect of multiple uncoordinated variations among other capitalistic states. Do we care about a cycle that only occurs once in each lifetime (at the most, twice)? As we will discover, the potential Grand Cycle is important for the more significant events that can include depressions, wars, and total global sociopolitical realignment. Obviously, such events lead to new currency systems and even standards as the post World War II era demonstrated.

Political Cycles

Nonuniformity among business cycles is associated with unique cycles within the business cycle. The most obvious is the political cycle. As the dominant currency standard through the twentieth century, all eyes focused on the U.S. presidential elections. This 4-year, man-made cycle has a profound influence on currency perceptions. Some believe a Democrat administration translates into a stronger currency, whereas a Republican administration is content to leave the greenback unsupported. In fact, wide variations in dollar parity appear under both parties. Still, we can expect a 4-year reaction in the dollar with each election. The 2- and 6-year congressional cycles can also tip the scales from one party to the next. Here, Republicans point out that the dollar gained its most significant prestige under a Republican Congress.

Political Uncertainty

Personal politics aside, sharp differences exist in monetary and fiscal policies between Democrats and Republicans. These translate into different world perceptions about the dollar. Down the road, the euro could become the dominant currency standard. If that becomes our reality, political cycles may be more difficult to gauge since each European Community (EC) member has different politics associated with different parties. However, no member is able to dominate the euro. Even Germany is subject to the will of its fellow members as majority rule takes precedence. Instantaneous jumps in currency parity can be attributed to expected and unexpected political events. From the discrediting of President Clinton during his unfortunate affair with Monica Lewinsky to the alleged kidnapping of Mikhail Gorbachev in August 1991, political events hit currencies hard —very hard! As Figure 8.1 shows, the U.S. Dollar Index spiked

Figure 8.1   September 1991 U.S. Dollar Index.

from 93.00 to 97.00 in a single session. If the kidnapping had been real, there is no way to determine how western Europe might have been affected. Hence, the uncertainty translated into a flight to dollars.

The reaction dissipated as quickly as it materialized when all was well with Gorbachev. However, the ferocity of the spike represented a $4,000 swing in the contract value in a single session. Within two days, the value reversed $5,000. All of this was on a single futures contract. Consider an 8 percent change in a $100 million Interbank transaction.

The 2000 U.S. Presidential Election is another illustration of political uncertainty and impact, as shown in Figure 8.2. The exceptionally tight preelection polls added to dollar volatility that was seen in late October. When the debate over Florida held the presidency in suspense, confidence in the U.S. political process was immediately reflected by a plunge in dollar parity. Although

Figure 8.2   March 2001 U.S. Dollar Index futures.

Europe's consensus was that the debate was a farce, currency traders were keenly aware of the consequences if the electoral process failed. When a quick resolution did not materialize, the U.S. Dollar Index plunged more than 8 percent from 118.00 to 107.50. Once the government was back on track, Europe felt a sigh of relief and the dollar resumed its former recovery.

Each of these political events can be categorized as random since they are somewhat instantaneous or at least highly unexpected. The more normal course of events changes market opinion based on an anticipated outcome. For example, when Bill Clinton ran against Bob Dole, the outcome was widely expected. The election anticipated another 4 years under a Democrat administration.

When an unexpected political development impacts currencies, the initial outcome is reactionary. We see an instantaneous consensus driving the market. The reaction is usually followed by an analytic phase that either corrects the reaction or confirms it. Once a trend is in place, currency parity pursues a direction until its value is normalized. So what is normal? Normal is reflected by a moderate to wide trading range that establishes a reasonably stable average. The range is usually less than 2 percent.

Not all major political events significantly change the course of currency trends. One of the most striking examples was the Gulf War that began on August 2, 1990 with Iraq's invasion of Kuwait. The U.S. Dollar Index immediately shot up as initial insecurities moved traders toward the United States. The range was only 100 points and the close on August 2 was only 32 points above the previous day. As shown in Figure 8.3, the Dollar Index was in a strong downtrend and the initial reaction was overcome by an analysis that moved the consensus back to the existing trend. In fact, a potential war with Iraq was viewed as unfavorable for the dollar based on the enormous expense and uncertain outcome—not to mention rocketing oil prices.

When Japan, Germany, and the United Kingdom pledged financial support for the U.S. intervention, the dollar made a brief recovery and nestled into a 1-month trading range. However, 85.50 support was violated and the U.S. Dollar Index took another tumble to 81.50. In late November, President Bush attempted a diplomatic solution after considerable saber rattling. Again, the move was viewed as favorable to the dollar. Iraq's

DXZ90 MovS=82.62 MovS=82.58

August 2, 1990, Iraq Invades Kuwait

Japan, Germany, UK say
they will support U.S. with
money.

Diplomatic solution
attempted, but fails.

Figure 8.3 December 1990 U.S. Dollar Index futures.

rebuff and insistence that Kuwait was annexed quickly dropped the U.S. Dollar Index back toward mid-November lows.

Once again, we see spikes or reactions within the trend. In each instance, the predominant price direction resumes. In retrospect, we know that the dollar was fundamentally realigning against the world's major currencies. What was causing the steady decline? Actual dollar weakness appeared in the first quarter of 1990. As we know, the United States was recovering from the crash of 1987 and the drought of 1988. Economic pressures combined to create the infamous double-dip that many political analysts claim was George H.W. Bush's downfall. The Fed began tightening to slow the rate of recovery that developed from 1988 forward. As shown in Figure 8.4, the 30-year Treasury bond moved sharply lower, which maintained a healthier dollar parity. When the Fed realized it might have overcompensated, it allowed rates to fall. The January 1990 mini-crash in U.S. stocks

Figure 8.4   December 1990 U.S. Dollar Index futures.

impinged upon real-estate values and represented an additional catalyst for leaving the dollar. To combat the second recessionary wave, the United States was forced into lower interest rates as illustrated by the T-Bond trend toward the end of 1990 (see Figure 8.5).

These illustrations serve two main purposes. First, we see that political influences within potential political cycles can spike prices higher or lower. These are not cyclical, but random. Then, we discover that the U.S. administration is only as influential as the Fed allows. So who's in charge here? An interesting personal anecdote partially answers the question.

Who's in Charge?

During President Clinton's State of the Union Address in 1999, he stated,

USZ90 MovS=95'29 MovS=94'04

Figure 8.5 December 1990 U.S. Dollar Index futures.

I stand before you to report that America has created the longest peacetime economic expansion in our history—with nearly 18 million new jobs, wages rising at more than twice the rate of inflation, the highest homeownership in history, the smallest welfare rolls in 30 years, and the lowest peacetime unemployment since 1957.

After hearing President Clinton's inspiring words, I was surfing channels when I came upon Fed Chairman Alan Greenspan on C-SPAN. He was testifying about the State of the Economy with remarks that the rate of job growth was too fast and it was necessary to curb economic enthusiasm to avoid a resurgence of inflation. While Clinton was boasting about job creation, Greenspan was outlining his plan to slow job growth. While Clinton was hailing the decrease in our trade deficit, Greenspan was laying the framework for a weaker dollar and more expensive imports. As Figure 8.6 illustrates, Greenspan did, indeed, allow rates to climb and the dollar responded by losing parity.

Who is in charge? When it comes to monetary policy, the Fed's inherent autonomy places it in charge. Ultimately, the Fed Chairperson is in charge and the President can only hope for his or her cooperation.

This same relationship holds true for Europe. If the French control the European central bank, expect to see a French bias in interest rate decisions. As the media mogul Rupert Murdock stated, "Europe is made up of so many diverse cultures and histories that to slam it together with a government of French bureaucrats answerable to nobody . . . I cannot see anything but a benefit by waiting." He was referring to Prime Minister Tony Blair's referendum to move from the sterling to the euro. Despite Murdock's assumed U.S. citizenship, he reflected the thinking of

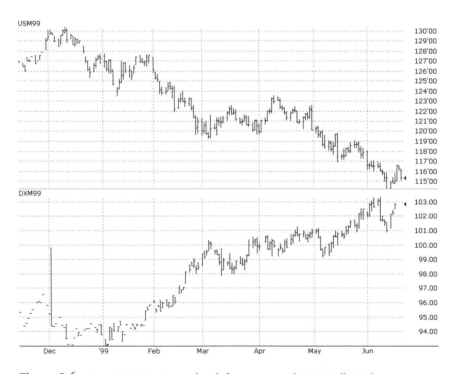

Figure 8.6   June 1999 U.S. 30-year bonds futures versus the U.S. Dollar Index.

a staunch Anglo-Saxon. With his media empire behind him, he had the wherewithal to present uncertainty about the euro's fate.

His point about French bureaucrats answerable to nobody was echoed through several member nations where an underlying defensiveness about sovereignty and economic control created an uneasy, although successful transition into the euro currency. Murdock correctly identified who is in control when he linked control of the euro to control over all economic policy. Thus, the monetary system is in control while the political cycle appears secondary.

Demographic Cycles

Aside from man-made business and political cycles, economies are responsive to demographic cycles that are a combination of man-made and natural selection. Although I cannot recall the exact source, I was attracted to the phrase *demographic congestion*, which referenced the population skew resulting from World Wars I and II. The baby boom experienced from 1945 through 1955 added 30 million Americans to the population—not to mention an equivalent amount throughout western Europe. This population bulge came of age during the 1970s. Marked by the Vietnam War, Peace Movement, Chicago Seven, inflation, stagflation, presidential resignation, and a host of other tumultuous events, baby boomers were slow to wean from their predecessor generation. This was evidenced by a reliance on the World War II leaders through the George H.W. Bush years. Late marriages and conservative propagation standards limited the offspring by approximately 40 million. Let us not forget that baby boomers were reared under the cloud of nuclear holocaust and a pending population explosion. Thus, Generation X was substantially smaller than baby boomers.

The population recovery from back-to-back world conflicts took approximately 60 years. Depending on where generational lines are constructed, skewed population transitions might diminish with Generation NeXt or Y. This becomes critical for fiscal and monetary planning because the tax base depends on a working population. Productivity and economic elasticity relies on a dependable labor market. The most serious long-term threat to economic stability is often a clash between generations—those who work and those who can no longer work, not to mention those training to work.

Putting demographics into monetary perspective, suppose the global population were to shrink by 10 percent. Depending on which demographic segment (upper, middle, or lower income) was reduced the most, the amount of currency required to service this smaller population would decrease in real terms. Inflation could cause the decrease in purchasing parity, but we would need fewer goods and services. We will need to house 30 million fewer Americans with Generation X. This suggests that as baby boomers retire and sell primary residences, we will see a momentary housing glut. When the larger Generation Y fills in, the baby boomer stockpile may be absorbed.

As baby boomers retire, Generation X will still be building wealth. This means that a larger population will be withdrawing from retirement accounts than is putting in. Until the following generation(s) comes of investing age, the system will be burdened by the demographic discrepancy. As long as there is not another world conflict, skewed demographics should become more standardized in terms of population and wealth. That is the goal. However, it is worth considering how changing demographics can impact money supply, currency demand, the demand for goods and services, labor availability, investing patterns, supplies of goods and services, world commerce, and (of course) politics.

The Four Attributes of Cycles

Numerous texts and opinions adhere to the Axiom of Cyclical Behavior that states all things are cyclical—from ordering the cycles of day and night, light and darkness, summer, fall, winter, and spring, sunspots, birth and death. The list goes on. Cycle advocates generally insist that all market moves are cyclical. However, the cyclical theme has many variations. From a technical viewpoint, cycles exhibit four attributes:

- Phase/interval
- Amplitude
- Frequency
- Regularity

Some may be familiar with these terms from high school or college physics. Cycle analysis is also included in natural sciences, math, economics, statistics, and many other disciplines including electronics and ham radio. Phase deals with the distance from peak to peak or trough to trough. In currency trading, the phase is measured along a horizontal access as time. If you are day trading, you may see a 5-minute interval. This implies that the distance from peak (high) to peak is 5 minutes. An important consideration when measuring phase is the potential for phase shift. Unlike the alteration of light when the wavelength is shifted by motion toward or away from the viewer, phase shift in currency analysis focuses on the regularity of the phase.

For example, a perfect sine wave is predictable because its components of phase, amplitude, and frequency are fixed. It is a perfectly regular wave. Currencies do not display such consistency. Cycles are irregular. Even a seasonal cycle can shift its peak or trough by days, weeks, or months. This adds a level of complexity to wave or cycle analysis. Figure 8.7 shows a standard cycle illustration with the attributes annotated.

When a cycle is regular, the frequency is directly related to the phase. This is to say that a consistent phase will produce a known frequency of cycles (waves) over any given period.

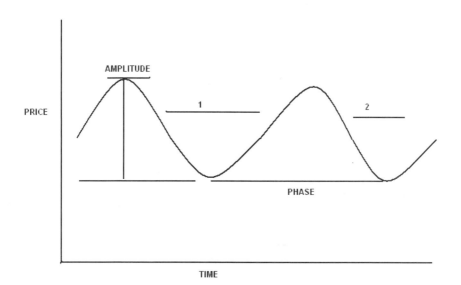

Figure 8.7 Cycle with amplitude, phase, and frequency.

Markets from stocks to bonds to wheat to currencies do not exhibit such regularity. Of course, it would be wonderful if we could find such a regular market. The problem would be finding traders to take the opposite side!

The real world produces cycles resembling Figure 8.8. Even this illustration may be too regular to accurately present the gyrations experienced by currency traders from peaks to troughs. More importantly, the cycle will depend on the time interval selected by the trader. For example, you may be concerned with intraday cycles or even intrahour cycles, if such exist. A common theory is that currency trading exhibits cycles related to our eating habits. When traders get the urge to eat lunch, the market allegedly slows down. However, a slower market does not necessarily mean the cycles will slow or even change. Still, some base their trading decisions on the time of day—for example, buying on the open and selling by lunch, always selling the close, or other intraday timing based on the assumption that some type of cycle exists.

As we will examine further, several theories have been developed about regularity in irregular cycles. Among the most popular is the Elliot Wave, which presumes markets experience

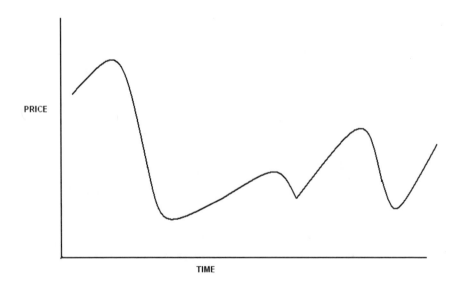

PRICE

TIME

Figure 8.8   Irregular cycle.

five waves within each major cycle. Theories such as the Elliot Wave identify cyclical patterns within cycles that are broken down into minor, interim, and major waves. Those who have been frustrated by the myriad cycles within cycles may claim that the minor, interim, and major cycles are simply excuses for missed trades after the fact. That is to say that the minor cycle was intersected by the interim cycle to produce an opposite result from what was expected. Unfortunately, double-talk is a trademark of technical analysis. Few technicians, whether wave enthusiasts or point and figure chartists, want to admit that they are or were completely lost.

Secular Trends

Although there is no question that markets experience cycles, overall movement is not exclusively identified by cycles. The term *secular* is not a reference to the nonspiritual nature of price movements since most traders are known to pray when things are going well or not so well. Secular trend refers to the overall trend inherent with the passage of time. It is the trend of the ages. Inflation is the most obvious example of secular trend that affects currencies. Purchasing parity deteriorates over time. Although the interim value of a currency can seasonally or cyclically move up or down, the waves will move along the secular trend.

In some instances, secular trend is associated with structural changes such as those linked to technological advances. For example, the price per mile driven is comprised of several components that include the price of fuel, fuel efficiency, and vehicle cost including depreciation, financing, and maintenance. Any single component will alter the cost per mile. Inflation will change the real cost per mile. It should be obvious that increasing efficiency from 9 miles per gallon to 27 miles per gallon is a threefold increase. However, if gasoline moves from 35¢ per gallon to $1, price inflation matches fuel efficiency. If interest rates soar to 20 percent, financing costs move in tandem. The price of the vehicle must also be considered. The question is whether technology is structurally altering the secular trend in mileage costs. This is measured by plotting costs over time to determine what trend exists.

Figure 8.9 illustrates a secular trend. Although it is unlabeled, we could compare this to the price per mile example whereby drops in gasoline or increases in fleet mileage would constitute a downward cycle, while rising gasoline would turn the slope upward. The secular trend, however, rises because the overall price trend (based on inflation) is higher. Let's face it. We are not going to see 25¢ per gallon unless we discover a new way to pump and refine oil or there is a massive currency realignment represented by a huge deflation. The secular trend is also rising because vehicle prices are moving up with inflation. This increases depreciation expense.

Currencies pose an interesting augmentation to the secular trend concept because values are relative. Although purchasing parity may deteriorate with inflation, observation proves that world currencies tend to inflate together at varying rates. It is this variable relative inflation that provides such exciting profit opportunities for the longer-term trading philosophy. At any given moment, secular trends among currencies will shift. In some cases, the upward or downward bias (slope) can be very short lived when compared to other commodities.

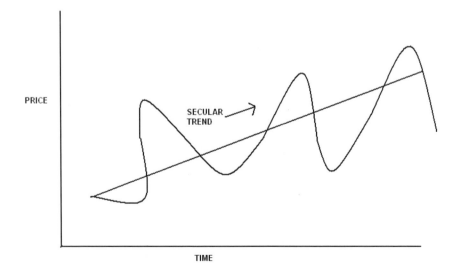

Figure 8.9   Cycle around secular trend.

As an aside but valid illustration, consider world grain prices from 1970 through 2002. Between 1972 and 1973, U.S. grains (corn, wheat, and soybeans) attained their highest price levels for the 32-year period. Despite 3 decades of inflation, the price for corn dropped below the averages seen during the 1970s. The secular price trend for farm products, regardless of some significant spikes, has been down. When adjusted for inflation, farm prices sank to the lowest levels ever recorded in modern history! Of course, this was due to structural changes in agriculture that tremendously boosted efficiency while lowering costs. Better seed, more efficient tractors, smarter planting techniques, and a host of other technological advances helped farmers quadruple yields per acre. This technology was not unique to the United States. Global efficiency caused prices to sink on a purchasing parity basis, as illustrated in Figure 8.10.

Figure 8.10 Soybean futures monthly chart (in dollars).

Since U.S. agriculture accounted for the largest portion of Gross Domestic Product (GDP) export revenue during the 1970s, we saw another structural change as the U.S. economy moved away from agriculture and toward high-tech goods and services. This meant that any currency models using agricultural exports as a GDP forecasting factor had to be constantly adjusted as agriculture's role diminished. For anyone attempting to construct a currency model based on GDP, this information is vitally important.

In Chapter 3, we reviewed fundamental elements of national wealth. In particular, we gave an example of the Japanese rise to the second largest world economy from 1970 through 2000. During this enormous increase in economic prowess, the yen displayed a secular rise against the dollar, as shown in Figure 8.11.

By late 1996, the secular Japanese trendline appeared to be broken. When Japan's economy became overextended, the yen

Figure 8.11   Japanese yen perpetual futures from 1983 to 2002.

responded in kind. Strategically, an investor would not necessarily hold the yen from 1985 through 1996. However, this powerful upward bias did suggest that Japan was a better place to invest dollars over that extended period. The Nikkei 225 exhibited exceptional upward momentum that surpassed U.S. equity performance during the 1980s. Consider the double-whammy achieved by those who rode the wave of Japanese stocks higher while also increasing yen/dollar parity.

The adage "what goes up has to come down" is more a cliché than a reality in currency markets. This is all the more true when considering that new currencies are created out of old, such as the euro. However, the reverse double-whammy was experienced after the Japanese stock market began faltering in the 1990s. By 1996, Japan's economic situation appeared increasingly gloomy while U.S. stocks were enjoying the last leg of an extraordinary bubble. As shown in Figure 8.12, the Nikkei 225

Figure 8.12 Nikkei 225 futures versus yen monthly futures.

broke its secular uptrend and was in steady decline despite brief recoveries. By the same token, the yen is plotted along the same timeline to illustrate how yen/dollar parity moved hand in hand with the overall economy as reflected by Japanese corporate performances.

A behavioral generalization might be drawn from Figure 8.12 since we see that the secular trends of the currency and stock market follow similar downward slopes. However, notice how the yen peaked in 1995 while the Nikkei 225 made interim lows. Thus, the observation must be tempered with the length of the perspective. In addition, observe how the yen was climbing from 1990 through the first half of 1995 while Japanese stocks were essentially in a wide trading range. It is true that half the whammy would have been achieved as yen parity increased on Japanese equities, but the risk of a fall in equity value was highly prevalent.

Tools for Identifying Behavior Characteristics

Now that we have examined basic price behavior characteristics, the next step in understanding currencies requires closer examination. The first objective is to feel comfortable with the components of random, sequential, seasonal, cyclical, and secular trends by more fully understanding tools for identifying these behavior patterns. Toward the mid-twentieth century, a number of respected market practitioners began experimenting with technical trading models. The speculative post World War I period created a group of technical market wizards whose reputations stimulated interest in this emerging field. Among popularized names were mysterious successes like W. D. Gann, Elliot, and even J. P. Morgan. By the 1940s, mechanical calculators were encroaching on the slide rule and rudimentary statistical models began to gain popularity.

Like the lost Ark of the Covenant or the Holy Grail, the works and achievements of these early technicians are highly cryptic and shrouded in secret. Every once and a while, investors are treated to a new revelation about an old system or market guru, but success rates have been dubious and scandals have been plenty.

The crux of the old masters was that they allegedly identified extremely consistent price patterns that were based on various mathematical principles. These include variations on prime numbers, the natural spiral, and Fibonacci sequences, to name a few. With 20/20 hindsight, many of these patterns appear to fit. The problem has been developing a rigid set of standards by which the math can be applied among several markets. Over the course of centuries, mathematicians and investors have tried to find the secret perfect order to markets. However, prevailing scientific evidence seems to demonstrate that no such perfect order exists. Still, you are likely to encounter several applications using relationships derived from natural sequences such as Fibonacci including Elliott Wave and Gann Squares.

Fibonacci Ratios

The Italian mathematician Leonardo Fibonacci lived around the turn of the eleventh century. He discovered a natural pattern by adding consecutive numbers in sequence as follows:

1, 2, 3, 4, 5, 6, 7, 8, 9

$1 + 2 = 3$
$2 + 3 = 5$
$3 + 5 = 8$
$5 + 8 = 13$
$8 + 13 = 21$
$13 + 21 = 34$

Fibonacci sequence = 3, 5, 8, 13, 21, 34, . . .

This sequence appeared to explain many of the patterns observed in nature. From this, some market theoreticians believe an order to market behavior can be found. The Fibonacci sequence presents a ratio that exists between consecutive values known as the Golden Ratio of 1.618 or, conversely, .618. Thus, the separation between the sequenced value is represented by a multiple of 1.618.

There is no question that nature follows the Golden Ratio. From the pattern of petals in a sunflower to the mating pattern of rabbits, the Golden Ratio is repeated. The natural scale is a function of the Golden Ratio that implies that all of Western music is based on the Fibonacci sequence. In conjunction with this, physicists believe a relationship might exist between the Golden Ratio and their quest for perfect symmetry, which they believe is the ultimate design of the universe. Esoteric concepts aside, you may find yourself calculating stops and profit objectives based on the Golden Ratio.

Figure 8.13 uses a charting utility that automatically superimposes Fibonacci ratios on a price pattern. Understand that the drawing is retrospective (after the fact).

Using the 1998 low, the ratio projected the 1998 consolidation between 98.00 and 102.00 while providing support/resistance projection at 110.00 and 121.50. At first glance, the projections are amazingly accurate. However, the objectives required a minimum of two points to draw—presumably the 1998 low and 102.00 resistance. Further, there was no way to

Figure 8.13   The U.S. Dollar Index with Fibonacci overlay.

know that the projection would be to the upside until the second point was observed.

The Fibonacci ratios also provide objectives for retracement. In other words, the eventual downtrend should achieve the same levels as observed on the way up. This projection runs into difficulty if a secular trend intervenes. Skilled practitioners know how to adjust for any secular trend that may have modified the prior objectives. A trend is computed as a line's slope. We tend to think of trendline more visually since our contact is usually as a line drawn on a chart. Slope is calculated as the change in vertical distance (price) divided by the change in horizontal distance (time). Since time is assumed to be a constant (1 day on a daily bar chart), the calculation is more vertically dependent. Now we know why we needed high-school calculus.

$$\Delta Y/\Delta X = \text{Slope}$$

Traditional trendlines are linear and customarily require a minimum of three points. As chartists know, slope can frequently change and requires constant vigilance to make sure lines are properly updated. There is a human tendency to attempt to bend the trendline if our subconscious seeks a particular outcome—that is, we want to remain long or short. It is well established that investment markets are not linear. Since they are not linear, new approaches seek to more precisely gauge market behavior that include curvilinear applications such as neural networks.

Moving Averages

Even with more sophisticated and powerful statistical tools, we still face the basic task of sorting out random noise and deciding what strategies to apply. If you haven't guessed by now, the most fundamental technical tool has been the moving average. Depending on its application, the average can be used to identify all five market behaviors. The debate arises as to how moving averages should be applied and whether they are, in any way, predictive. As mentioned, statistical texts are devoid of any relationship between moving averages and trading decision rules.

The fact that such averages lag current price is inherent in the math. When the velocity of any price change is sufficient, the moving average will turn down within the time permitted by the average's construct—short, medium, or long interval.

For the day trader, the moving average can discern intraday price direction. For the seasonal trader, we can see whether fiscal periods consistently influence particular currencies. Cyclical traders are able to measure amplitude, phase, and frequency, while secular enthusiasts will see overall price direction without necessarily consulting an average. In each instance, predictive capability depends on behavioral consistency. Is there a reliable seasonal pattern to the dollar, euro, yen, or sterling? Can we say with sufficient certainty that one can buy the yen on the second Tuesday in February and sell on the first Monday in April and always make a profit? Can we assume that a price above a 30-day moving average will continue in the direction of the breakout or bust?

Statistical Probability

We answer the question by simply observing behavior and creating a historical reference. Here, the important tool is statistical probability. Like the moving average, probability can be used to describe all five behaviors. However, probability can standalone or be used in conjunction with moving averages to derive more accurate predictive capabilities. The analogy is frequently drawn between investing and gambling. In fact, many sophisticated individuals believe one is simply a derivative of the other—that is, investing is a derivative of gambling. With this cynicism in mind, a great deal of effort has been spent on developing gambling systems. Thus, this bastard cousin has provided some insight into trading methodologies.

Just because price movements appear random, it does not mean you cannot profit. Gaming theory establishes betting formulas based on observed or calculated probabilities. When playing card games, you know each deck has 52 cards and the probabilities of encountering any single card is 1 out of 52 in a fair shuffle. Two decks expand the probability domain to 2 out of 104. The difference is that you are taking a combination of 104 cards taken 5 at a time for blackjack. Cards have fixed odds, whereas currencies do not. Still, currencies have observed behavior from which odds can be derived. Using a technique called *Monte Carlo simulations*, observed events are distributed into frequency distribution called *histograms* or tabulated into expected outcome tables. A simple example is the observation of consecutive up or down strings. How many up days do we see in a row before experiencing a down day when marked to the close? After measuring the data over a number of years, we may find the probability of 4 up days in a row is .1. Using this observation, we adjust our exposure parameters to take into account the probability of 4 up days in a row.

Those familiar with blackjack know about doubling down. Based on probabilities, the process of doubling one's bet on each draw is supposed to provide a positive result once you hit. The problem is whether you hit before you go broke. The practice is the same as the theory. Probability combined with a known exposure yields a desired result. For the currency trader, the application goes a step farther. What is the observed frequency of an upward move after interest rates are raised by .25 percent? Taking all increases in U.S. interest rates and those in other countries, we generate an expected outcome table. The table can go out 1 day, several days, 1 week, or even 1 month. As always, the objective is to identify a pattern within certain probabilities.

Although winning or losing strings may represent random behavior, compiling the probability that changes in short-term interest rates will influence currency parity seeks to measure sequential events. Sequential events present themselves as if-then logic. If interest rates rise, then the U.S. Dollar Index will rise within the following probability parameters. If the GDP declines by one-tenth of a point, then the euro will rise by X with a probability of Y. The value of the probabilistic relationships cannot be overestimated. It is simply enormous. Tens of millions (if not hundreds of millions) have been spent in computing power, man years, and data acquisition to compile event-driven probability tables. Referencing Chapter 4, virtually every piece of fundamental data has some probability of influencing currency parities.

The release of the Fed Beige Book represents a fundamental event. However, it is the information portrayed by the Beige Book that determines the influence on currency parity and interest rates. This means that each piece of datum must be explicitly tested for unique influences and probabilities. Retail sales, inflation figures, durable goods, and a host of other statistics serve to confirm or deny price direction forecasts.

The world of probability has mutually exclusive events, related or dependent events, and multidependent events. We know a coin flip represents a 50/50 probability. When flipping twice, what is the probability of getting heads twice in a row? Each flip is independent, but multiple flips have a combined probability of achieving heads several times before tails appears. In the case of market analysis, there are probabilities associated with each fundamental event, but we also have the ability to measure the influence of combined events—such as a rise in interest rates coupled with a decline in GDP.

Moving to seasonal patterns, the question is the same. What is the probability seasonal patterns will repeat? For example, does the euro always rise against the dollar in the spring? Here, we can simply plot the spring performance over each year and compile the behavior. From this compilation, we see how many times the relationship holds true. At the same time, we want to know what the variation in performance is. For example, spring lasts 3 months. How do we define a rise or fall in parity? Is it at any time in the spring or in the middle, end, or even beginning? This is important because we discussed the possibility of phase shift— the propensity for seasonal patterns to wander forward or backward by several days, weeks, or even a month. This variation has a measurable occurrence and, therefore, observed probability.

When applied to cycle analysis, probability is more frequently associated with the short-term fluctuations. Since the Grand Cycle is not likely to occur more than once in any modern lifetime, forecasting its probability of occurrence is not as immediately useful as predicting the price outcome over the next several days, weeks, or months. Realistically, we know that currency trades last less than 2 days in the cash market and less than 18 months in the futures and related options. This means that we are interested in cycles that may impact parity direction and distance within a short timeframe. Unless your objective is to determine the secular parity trend relative to dollar-, euro-, or yen-denominated investments, the probability that we are in a 60-year bull or bear market transition is irrelevant.

Observing the long-term sterling chart in Figure 8.14, we see the longer-term cycles that are identified with irregular phases lasting between 2 years and several years. Within these longer cycles, there are interim cycles. An investor holding a sterling-denominated investment from 1981 through 1985 lost more than half his value in adverse currency parity. This would make that cycle a very important consideration. However, this is not currency trading.

The trader is interested in determining the pattern within a tradable period. What we discover from the empiric approach is that all currencies operate on a fiscal basis. A calendar year is available for every country. Each season is 90 days trisected by 30-day monthly intervals. The average for bisecting each period falls at approximately 45 days. This means that the average interim trend, whether seasonal or cyclical, should be identified by a 45-day simple moving average.

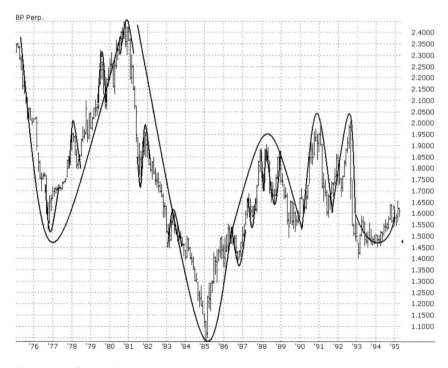

Figure 8.14   Sterling perpetual with cyclical overlay.

Examining the years 1976 through 2001, we see that a super-imposed 45-day moving average appears quite capable of track-ing the interim trend. Notice the consistent seasonal pattern is an approximate 90-day period beginning in mid-June and ending in August. Throughout the quarter century represented, this period displays a relatively trendless market. Even where a trend existed in 2000, 1998, and 1994, wide swings appeared within the trend channel. See Figures 8.15 through 8.40.

By identifying this seasonal tendency, we can attempt to con-struct an option strangle strategy beginning in late June and car-rying through the summer. During the remaining periods, we see a strong trending potential that, again, is identified by a definitive 45-day moving average slope. Upon closer examination, we see that trendless periods are represented by a 20 percent decrease in slope. The exceptions are 1980, 1982, and 1984. In all other years, the slope change signals a transition. Note, however, that the three exceptions were years where the overall trend did not change direction. The behavioral personality of sterling is some-what revealed by the simple application of the 45-day simple

Figure 8.15   December 1976 sterling.

Figure 8.16   December 1977 sterling.

Figure 8.17   December 1978 sterling.

Figure 8.18   December 1979 sterling.

Figure 8.19   December 1980 sterling.

Figure 8.20   December 1981 sterling.

Figure 8.21   December 1982 sterling.

Figure 8.22   December 1983 sterling.

Figure 8.23   December 1984 sterling.

Figure 8.24 December 1985 sterling.

Figure 8.25 December 1986 sterling.

Figure 8.26	December 1987 sterling.

Figure 8.27	December 1988 sterling.

Figure 8.28 December 1989 sterling.

Figure 8.29 December 1990 sterling.

Figure 8.30   December 1991 sterling.

Figure 8.31   December 1992 sterling.

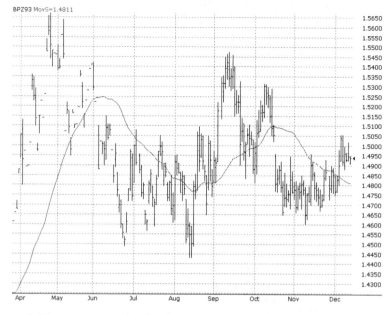

Figure 8.32 December 1993 sterling.

Figure 8.33 December 1994 sterling.

Figure 8.34   December 1995 sterling.

Figure 8.35   December 1996 sterling.

Figure 8.36 December 1997 sterling.

Figure 8.37 December 1998 sterling.

Figure 8.38   December 1999 sterling.

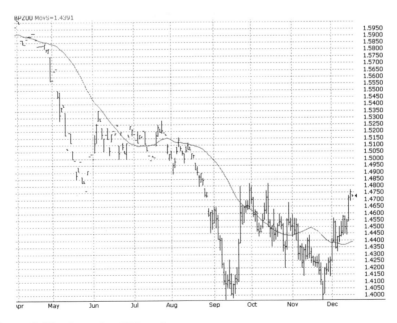

Figure 8.39   December 2000 sterling.

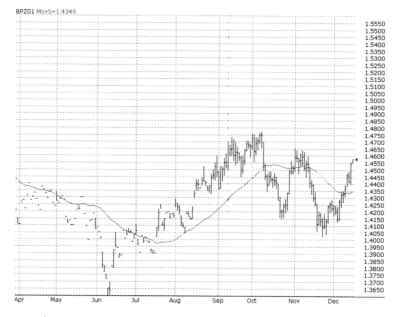

Figure 8.40 December 2001 sterling.

moving average. It is worth noting that the simply moving average theme has many variations. These include logarithmic moving averages, lagged or advanced moving averages, and weighted moving averages where the value of the closer days is indexed or weighted higher than the earlier days within the series.

Determining Slope Change with a Protractor

Assuming you are married or have a significant other, your companion probably falls within two categories: those who allow years of past early life experiences to pile up in drawers and closets or those who incessantly clear out everything that has not been nailed down or specifically scheduled with your insurance carrier. For those in the junk collector category, rummage around your piles and attempt to find your high-school geometry protractor. For those readers who are seasoned and/or addicted chartists, the protractor is probably embedded in your left or right hand.

The tricky part is remembering how to use the protractor. Fortunately, our application is relatively simple. Placing the crosshairs on the flat part of the 45-day line, we can measure the trendline slope and its rate of change. Referencing Figure 8.41, we can see that the market enters its trading range after a 20-degree decrease in the rate of descent.

When the slope increases by 20 percent (in either direction), either a new trend develops or the old trend resumes. It may be necessary to draw horizontal reference lines from which you extend the 45-day line to get an accurate reading.

Determining Slope Change with the Moving Average

Practitioners of the moving average crossing technique will argue that the protractor exercise is not necessary. Simply use

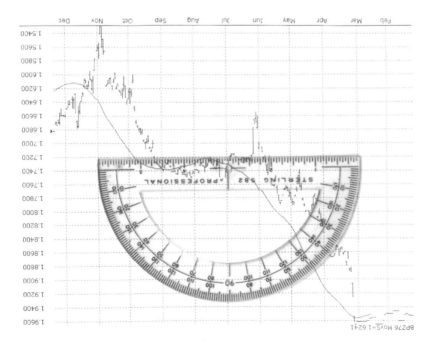

Figure 8.41   December British pound.

the price as the reference. As we discussed, when the price crosses the average to the upside, the assumption is that the trend is up. An opposite crossover presumes the trend is down. Observing the summer seasonal, we see that the crossover method is subject to several false buy-and-sell signals when the market is trendless. This is why more conservative (or less funded) currency traders prefer to confirm the crossover with a change in slope. Since most trends last several months and account for more than 10 percent of swings in sterling/dollar parity, the sacrifice of a few points in favor of slope confirmation should not be unbearable.

As Figure 8.42 illustrates, the distance captured by the 45-day average from July through October 2001 is more than enough to offset the near zero losses encountered during the flat period from early October to mid-November. The two entries/exits are approximately the same price. The early October trend change dropped from 1.4700 to 1.4500 before the moving average was violated. This distance represents the efficiency of using the 45-day moving average as a decision rule for buying and selling. This

Figure 8.42   Profits from July through October 2001.

is only the efficiency represented by the single event. In order to have a more realistic view, we would need to measure every crossover and compute the efficiency for each. Then we must analyze the overall efficiency for its own characteristics, such as the average, median, and standard deviation. This same retrospective is easily performed on all the available years in any currencies currently traded.

Over the years, technicians have determined that the use of two moving averages with different periods can be more effective in determining a slope change. For example, a 45-day average might be combined with a 60-day average to determine when the near-term velocity alters course sufficiently to violate the longer-term average. The assumption is that the longer-term average will have a more moderate slope during a trend since the rate of change represented by the average is over a longer period. In fact, this is usually the case.

A 60-day average represents 2 months and is considered extremely effective because it takes into consideration a new month of economic data and a corrected month of data. As many currency watchers know, the United States releases new monthly statistics while revising the prior month. This is also the practice for quarterly data. Sometimes the revision is as influential as the original data. Thus, a 2-month average attempts to smooth out monthly sequential data. Figures 8.43-8.58 presents individual charts for the December U.S. Dollar Index futures from the 1986 expiration through 2001. The dashed line represents the 60-day moving average and the solid line represents the 45-day moving average.

Like the pound, we can discern a seasonal propensity toward trendless parity. Understand that the U.S. Dollar Index is a weighted composite of several currencies. Therefore, it will not precisely reflect a parity change specific to only the yen or only the euro. Still, we see how interim trends are accurately tracked by both averages. In addition, the crossover of the averages provides an efficient method for identifying a change in trend.

Although the years are not connected in a continuous chart, we see a secular downtrend in the U.S. Dollar Index from a 1985 high above 127.00 to 1988 lows around 88.50. This approximate 30 percent decline is indicative of the multiyear decline or rally. In June 1988, we see a roller-coaster ride from the 88.50 lows to

Figure 8.43 The 1986 U.S. Dollar Index futures historical perspective.

Figure 8.44 The 1987 U.S. Dollar Index futures historical perspective.

Figure 8.45 The 1988 U.S. Dollar Index futures historical perspective.

Figure 8.46 The 1989 U.S. Dollar Index futures historical perspective.

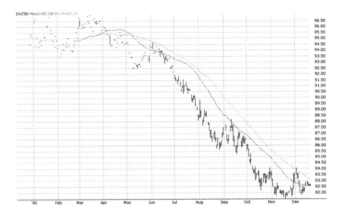

Figure 8.47 The 1990 U.S. Dollar Index futures historical perspective.

Figure 8.48 The 1991 U.S. Dollar Index futures historical perspective.

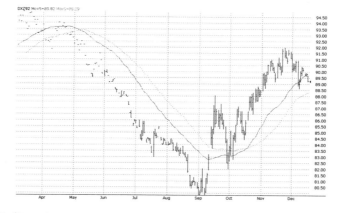

Figure 8.49   The 1992 U.S. Dollar Index futures historical perspective.

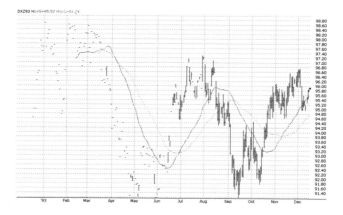

Figure 8.50   The 1993 U.S. Dollar Index futures historical perspective.

Figure 8.51   The 1994 U.S. Dollar Index futures historical perspective.

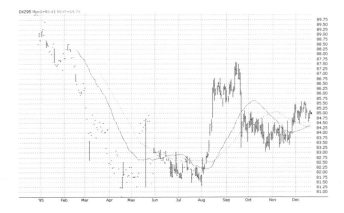

Figure 8.52   The 1995 U.S. Dollar Index futures historical perspective.

Figure 8.53   The 1996 U.S. Dollar Index futures historical perspective.

Figure 8.54   The 1997 U.S. Dollar Index futures historical perspective.

Figure 8.55 The 1998 U.S. Dollar Index futures historical perspective.

Figure 8.56 The 1999 U.S. Dollar Index futures historical perspective.

Figure 8.57 The 2000 U.S. Dollar Index futures historical perspective.

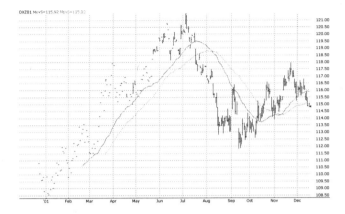

Figure 8.58   The 2001 U.S. Dollar Index futures historical perspective.

a 99.50 high—a 12 percent rise followed by a plummet almost back to the starting point. In 1989, we experienced a similar pattern; however, the lows were higher than the previous year. By 1990, the downtrend was firmly back in place. From a fundamental perspective, what caused such incredible parity swings in the Dollar Index?

Examine Figure 8.59 that compares 1987 30-year T-Bonds with the Dollar Index. There are several distinguishing features. During a period of stable long-term U.S. interest rates, the dollar fell from January to February 1987. February saw a stable dollar, but the dollar appeared hypersensitive to interest rates in March when a minor decrease in rates (rise in principle) was concurrent with the dollar's drift lower. When interest rates shot up in April, the dollar continued to lower. This would seem contrary to popular theory that the dollar moves inversely to interest rates.

Of course, we know the Fed was concerned about reigniting inflation with lower interest rates as the fall of 1987 approached. Greenspan applied the brakes, as shown in the impressive bond decline in the beginning of September and the beginning of October. However, by October 10, the stock market became overburdened and finally crashed on Black Monday on October 19, 1987. In a panic to add liquidity, the Fed poured huge money into the system while precipitously cutting rates. But the dollar was unresponsive. Although stocks recovered from the crash in 1987, the economy moved in segments toward the eventual

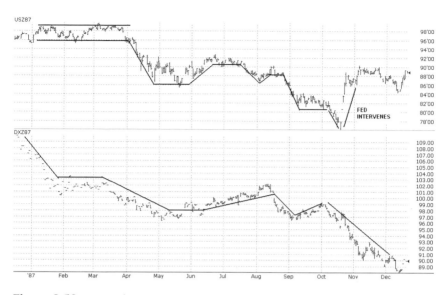

Figure 8.59 December 1987 U.S. 30-year T-Bond futures versus December 1987 U.S. Dollar Index.

boom enjoyed under the Clinton Administration. From 1987 through 1990, the recovery remained tenuous. For example, a bottom in real estate culminated in 1993. Keep in mind that the Gulf War was fought in the intervening period and the U.S. stock market suffered through several corrective hiccups. All of this impinged on a smoothly trending dollar.

This was a difficult period for currency traders because they were in the process of constructing new rules and strategies. If the positive correlation between rising interest rates and a rising currency failed to prove true, it would have been back to the drawing board. Examine how the U.S. Dollar Index declined smoothly just below the 60-day moving average through 1990. This nearly perfect trend became one of the most exciting speculative rides of that decade. From December through April 1991, the dollar rallied only to experience a similar decline.

Each year displays its unique characteristics; however, we are able to see seasonal and even cyclical patterns—not to mention the secular trends. Before examining a continuous chart, it is worth noting that the concept of currency value was being structurally questioned. We are all familiar with inflation. The 50¢ ice cream goes to $1.50. From $1.50, it moves to $3.50. This process continues regardless of a major deflation. We know inflation erodes monetary value, but governments were not sure how to measure overall value because the typical basket of goods and services used to measure value was clearly changing. From diet to smoking habits, consumers were not following the path of predecessors. You can be confident that the next generations will also change their patterns.

Efficiency in delivering goods and services and, in particular, high-tech information processing altered valuation standards in the industrialized nations. In fact, the first Bush Administration considered changing the Consumer Price Index (CPI) as a way to more accurately reflect the dollar's value. Since so many goods and services were substantially linked to the CPI, it would have been an enormous undertaking with dire consequences for some and extraordinary benefits for others. A lease with rent escalations linked to the CPI could have been held in limbo or even retrogressed. Labor contracts might have automatically retrogressed. Employers and leaseholders might have had huge windfalls.

The troubles during the 1980s and 1990s are reflected in the monthly continuation chart shown in Figure 8.60 where we take the behavioral analysis a step farther. Here, the chart has a numbered trend overlay from 1 through 5 coupled with concentric Fibonacci arcs produced from the first wave. Whether it is by coincidence or not, we have a 5 count that corresponds to the Elliot Wave theory that breaks interim trend patterns into a series of 5 up and 5 down. Don't jump to conclusions when observing the subsequent upwave. Elliot Wave theory also identifies major and minor series along with transition waves.

This brings us to another form of behavioral analysis. From 1986 through 1987, the trend was down. From 1988 through 1990, the trend was up. From 1990 to 1991, the trend was down. The next 2 years were bounces. From 1993 to 1994, the trend was erratically up. From 1995 into 1998, the trend was up. During half of 1998, the trend was down. The pattern is an approximate 2-year cycle with phase shift that is remarkably coincidental with the Fibonacci ratios.

Taking a fundamental perspective, our curiosity should take us to the interest rate correlation. Using the T-Bill continuation chart

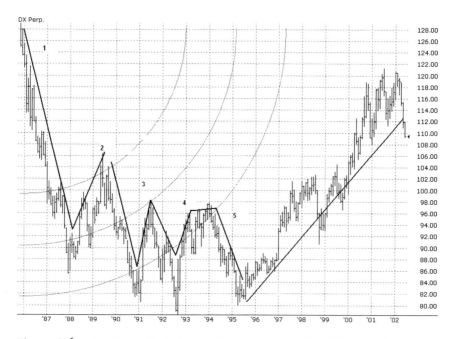

Figure 8.60   The U.S. Dollar Index from 1987 to 2002 monthly with Fibonacci arc overlay.

as a reference, we see a comparison to the U.S. Dollar Index. This analysis is in a vacuum because we are only examining the local (U.S.) short-term rate rather than the relative interest rate, as explained in previous chapters. This is a flawed picture because it is the relative rate that determines parity differentials. However, this is the U.S.-centric view that is habitually applied by both U.S. and foreign currency traders. See Figure 8.61.

Heavy lines are used to distinguish when there is divergence in the interest rate correlation. The monthly perspective shows interim trends that do not follow interest rate patterns. This is why evaluation must be tempered with the high probability that normal relationships will not hold during different timeframes.

From 1995 through part of 2002, the dollar dominated the world currencies along with the U.S. 8-year economic boom. Although U.S. good fortune reigned, other nations were not doing as well. Another new world assumption that what was good for the United States was good for the world was crushed along with the Japanese stock market.

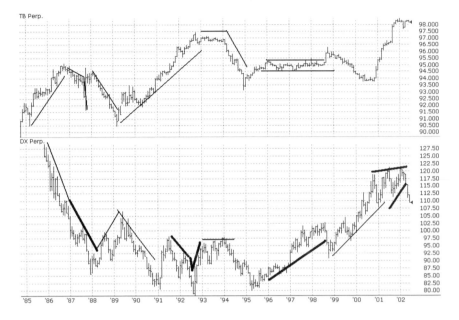

Figure 8.61   T-Bills versus the U.S. Dollar Index from 1985 to 2002.

Figure 8.62 shows the Nikkei 225 Index against the U.S. Dollar Index. We see the Dollar Index's rise with the Nikkei's fall. The strong dollar did not help the Japanese export economy, as we would have concluded. We know, however, that Japan attempted to stimulate with near zero interest rates. This practically removed the interest rate consideration since you can't go lower than zero. Reading currency commentary from 1997 through 1999, there was a quest for the yen's bottom. It briefly materialized in mid-1998, as Figure 8.63 reveals, but the yen failed to hold on.

Following the dollar, sterling, and yen, we discern reasonable differences in behavior associated with particular economic performances. This brings back the concept of the wealth of nations. Secular trend seems to be defined by the wealth factor, while intermediate movement correlate to sequential events or seasonal patterns. What is prominent about our brief behavioral examination is the propensity for major interim and secular trends. These significant parity realignments represent tremendous profit opportunities—one of the essential themes of this text.

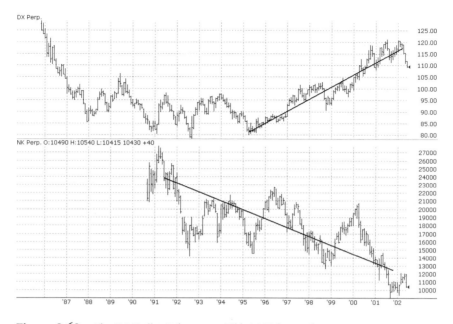

Figure 8.62   The U.S. Dollar Index versus Nikkei 225 futures from 1987 to 2002.

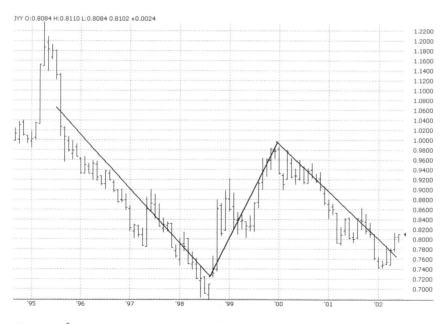

Figure 8.63   Japanese yen cash from 1995 to 2002.

Chart Analysis

As illustrated, 45- and 60-day simple moving averages are capable of filtering out noise and identifying parity trends lasting a few weeks to several months. In addition, flat averages alert us to trading range conditions. Changing slopes signal turning points by decelerating. Very steep slopes after a more moderate slope frequently signal an overbought or oversold condition. Patterns identified by moving averages do not represent the totality of those used to discern profit potentials. In fact, the largest body of behavioral methodologies examines very specific subpatterns for clues to more immediate price movements lasting a few days or weeks. Invariably, you will be introduced to chart patterns that are hailed as sure-fire ways to accumulate a million bucks. However, chart interpretation is as much an art as it is a science.

Some intuitive chartists can seemingly predict the very next sequence of events by evaluating prior events. Unfortunately, chart patterns tend to be like the psychological Rorschach test that uses inkblot interpretation as a diagnostic tool for identifying schizophrenia. Everyone sees pictures a bit differently. Thus, chart pattern recognition tends to be extremely subjective. Still, there is general agreement about certain patterns that appear to lead to other behavior. Most investors have come in contact with chart interpretation in one form or another. This experience probably introduced concepts such as trendlines, head and shoulders, flags, pennants, rounded bottoms or tops, double tops or bottoms, *W* and *M* formations, gaps, island reversals, and more.

Rules for Formation

Missing from many chart analysis books is an explanation of the behavior behind the patterns. It is assumed to be sufficient to simply identify the alleged pattern and its expected result. The problem with this identification-by-rote approach is that interpretation becomes more accident prone. For example, the word *pattern* is frequently interchanged with *formation*. A common misunderstanding exists that formations and patterns are the same. In fact, a formation is a component of a pattern. Traditional charting makes this distinction because a formation by itself is not predictive enough. Only after a formation repeats do we see a behavioral pattern that presumes some predictability.

Consider a top formation, which is numbered with 1 and 2 in Figure 8.64. In this illustration, a top has formed twice. The repetition of a top formation creates a double top pattern. If the top were to repeat a third time, we would have a triple top pattern that might also be interpreted as a trading range consolidation if the tops and bottoms were symmetrical, repeating at the same levels. Depending on its configuration, a consolidation can be a pattern or a formation. Although Figure 8.64 paints a clear picture of symmetrical tops, it does not explain the dynamic that creates such a formation. As we know, charts are nothing more than a pictorial record of prior behavior between buyers and sellers. From this viewpoint, why do prices rise and fall to paint the top formation?

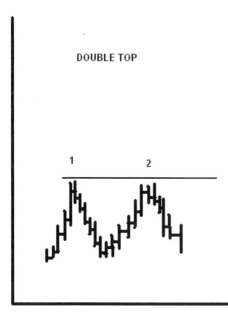

Figure 8.64   Double top pattern.

The first top labeled 1 tells us the following technical rule:

Rule for rising formation—Buyers continue to be willing to buy
at increasing prices. Sellers are only willing to sell if they are
offered higher prices.

As simple and obvious as this rule may seem, it is critical to
any understanding of technical chart analysis. What we see
directly reflects the *psychology of the market*—a phrase frequently bantered about over after-trading drinks or at cocktail
parties. You may even encounter market psychoanalysis at how-
to trading seminars and lectures. The next technical rule defines
the formation of top 1 as follows:

Rule for top formation—Buyers are no longer willing to buy on
rising prices.

The top represents buyers' exhaustion. It is not that sellers
are not asking for higher prices; it is simply the absence of buying interest. However, at some point sellers realize that the only
way to tempt buyers back is to offer more attractive prices.
Hence:

Rule for declining formation—Sellers are willing to sell at falling
prices. Buyers are only willing to purchase if offered lower
prices.

When a market experiences a complete cycle from low to top
and back to the same low, we see a top formation. The rule is:

Rule for bottom formation—Sellers are no longer willing to
accept lower prices.

In reality, tops and bottoms are ultimate tests of specific
prices that change the balance between buyers and sellers. They
represent psychological *break points*, or more appropriately
named *brake points* since they brake a rise or fall. When the
reaction is sudden or sharp, the top will appear as an inverted
V—hence the expression *V* top or *V* bottom. If the rise or fall is
precipitous and extends beyond the former turning point, it is a

V reversal. These formations occur when a rapid decrease in buyers (top) or sellers (bottom) is present. Thus, they are frequently associated with surprise sequential or nonsequential events. A monetary standard such as short-term interest rates might be changed or a monetary statistic may substantially deviate from expectations. However, V formations can occur for no other reason than when buyers or sellers reach a mass psychological limit —the price is more or less than buyers or sellers can accept, all things remaining equal.

V tops and bottoms are also associated with testing news. When an unexpected event occurs, chartists watch to see if it exhausts either buyers or sellers. Consider the expression "a picture is worth a thousand words." In our case, it could be thousands of dollars, reals, yen, or euros!

The Transition from Formation to Pattern

When a top is experienced at approximately the same level twice, the formation turns into the pattern. We discern that buyers are resistant to higher prices at the same level. Fundamentally, the market condition must change in the minds of buyers to induce them to raise the bar. A series of similar tops forms a *consolidation top*. The defining rule is:

Consolidation top pattern—Buyers reach an equilibrium limit beyond which they are unwilling to buy unless circumstances change.

Indeed, continuous resistance at the same price is a form of equilibrium as well as an obvious price limitation. The rule for a bottom pattern is simply the inverse—that is, an equilibrium limit beyond which sellers are no longer willing to sell unless market conditions change. The change in condition can either be a fundamental event or simply the absence of fellow sellers.

Other pictures of equilibrium are depicted when tops are maintained while bottoms are rising. This forms a wedge, as illustrated in Figure 8.65.

This pattern is associated with buyers and sellers coming together in a narrowing range. A closer consensus on price is

Figure 8.65   Ascending bottom asymmetrical triangle.

being achieved from the buyers' viewpoint. Although we have identified a uniform buyers' resistance, sellers are showing a reluctance to accept lower prices. This is indicative of a break-out. If the price moves above resistance, it proves that sellers have a greater influence despite the fact that buyers appear in control. Sellers are forcing the price higher by their unwilling-ness to accept the same or lower prices. These patterns have sis-ter patterns with rising tops, falling bottoms, and flat tops/ bottoms. Illustrations are similar. When a chart defines a series of rising tops and bottoms, we identify an uptrend and a channel. The channel is constructed from top to top and bottom to bot-tom. When the channel is drawn with parallel lines, it is a sym-metrical channel. There are converging channels where buyers and sellers are narrowing the upward range and diverging chan-nels where the range is widening on the way up.

Although many conclusions are drawn concerning the sig-nificance or implication of widening and narrowing channels, a case can be made that all patterns follow this general appearance sooner or later. Therefore, no reliable prediction exists. However, when these patterns are extensions of a previous breakout or bust, they form highly popular *flags* and *pennants*. As these names imply, a flag is a square consolidation after a vertical run-up or decline. Pennants are triangular consolidations developing from the same vertical formation. Flags and pennants represent decision-making periods. A consensus between buyers and sellers is reached after a major psychological dislocation. In the case of a run-up, a burst of buyers was suddenly willing to pay significantly higher prices. At the same time, the supply of sellers was exhausted. The consolidation brings buyers and sellers into balance until one or the other side realigns and forces the price higher or lower. Hence, flags and pennants are associated with continuation and reversal forecasts. The slope and form of the flag and pennant provide clues about the eventual continuation or reversal. Contrary to logic, a downward sloping flag is believed to signal a continuation up if the pole was up. This is because sellers abruptly disappear on a test of falling prices. An upward slope signals caution and a possible reversal because buyers' enthusiasm can quickly wane leaving a pool of sellers.

Pattern Recognition

When drawing a series of open/high/low/close bar charts, an infinite number of formations and subsequent patterns are possible. At some point, these formations and patterns must be pared down and correlated to potential events. A large number of currency traders strongly fall into the technical analysis camp and indulge in monumental chart-following pools. Charts may be self-fulfilling to the extent normal traders experience the same Rorschach interpretations. If we all come to the same conclusion, the market will be driven in the direction of that conclusion. In any event, currencies seem to lend themselves to chart interpretation, as attested to by Figure 8.66.

Putting it all together usually requires a vast search of hundreds of charts to illustrate each unique pattern. However, Figure 8.66 packs most of the popular patterns into a single euro currency chart over just 1 year. This exceptional example of conformity enables us to take each pattern and demonstrate how it may be applied to (hopefully) work. In this particular example, the pattern recognition was actually conducted in real time without the benefit of 20/20 hindsight. The identification was

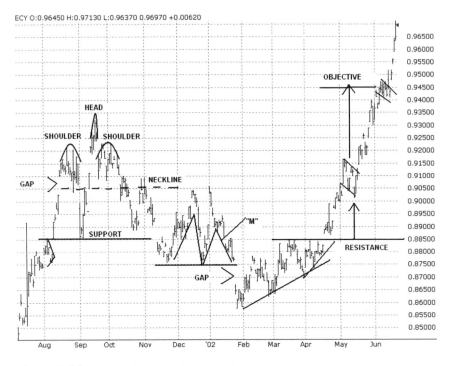

ECY O:0.96450 H:0.97130 L:0.96370 0.96970 +0.00620

Figure 8.66   Technical chart analysis euro currency cash.

used to advise traders who subscribed to the Commodity Futures Forecast® Service during 2001 and 2002.

Moving from left to right, the first pattern consists of a rapid rise culminating in a triangular consolidation. Alone, this pennant does not provide insight into the next direction. If the price had fallen below .87000, we would predict a setback to .86000 if the initial bust below the .87500 bottom of the consolidation did not instantly achieve the .86000 objective. However, there was a powerful breakout above .88500. Measuring the distance from .85000 to .87500, we get 150 points. A crude but popular method of calculating an objective is to add the 150 to the top of the consolidation, which gives .90000.

Gaps

As we can see, prices did touch .90000, but extended further to a high above .92000. In the process, a more radical dislocation between buyers and sellers gapped prices to a new consolidation between .90500 and .92000. The rule on gaps is that they eventually fill. That is, what goes up eventually comes down, and vice versa. Two types of gaps are available: breakaway and exhaustion. As the names imply, breakaway gaps see a continuation in the direction of the gap, whereas exhaustion gaps usually have a consolidation and a retracement. Many skeptics contend that gap identification is post facto. You don't know what it is until it's over. In Figure 8.66, prices consolidate and decline just enough to fill the gap. Once filled, bulls can regain confidence that the price will move higher. But how high?

Gaps are considered useful for answering this question. The term *measuring gap* is used to project to a new high or low. The distance traveled from the first gap is approximately 150 points. By adding this to the consolidation high, we get .93500 as our next upward goal. Amazingly, the next breakout above the gap achieves this lofty figure, but not before testing all the way down to .88500. The powerful bounce from .88500 signifies support that is identified by the breakout from the triangle and subsequent inability to fall below this same price level. The severity of each event also has significance. It means buyers are strongly opinionated about .88500 being a good parity for the euro against the dollar.

To be precise, the .88500 test violated an important subsequent level of .90500. Notice in the left consolidation labeled Shoulder that prices touched just below .90500 and moved higher. We have a hint that .90500 also represents support. At this stage, a review of the appropriate action helps clarify the exercise.

The breakout from the August pennant results in the following decision:

> *Buy September euro currency at market using an .87500 stop. Move stop to entry after .90000 (0.88500 + 150). Raise stop to .90000 after .91500.*

We see how the buying decision was generated and how we arrived at placing and moving protection. When prices fell below .90500, this position was stopped out with a 150-point profit from .88500 to .90000.

When prices dropped to .88500 and supported, there was no
action. Perhaps another chartist might have identified some
alternative action, but this interpretation was directionless.
After supporting, however, there was a new incentive to buy.
With prices jumping from .88500 to .89500, the action is:

> *Buy long December euro currency at market using an
> .88500 stop. Move stop to entry after .90500. Increase
> stop to .90500 after .92000. Raise stop to .92000 after
> .93500.*

The rationale behind this action should be identifiable on the
chart. Rather than offer a step-by-step explanation, trace the
logic to see if you would have come to the same conclusions.

This resulted in another stop out at .92000. We see this head
floating between .92000 and .93500. From there, the price gaps
lower and the right shoulder fills the gap. At this point, we are
not necessarily able to determine a new strategy. However, there
is significance to .90500 as support. The appearance of two
shoulders with a higher exhaustion head alerts to the possibility
that 9500 is a neckline. The problem with this interpretation is
the rise to the head takes place in September after already vio-
lating this alleged neckline. Thus, purists would deny the existence of a true head-and-shoulders formation. However, real-
world applications find us bastardizing charting rules all the
time. We bend and make exceptions because other aspects of
trading action suggest such liberties. Hence, charting is far from
an exact science or even a disciplined art.

The distance from the top of the head at .93500 to the neckline of .90500 is 300 points. This measures for our downside
objective that is .90500 less 300, or .87500. The next downside
would subtract another 300 points to produce .84500. The strategy is as follows:

> *Sell short December euro currency at approximately
> .90500 using .91500 stop (150 points). Lower stop to
> entry after .89000 (150 points). Drop stop to .89500
> after reaching .88500 former support (in case support
> holds and a rally follows). Take profits at .87500, can-
> celing stop.*

Penetration Adjustments

At this stage, we can introduce the concept of penetration adjustments. Although the term and practice may sound like an excuse for missed transaction, it is actually a widely applied technique for adjusting objectives. Generally, objectives appear to line up with the chart grid. Chart grids, by nature, divide the vertical into even numbers falling at regular intervals. This can tease the eye and mind into selecting exact grid numbers such as .80500. To overcome this propensity, chartists apply an adjustment for penetration. Usually, it is in the conservative direction when setting profit goals while allowing some extra leeway when setting stops. Assume the euro adjustment was 5 points. Instead of seeking .87500 exactly, we would look for .87550.

In our example, we would have taken our profits at .87550 in late November. If no adjustment was made, we would have been stopped at .89500 for a 100-point gain. With the adjustment, we achieved our objective.

The move above .88500 brings us back long with an .87500 stop. We move stop to entry after reaching .90500 (or .90450 with adjustment). After the market retreats, we are stopped at our entry for a breakeven plus costs. Now, the market supports at .87500 again. Here, we are on the sidelines waiting to see if .90500 offers resistance. If it does, we sell seeking .88500 as a first goal (former support) and .87500 as a second goal.

A more astute chartist might have bought on a breakout above .88500 (former support assumed to be new resistance) using an .87500 stop. The first objective to move stop to entry would have been the .90500 neckline that is assumed to be resistance. The result would probably have been a breakeven after the setback. However, a breakout above the neckline would have generated a handsome profit as the stop was ratcheted higher.

The January 2002 decline became a challenge of .87500 support. This converts .88500 former support into the resistance line. We have an *M* pattern that says a dip below .87500 will result in a drop to 50 percent of the distance from .90500 resistance as a first goal. Indeed, prices gapped below .87500 and touched below .86000—right on target. Unfortunately, the gap foreclosed our participation.

M Pattern and W Formation

It is worth mentioning that an *M* pattern is obviously a double top, whereas a *W* formation is a double bottom. The significance is at the extremes—that is, the tops of the *M* or bottoms of the *W* and the base of the *M* or height of the *W*. A bust below or breakout above either level is considered a continuation with the first objective equal to 50 percent of the height of either pattern. Although the letter may not be perfectly symmetrical, the tops and bottoms should conform. Once the downside objective of .86000 is achieved, we wait to see the next pattern. Our new assumptions are that .87500 will offer resistance—the bottom of the *M*. This leads to a sell if .87500 holds and a buy if it is exceeded. The buy would have been stopped at .86500 for a 100-point loss. The sell would have succeeded. Which would you have done? Try to be honest with yourself. Remember what Shakespeare said, "To thine own self be true."

The decline below .87500 stops just below .86500 and rallies just under .88500 resistance. We can identify a pattern of increasing lows and highs. At the end of March, the dip to .87000 provides the points necessary to construct a trendline. From March through mid-April, .88500 resistance continues holding to from an asymmetrical triangle. Our anticipation is a breakout above resistance with the following strategy:

> *Buy at .88450/50 using .87000 stop. Move stop to entry after making .90000 (.88500 + 150 points). Raise stop to .89950 (.90000 adjusted by 5) after reaching .91450 (.91500 adjusted by 5).*

When we reach .90000, buyers and sellers have a brief argument where sellers bring the price down to .90000 in a downward sloping flag. This behavior reflects the anticipation of the .90000 and .91500 objectives. Some buyers (longs) who set their exit objective at .91500 added to selling liquidity. In the meantime, other buyers are waiting for the dip to .90000 to reenter, enter for the first time, or add to existing positions. It is also worth noting that the .90000/.91500 range correlates with the head-and-shoulders neckline assumed to be .90500.

This becomes a continuation pattern as long as the .90000 support holds, which it did. The projection is to .94500 that measures the distance from .88590 former resistance (the breakout from the asymmetrical triangle) to .91500 (the top of the flagpole). Behold! The next leg higher does stop at approximately .94500 and we see the same type of consolidation—probably for the same reasons. The next projection is .97500, moving the stop up by the full objective plus 50 percent.

I have always believed that chart analysis should become part of a medical school's Department of Psychology curriculum. What we are doing is making predictions based on mass psychology patterns reflected in chart formations. We see areas where buyers or sellers become reluctant to participate. We understand that measurements made by John could be the same as those of Mary, who is following the advice of Jane, who was talking to her husband's broker Bob. No matter what sequence leads to the reflected behavior, we assume these formations and patterns have consistency.

Charting is as much a metal exercise as it is a method of trading. Talk to any chartist and you will find he or she takes as much pleasure in the exercise as in the results. This is why so many chartists consistently lose during their "practice" in the hopes that some day they will get it perfect. In the meantime, they enjoy the process.

Gender and Chart Analysis

A confession is required before moving forward. As much as my male ego is bruised by this reality, I have found that women are inherently better traders than men. This discovery was made by sending a questionnaire to Commodex® System subscribers. Commodex is a daily futures trading system covering all major U.S. commodity, financial, and energy futures. Although women were a far smaller percentage of the polled sample, the results were statistically significant after adjusting for proportions of men versus women. The ladies consistently reported profitable results, whereas the men were frustrated in a performance never-never land.

I happened to run into a psychiatrist and asked why women outperform the men. The explanation was enlightening. Commodex is an automatic daily system that issues exact buy and sell signals with accompanying stops. It is like following a trading roadmap. The doctor explained:

> *"If I have two patients, one male and one female for whom I prescribe the same medication to be taken one every four hours, and the fourth hour is at 2 A.M. in the morning, the female gets up and takes the pill while the male sleeps until 7 A.M. and takes two pills."*

In short, women have a discipline to follow directions, while men always want to challenge the rules. When attempting to follow charts, discipline is critical. All too often, a pattern will be violated and the action hesitated. He who hesitates is lost. However, always look before you leap. Hesitation or taking the plunge can be an easier decision if the patterns have logic. It is simple enough to understand that a double top means that buyers have reached their interim limit more than once in the same spot. However, a head and shoulders is a bit more complex. The right and left shoulders show the buyer's limit, but the head is an anomaly.

When tracking this pattern, we see that the head is formed by a minority of buyers who express overenthusiasm after the recovery from the left shoulder. Without an increase in buyers, the head fades back to the right shoulder. Those who created the head are now sensitive to their losses. When the right shoulder fails, not only do the buyers from the head sell, but the buyers from the right shoulder also sell. This adds selling momentum and the neckline is violated.

The asymmetrical triangle shows a willingness of buyers to purchase at climbing prices while sellers are resisting lower lows. This makes the baseline or trend rise. Still, the flat top shows resistance is holding. When the supply of sellers who are willing to sell under the resistance line exhausts, buyers are forced above the resistance and we have a breakout. The reasoning behind objectives has to do with momentum. In futures, the margin gained by the first leg can be used to leverage the second leg. This means the distance traveled should be the same. In stocks or cash investments, the profit margin is doubled, enabling a doubling of wealth in the account and a carry to a second level that is equal to the first.

Stochastic Measurements

Some technicians do not want to know the reasoning behind the images. They only want to spot the formations and patterns so they can act. However, patterns are in the eyes of the beholder. This represents the supreme danger when using charts alone. Momentum indicators augment charting logic and provide some additional levels of alleged objectivity. Two popular momentum measurements use price differentials to determine whether relative changes are accelerating or declining. In engineering, a stochastic measurement uses differences in observations to derive a probability of future observations. Stochastic measurements are used for quality control on manufacturing lines. The concept was applied to commodities by George Lane using differentials in high, low, and close.

The popularization of the stochastic approach was labeled *stochastics*. However, there is no plural for stochastic nor is Lane's application to futures trading indicative of a stochastic methodology. Lane observed that uptrend closes tend to appear in the higher portion of the daily range until a top is eminent. At that point, closes lose momentum and begin to move into the lower portion of the daily range. Given this behavior, his formulas compute two component variables labeled %K and %D. The K variable is computed:

$$\%K = (CLOSE - LOW_{(day\ x)})/(HIGH_{(day\ x)} - LOW_{(day\ x)})$$
$$\%D = \Sigma\%K/C$$

Where C is a constant equal to the number of days in the %K series. Popular constants are 9 days, 14 days, and 21 days.

The formulas create smooth waves that track each momentum as a function of high/low/close differentials rather than absolute price. If Lane's observation is consistent, a reversal from a high coupled with a high %D and %K values indicates a divergence—a signal to sell or bring protection close in a bull market. The opposite applies to a bear market. Stochastic indicators can be plotted on a chart in conjunction with the absolute price to identify bullish or bearish divergence. This enables a visual correlation to current price patterns that can assist in deciding whether a market is overbought or oversold.

Missing from Lane's stochastic application is the probability distribution associated with divergent events. Normally, each observation would be tracked in a distribution to determine a success and failure rate within various performance categories. Without specific probabilities, the stochastic application operates as an independent oscillator with somewhat amorphous decision rules. For comparison, type *stochastic* into any Internet search engine. The results are far from what is described in the popular commodity application. Still, Lane's application is highly useful in identifying the velocity of narrowing daily ranges over the selected periods.

Figure 8.67 displays the same euro currency chart as Figure 8.66 with a stochastic study appended to the bottom. Overbought and oversold values are indicated by the vertical lines

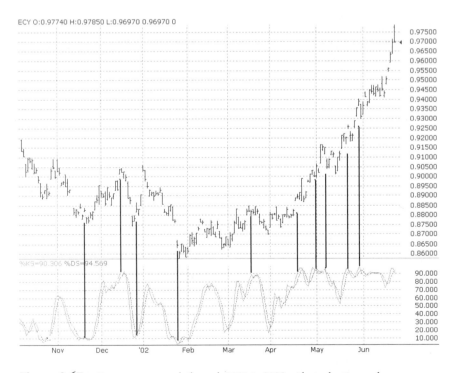

Figure 8.67   Euro currency cash through 2001 to 2002 with stochastic overlay.

drawn to reference the specific price correlated to the values. An initial reaction might be that the stochastic simply mimics the slope of the price line. Although this is true, the scale brings a new quantitative value to a price move. How do we know if a rally is overextended? The stochastic enables us to differentiate between high relative price values and low relative price values within the selected time criteria. Thus, a value above 80 suggests a powerful market in need of some relief while a value close to 0 implies a strong bear pattern that could reverse.

Stochastic lines also have formations with implied significance. The most frequent reference is to a divergence between the slow and fast or %K versus %D. Crossovers before an elbow (to the left of the bottom) is more indicative of a reversal because the near term has accelerated its advance. *Knees* and *shoulders* along with rising tops and bottoms or falling tops and bottoms appear. Lower %D bottoms when the price pattern has rising bottoms is indicative of a bear setup that culminates in a final top. The opposite is a general rule for bull setups. However, referencing Figure 8.67, we see rising tops and bottoms for both the stochastic indicators and price. This is why even Lane strongly suggests using the stochastic as an adjunct to chart interpretation rather than a decision process by itself.

Relative Strength Indicator (RSI)

Along with the stochastic is the Relative Strength Indicator (RSI) popularized by Wells Wilder, Jr. Like Lane's stochastic, price action is reduced to an indexed oscillator on a fixed scale from a hypothetical 0 to 100. This index is derived by dividing the average of rising days by the average of falling days. For example:

Relative strength = Average$_x$ of up days/Average$_x$ of down days

Where $_x$ is the interval. Wilder used 14 days for his RSI, which is calculated as:

$$RSI = 100 - (100/(1 + RSI))$$

This reduces the interval price movement to a standardized value to provide a basis for comparison. Is the current price relatively high or low? Has the price movement been relatively strong or weak? The 14-day RSI generally moves between 50 and 80 in bull currency markets and 50 to 20 in bear markets. Some traders consider these extreme values as independent buy or sell signals. Thus, an RSI over 80 would be a sell while 20 or less would be a buy.

Extreme bull and bear markets can trick the RSI into signaling overbought or oversold conditions prematurely. Since these powerful trends are the very moves many long-term traders seek to build their fortunes, the RSI must be very cautiously used. This is not to say that RSI values cannot be predictive in powerful markets. It is simply a caution that limit-up or very powerful trends will rapidly violate extreme RSI values.

For illustration, examine Figure 8.68, which plots the same euro currency period using an appended 14-day RSI.

In this example, the oversold band is drawn at 30 and the overbought is at 70. The late January 2002 reversal took place; however, the ensuing overbought signals were generated in a

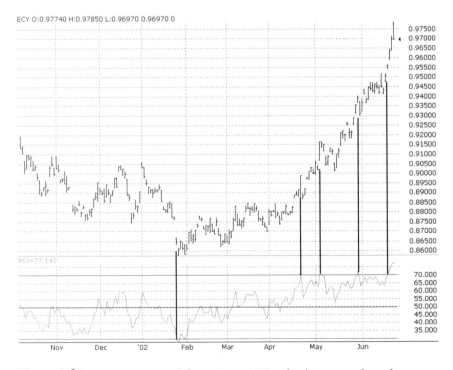

Figure 8.68   Euro currency cash from 2001 to 2002 with relative strength overlay.

strong uptrend. Each overbought signal from April forward would have been false. In particular, the last signal in June was over the 75 mark while prices continued higher.

The RSI also experiences divergence when its slope is contrary to the price trendline. If RSI peaks increase while the actual price experiences lower peaks, it represents a divergence sell signal. Since the RSI is a function of previous price, it cannot maintain any independence. This aspect of RSI and stochastic indicators represents a drawback when major longer-term moves occur.

Overbought and Oversold Dynamics

Index oscillators raise a more basic question: What exactly is an overbought or oversold market? These terms are frequently used, but rarely defined. The basic understanding is that buyers have accumulated too much position during a price rise. As they decide to unload, the market reacts downward. When too many sellers have driven prices lower, their attempt to cover (buy back) their position squeezes the market and bids prices higher. However, these explanations are too general to gain a real grasp of the overbought/oversold dynamic. The best example is represented by an auction. When there is interest in an auctioned item, we see large participation. A low price attracts many bidders. As prices rise, buyers drop out. At some stage, the process is reduced to two bids. We know that two interested parties can still fight each other for the prize, but whom will they have to sell to? When the item is finally won, the only person the winner could conceivably sell to would be his final opponent who was unwilling to pay his price. He has, in effect, overbought the item. This is the dynamic behind an overbought market. An oversold condition is the same phenomenon in reverse.

As we know, futures and options have a technical statistic called *open interest* that represents the number of positions existing between buyers and sellers. When open interest is rising, we have a true accumulation, as previously explained. In combination with price, open interest can give us a more accurate assessment of an overbought market. When a rising market generates unusually large open interest, we know selling will be congested. There are simply too many positions requiring liquidation relative to the pool of sellers. This truly defines a reversal situation.

Overbought reactions are more likely to occur as contracts approach expiration. This is because all buyers (or sellers) have a limited time window within which they can take their profits and run. Cash market accumulation is more significant because it results from either excessive investment cash flows or trade imbalances. When Japan was continuously accumulating dollars, it eventually poured money back into the United States through larger investments in real estate, stocks, and government paper. Japan's effort to unload dollars bid up the yen's value during their conversion efforts. In the end, both sides of Japan's transactions lost value.

Some analysts believe currency behavior is environmental. They claim currencies respond to the monetary structure more than to the whims of traders. As proof, they reference prior periods when currency parity was restricted to specific bands such as the snake and tunnel referenced earlier in this text. By caveat, global monetary institutions establish the rules and standards for currency fluctuation. Under a free-floating system, parity differentials and the speed of parity adjustment have no theoretical limits. From a practical standpoint, parity appreciation and deterioration are still limited, unless a country goes completely bankrupt.

Any behavioral currency study will show increasing volatility with each consecutive decade following free-floating parities. Even with the consolidation of western European currencies into the euro, we saw 30 percent swings against the dollar. Consider this change in relative value in conjunction with stock market volatility from 2000 forward. The rapid decrease in the dollar combined with the fall in U.S. equity values to produce a very harsh result for any western European investors holding U.S. equities. This double consequence resurfaced the question whether the world could experience another post-1929-style depression. Although the educated consensus believed the answer was no, the difference between no gold standard and free-floating currencies was not tested in a spiraling inflation.

For currency trading, volatility is good and stability is bad. For world peace, volatility is questionable and stability is preferable. This brings us to the subject of expectation.

Chapter 9

GREAT EXPECTATIONS

Is there a master plan? Watching the evolution of modern currency markets, one can only conclude that there was absolutely no plan whatsoever or the plan is so extraordinary that we simply cannot see it taking shape. Reading the works of Fed Chairmen Paul Volcker and Alan Greenspan, we see that neither was a proponent of the type of global monetary system that eventually evolved. In fact, Greenspan feared the very environment he helped to shape in the late 1980s through the beginning of the 21st century.

Any master plan is likely to have been the product of confusion after Nixon summarily closed the U.S. Gold Window in the early 1970s and proceeded to force the world onto a totally paper system. The Group of 5 (G5) that grew into the Group of 7 (G7) and morphed to G8 to G10 seemed intent on consolidating currencies by regions and standardizing valuation. If the training period involved greater volatility as the new world monetary order evolved, so be it. Many currency traders could become extraordinarily wealthy during the transition and subsequent maturing.

Influences on Expectations

A great deal of confusion and apprehension surrounded professional currency traders and brokers when the euro became a reality. Wonderfully popular currencies such as the German mark,

French franc, Swiss franc, and Italian lira were suddenly gone and replaced by a single currency. During its debut, the euro eclipsed the greenback only to lose substantial parity within the following year. Regardless of 30 percent variations, we should expect an eventual attempt to stabilize the euro, dollar, and yen parity in an effort to standardize monetary values. This is the ultimate globalization process. In effect, the world's regions should have currencies that maintain a 1:1 parity. Who knows—perhaps there will be a single world currency. The twenty-first century has taken shape as the proving ground for monetary unification. Thus, currency traders must be keenly aware of any suggestions that unified monetary standards should be developed. Hints that parity should be "brought to par" (even money) will signal an eventual end to the opportunities and a return to fixed parity ratios.

Resistance to Consolidation

Reducing the variety of currencies requires consolidating monetary regulation. Herein remains the resistance to a single world currency. To give up one's currency is similar to relinquishing sovereignty. What makes a nation unique? Is it not the government as well as the populace? If a foreign body—albeit democratic in nature—controls the currency, it also controls the economy. This reluctance to relinquish control over monetary policy remains regardless of the European success or failure. The famous line "things are not as they seem" is particularly applicable in currency markets where the appearance of agreement is actually the beginning of separatism. In short, the world competes.

Concepts of national wealth described earlier have become much more inflammatory. In fact, the challenge of Western ideology by fundamentalists like radical Islam and China's autonomy movement is based on economic principles rather than religious zeal. What is wrong with the United States and western Europe? In a word, everything! The formula for "two chickens in every pot and two cars in every garage" prescribed by President Hoover has an underlying implication of a lower standard among less fortunate nations. From a resource standpoint, the entire world cannot enjoy the same lifestyle as the U.S. or European middle class. According to environmentalists, our globe would be reduced to a spinning cinder. Thus, the world is divided into the haves and have-nots based on resource allocation substantially controlled by the West.

As the oil supplier to the world, the Middle East has the potential to redistribute wealth, but not resources. With all the oil, the Middle East has remained woefully underdeveloped, poor, and backward by industrialized standards. Radicalism has recognized this and challenges the disequality. Unless Western greed is slowed, the entire world will suffer. The West lacks the discipline to curb its appetite for more. However, the West expects sacrifice and conservation from the less fortunate. Save the rain forests! Fine. Whose rain forests should we save? At what cost? Who pays the bill?

Although China has taken draconian measures to stem its population growth, the U.S. insists on building higher living standards while imposing lower standards on other regions. This establishes an adversarial agenda.

Prospective currency traders wonder what to expect. Is it possible that the world will go to a single currency within a lifetime? Even a move for a triparity system would be a totally new paradigm. Intriguingly, isn't a single currency standard similar to going back to gold? After all, gold was the universal world monetary standard—with a little help from the sterling. Figure 9.1 plots monthly gold performance against the U.S. Dollar Index to demonstrate that structural relationships can still change.

From 1985 through 1987, gold prices were rising while the U.S. Dollar Index fell. The next inverse relationship was seen from 1987 into 1989 with gold falling while the Dollar Index rose. Despite some spikes, gold's secular trend from 1990 through 1992 was down and the Dollar Index displayed an erratic pattern with a downward bias. Although this break with the normal relationship was sporadic, it confirms the metal's capability to divorce from dollar parity. From 1993 to 1996, gold moved up while the dollar moved in both directions. From 1995 into 1996, gold tracked the dollar, which was a contradiction. Normalcy returned and the brief divergences could be explained; however, gold's rise from 2001 forward served as a warning that the Dollar Index would change direction or gold would fail.

If gold tracks the dollar so well, is it not a de facto monetary standard? A problem arises from the fact that direction is not

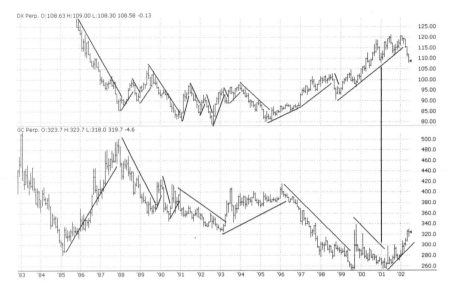

Figure 9.1   The U.S. Dollar Index versus gold from 1983 to 2002.

value and value does not determine direction. The inflation equation was absent from gold for more than 15 years. If enough gold was available and its supply was sufficiently diverse, it could operate as an official reserve asset. This would preserve an official monetary link. Without this requirement, gold remains one level removed from currency and monetary systems.

In the words of Alan Greenspan, gold cannot be created or destroyed like a book entry. Gold has the ultimate accountability. Perhaps this is why modern governments abandoned the gold standard. Too little flexibility and too much inventory control meant no cheating—just maneuvering. Although the chart proves the directional correlation, parity has significantly changed. The dollar has undergone 3 decades of severe to mild inflation while gold prices fell from a 1979 high above $800 per ounce to unthinkable lows below $300 20 years later. Thus, one might assume the dollar has actually appreciated in purchasing parity based on absolute parity.

The gold's importance (and, to a lesser extent, silver's) remains the previous monetary representation and the potential for a renewed link. Currency markets and monetary systems are in constant flux because economic requirements change with lifestyles, demographics, and technology. Are Internet expenses reflected in the Consumer Price Index (CPI)? Do we count AOL access within the basket of goods and services defined by the CPI? Have we taken just-in-time inventory replenishment into account when determining economic efficiency and overall productivity?

A chapter on great expectations is necessary because currency trading will change over the next several decades. Without expectations, there cannot be anticipation or preparation. Speculative potential comes from two sources. First, the monetary divorce between a fixed standard (like gold) and currency enables the supply and demand to fluctuate. This provides parity variation within short time intervals. Secondly, the political environment permits private citizens to pit skills against governments. To be exact, a third opportunity lies with financial invention that brings the Interbank, currency futures, and related options to the general investor. Our ability to trade currency relatively unencumbered is a privilege rather than a right. Too many scandals or too much speculation could precipitate greater regulation, more restriction, and less profit potential.

The Political Environment

Over the next several decades, political structures will go through profound changes. Once again, alliances are being reformulated with Russia joining the West in new efforts toward capitalism, democracy, and free trade. Just as quickly as Japan rose to global economic dominance after World War II, Russia and her Commonwealth of Independent States (CIS) can dominate in the next century. This suggests that the ruble or any derivation thereof will be a significant currency to track and trade. Behind or alongside of the ruble we will see China's yuan. Descriptions of currency behavior that relied on the euro, sterling, and dollar are equally applicable to the ruble and yuan. It is simply a matter of data and time.

Renaming the Third World to *emerging economies* was clairvoyant when considering the pace of economic progress that currently exists among certain poorer economies. The reality is that

emerging economies will provide the greatest growth potential
and, hence, better currency-trading opportunities as long as the
currencies are available for speculation. This is a key point. What
will be available for speculation over the next several decades?
For example, the euro was experimental. Its transition took place
in two stages. The euro was introduced as a book entry in tandem with existing western European currencies. It became real
cash and coin in 2002. The survival as a book entry demonstrates
the potential for converting to an all-book entry system. This
form of cashless society has been planned and designed with the
first credit-card transaction. However, today's information-
processing technology brings the prospect of cashless existence
within reasonable expectation and reach.

Any exercise in foretelling the futures of currency markets is
mentally stimulating, but not necessarily applicable to making
a profit. Still, it is important to maintain flexibility so that trading strategies can be quickly molded to suit the investment environment. As certain economies emerge, determine the economic
foundations of the region. For example, the ruble is likely to have
a high correlation to oil prices as Russia and its sister states
develop their vast petroleum resources. This oil link will be
emphasized by ruble/dollar parity as long as oil is primarily
priced in dollars. However, duel pricing in dollars and euros
means that a four-way parity will exist between oil and the three
currencies: the ruble, dollar, and euro.

This means great profit expectations will exist in arbitraging
oil against these currencies. Although the ruble is not a widely
traded currency futures or options contract, popularity can
change in a matter of months. You must be prepared. Figure 9.2
charts the ruble as it declined from 2000 through 2001. It should
be obvious that any goods purchased from Russia for future delivery would have been paid for with a cheaper ruble.

The lead time for some contracts is 18 months or longer for
materials such as nickel, zinc, lead, platinum, and palladium.
With the proper strategy, this parity decline represents money.

If Russia is capable of mobilizing its huge natural resources,
we could actually see a destabilizing deflationary spiral. The
costs for extraction and processing are likely to be lower in the
CIS relative to the West. This can drive Western producers out of
business and make Europe and the United States more depend-

RUY O:0.031760 H:0.031770 L:0.031760 0.031760 0

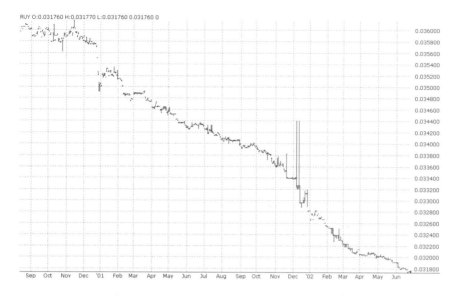

Figure 9.2 The ruble from 2000 to 2001.

ent on CIS raw materials and energy. How might the ruble chart change? China's massive population resource represents another challenge to the West. Far cheaper labor with a lower standard of living represents a threatening one-two punch for Western economic survival. If Japan was any indication of things to come, a China molded after the Japanese economic model would be a formidable economic rival.

Of course, autonomy represents a course of conduct if western Europe or the Americas feel threatened. Aside from energy, the continental regions have reasonably diverse natural resources to survive without trade at the raw material level. We could always revert to isolationism and protectionism. However, this flies in the face of globalization. Which will it eventually be: a global economy or three to four regional economies?

The Impact of Techonology

Along other lines, what great expectations might we have for trading systems, facilities, and accounts? As computers become less expensive and more powerful, the ability to place an instantaneous arbitrage recognition system on every desk becomes easier and more probable. This raises the question of market efficiency. According to the theory previously discussed, the more players who share the same information at the same time, the more efficient markets become. In turn, efficiency reduces profit opportunity. We cannot identify market dislocation if it becomes instantaneous and minute. Alas, will technologies foreclose our dreams of riches?

Indeed, efficient systems can reduce profit potential. That is why the opportunity is now rather than later. For example, electronic transactions are becoming far more efficient and popular. The concept of Internet money; exchange parties such as PayPals™, MasterCard®, Visa®, American Express®, Discover®, Novus®; and an expanding list of participants point to eventual standardization. If U.S. consumers shop the Net for ink cartridges and the best price is from India, the transaction will be consummated and the exchange will automatically be converted. The daily currency trading focus could easily become daily Internet cash flows rather than money supply, employment, or monetary statistics. Again, flexibility is essential if you are to participate in the profit potentials generated by such an eventuality.

One prediction is more apt to be absolute. Currency trading volume will exponentially grow in coming years and decades unless or until monetary systems become consolidated. Given the time required for Europe to finally adopt a single currency, it is not overly probable that readers will need to find a different forum for similar wealth-building resources. From more than $1 trillion per day in transaction value, the next 50 years will generate 5,000 times that amount in value. Even if we see a major deflation, the purchasing parity associated with daily currency transactions will soar. This is inevitable and highly encouraging for anyone seeking to profit from currency markets.

Multicurrency Arbitrage

It is also worth mentioning that new financially engineered vehicles such as single stock futures and options will open up as many

channels for multicurrency arbitrage as potential currency consolidation may shut down. Stocks valued in more than one currency have not been easily arbitraged because selling short has
been encumbered by the former process. However, the ability to
sell leveraged futures and options opens up three- and four-way
currency arbitrage between every stock that is traded abroad. The
possibilities are almost endless and incredibly exciting.

From the late 1980s into the 1990s, investors were seeking
better returns from South and Central America. Strengthening
trade between the Americas represented new support for Latin
American stocks, government debt, and currency parity. The
Brazilian Social Security system was even heralded as a model
for the United States—semi-privatization became part of the
Bush campaign platform. Figure 9.3 shows the deterioration in
the Brazilian real as South American economies faltered after the
turn of the century.

Little doubt exists that a short sale would have yielded a
handsome gain. Any appreciation in Brazilian stocks might have
been offset by losses in parity unless the equities were hedged.
Note how the technical *M* pattern establishes a renewed sale in
May 2002 when the baseline is broken. Pouring money into

Figure 9.3   Brazilian real cash.

emerging Latin American companies was ill advised after the
bust, but this is with the benefit of the chart. However, a consolidation of equity and currency strategies could have provided
a double profit opportunity by using negative parity to one's
advantage. This same pattern was available from the Mexican
peso, as illustrated in Figure 9.4.

Unlike the Brazilian real, the peso was more responsive to
U.S. trade. Notice the opportunity for selling strangles from
November through May 2002. The strong dollar link plunged the
peso when Latin American investors began running to the dollar
after Argentina's system began crumbling. Again, we observe
enormous profit potentials. With any Latin American recovery
comes the opposite secular parity alignment.

All examples point in a single direction. Increasing world
commerce coupled with powerful competitive forces will drive
currencies. Whether this driving force is reflected in changing
government interest rates or basic cash flow will only be relevant
to the trading rules that develop. We have seen how the interest
rate correlation can fail and we know that trade imbalances can
be overcome by interest rate differentials. These relationships are

Figure 9.4   Mexican peso cash.

bound to bounce back and forth to create a challenging dynamic. You must be able to spot when trading consensus changes. This will be apparent in the hue of articles and expert commentary.

Just as traders watched aggregate money supply figures in the 1980s and changed focus to the Fed short-term rates in the 1990s, we can see another focal point emerge—or a combination of overemphasized data. When the consensus locks into new thinking or reverts back to the old, you should follow the crowd. Remember how volume and open interest commands a market. You know the rules of the auction and its dynamics. You know how to identify overbought and oversold markets regardless of the cause.

Practical Considerations When Developing Expectations

You should make some practical considerations after you have evaluated the efficacy of currency trading. For example, decide how you will open your account. Today's Internet provides an excellent resource to locate firms that handle various types of currency transactions. If you decide to trade cash currencies, it may be wise to seek a registered firm that transacts other forms of investing. If a firm is a member of Nasdaq or the National Futures Association (NFA), you have more confidence that certain regulations will be followed, whether required by cash markets or not. Selecting a trading firm is one of the most neglected processes conducted by the general public. Some of this neglect is due to ignorance, whereas some results from being sold. Hence, you should have great expectations of your broker and clearing firm.

Take the time to do the research. Here are important considerations:

- **Type of execution facilities.** Will you be trading electronically or placing your orders by phone? If you will trade electronically, what type of access does the prospective firm provide? How are you protected against system failures, negligence, and rouge trades? What are the error-reporting and correction policies?

- **Registration status.** Is the firm a member of a self-regulatory body such as Nasdaq or the NFA? If so, do some research. Has the firm or the particular broker ever been sanctioned? If yes, for what and how was it resolved? Go on the regulators' Web sites and investigate. Use the information hotlines to make your inquiries and take notes. Make sure you're dealing with a sound firm.

- **Financial qualifications.** Many firms including venerable names like E. F. Hutton and Drexel have failed. If you are trading with such a firm, the experience can be a disaster. Check a firm's financial statements and find out if the firm takes positions for its own account. Firms that trade are vulnerable to meltdowns. Keep this in mind if you open an account with a firm that trades alongside customers.

- **Money management.** You may decide to use the services of a money manager or professional currency trader. If you do, check the trading record *for real*. Don't simply take their word for it. You know how to get a chart and read the results. See if the profits match the history. Find out if the record is audited and by whom. Has the record been filed with the regulators? Are there filing requirements?

- **Costs.** If you will be trading in cash markets, find out the cost. Will you be paying a fixed spread or will it vary? The spread will be expressed in the number of pips—that is, *10 wide*, meaning 10 pips. If you are transacting futures and options, what are the commissions? A typical full-service charge for the year 2002 was $60 to $70 for U.S. execution. Full service is advisable if you need assistance in placing your orders or interpreting markets. Discount costs vary and can be as low as $5 per side ($10 per round turn, in and out) or as high as $30. The difference is in the amount of service and the size of the firm. Don't be penny-wise and pound-foolish. Remember that you usually get what you pay for!

- **Up fronts.** Beware of loading and up-front charges. These are fees above and beyond costs. Although an up-front fee may be reasonable if you are entering an investment partnership that has initial startup costs, do not pay loading fees for options or more general transactions. An option should cost no more than the quoted price. If you are offered an option at a premium to the actual offer, forget it. You're better off paying the commission (usually).

- **Be prepared.** Our new investment environment imposes more rules and regulations on the honest as a result of the dishonest. This means it can take considerable time to properly fill out all forms and have your account open. Credit and identity checks can delay this process several weeks, if not months. Since currencies can move very far very fast, you must be prepared. Therefore, it is advisable to have an account open and funded even if you do not intend to immediately trade. This ensures that you are prepared when a profit opportunity develops.

Enjoy Yourself

The process of currency trading is intended to make money. In addition, it should be an enjoyable experience. Your expectation of profit should go hand in hand with your expectation of having fun learning and trading. If you don't expect to enjoy yourself, you probably won't.

As suggested, the process can be (or is) stressful. Fast action translates into big gains or losses in unusually short periods. If you are winning, it is exhilarating. However, if you are losing, the vital objective is to limit your exposure. Do not expect to make millions in an instant. Such luck (or skill) is extremely rare. It is true that the ability to make huge gains today is greater than ever. Volatility and uncertainty abound. Trends are a consequence. However, patience is a virtue. A carefully researched and planned strategy should win. A haphazard attempt will be a costly experience.

Great expectations are the result of several decades of wealth accumulation during the 1980s and 1990s. This precedent generated a hunger for better returns. However, the equity bubble did eventually burst. Investments move with greater speed and more sensitivity. This means you need to seek the best possible returns for the amount of exposure required. Diversification into currency markets is a big endeavor for many investors. Ultimately, the decision depends on trading capital, economic environment, and risk aversion. An 80-year-old man on fixed income is not a candidate for currency trading unless the excitement is doctor prescribed. An 80-year-old man who is highly self-sufficient should enjoy the action and income potential.

Many excellent resources are available for learning more about these exciting markets. Since these resources are almost as volatile as the markets themselves, the best course is to investigate currency trading on the Internet and through various book distributors. As the field gains popularity, more information will become available. Virtually all exchanges have information sites and telephone numbers. Use these free resources.

Few experiences are as amazing as riding an enormous currency trend. I hope you will have an opportunity to personally describe your own.

Appendix A

WORLD CURRENCIES

Country	Currency	Symbol	Subdivision	ISO-4217 Code	Regime
Afghanistan	afghani	Af	100 puls	AFA 004	float
Albania	lek	L	100 qindarka (qintars)	ALL 008	float
Algeria	dinar	DA	100 centimes	DZD 012	composite
American Samoa	See the United States of America.				
Andorra	Andorran peseta (1/1 to Spanish peseta) and Andorran franc (1/1 to French franc)				
Angola	kwanza	Kz	100 lwei	AOK	(replaced)
Angola	kwanza (kwanza reajustado,–2000)	Kz	100 lwei	AON 024	m.float
Angola	kwanza (new kwanza, 2001–)	Kz	100 lwei	AOA 024	m.float
Anguilla	Dollar	EC$	100 cents	XCD 951	U.S.-$ (2.7)
Antarctica	Each Antarctic base uses the currency of its home country.				
Antigua and Barbuda	dollar	EC$	100 cents	XCD 951	U.S.-$ (2.7)
Argentina	austral (–1991)	double dashed A	100 centavos	ARA	(replaced)
Argentina	peso (1991–)	$	100 centavos	ARS 032	U.S.-$ (1.0)
Armenia	dram		100 luma	AMD 051	
Aruba	guilder (aka florin or gulden)	Af.	100 cents	AWG 533	U.S.-$ (1.79)
Australia	dollar	A$	100 cents	AUD 036	float
Austria (–1998)	schilling	S	100 groschen	ATS 040	euro—13.7603
Austria (1999–)	See European Union.				
Azerbaijan	manat		100 gopik	AZM 031	
Bahamas	dollar	B$	100 cents	BSD 044	U.S.-$ (1.0)
Bahrain	dinar	BD	1,000 fils	BHD 048	US-$ (lim.flex.)

284

Country	Currency	Symbol	Subdivision	ISO-4217 Code	Regime
Bangladesh	taka	Tk	100 paisa (poisha)	BDT 050	composite
Barbados	dollar	Bds$	100 cents	BBD 052	U.S.-$ (2.0)
Belarus (–1999)	ruble	BR		BYB 112	replaced, 1000 BYB = 1 BYR
Belarus (2000–)	ruble	BR		BYR 112	m.float
Belgium (–1998)	franc	BF	100 centimes	BEF 056	euro—40.3399
Belgium (1999–)	See European Union.				
Belize	dollar	BZ$	100 cents	BZD 084	U.S.-$ (2.0)
Belorussia	This is the old name of Belarus.				
Benin	franc	CFAF	100 centimes	XOF 952	French franc (100.0)
Bermuda	dollar	Bd$	100 cents	BMD 060	U.S.-$ (1.0)
Bhutan	ngultrum	Nu	100 chetrum	BTN 064	Indian rupee (1.0)
Bolivia	boliviano	Bs	100 centavos	BOB 068	float
Bosnia-Herzegovina (–1999)	B.H. dinar		100 para	BAD 070	
Bosnia-Herzegovina (1999–)	convertible mark	KM	100 fennig	BAM 977	DM (1.0)
Botswana	pula	P	100 thebe	BWP 072	composite
Bouvet Island	See Norway.				
Brazil	cruzeiro (–1993)		100 centavos	BRE 076	(replaced)
Brazil	cruzeiro (1993–94)		100 centavos	BRR 076	(replaced)
Brazil	real (1994–)	R$	100 centavos	BRL 986	float
British Indian Ocean Territory	Legal currency is the British pound, but mostly U.S. dollars are used.				
British Virgin Islands	See United States.				

Country	Currency	Symbol	Subdivision	ISO-4217 Code	Regime
Brunei	ringgit (aka Bruneian dollar)	B$	100 sen (aka 100 cents)	BND 096	U.S.-$ (1.0)
Bulgaria	leva	Lv	100 stotinki	BGL 100	German mark (1.0)
Burkina Faso	franc	CFAF	100 centimes	XOF 952	French franc (100.0)
Burma	This is now Myanmar.				
Burundi	franc	FBu	100 centimes	BIF 108	composite
Cambodia	new riel	CR	100 sen	KHR 116	m.float
Cameroon	franc	CFAF	100 centimes	XAF 950	French Franc (100.0)
Canada	dollar	Can$	100 cents	CAD 124	float
Canton and Enderbury Islands	See Kiribati.				
Cape Verde Island	escudo	C.V.Esc.	100 centavos	CVE 132	composite
Cayman Islands	dollar	CI$	100 cents	KYD 136	U.S.-$ (0.85)
Central African Republic	franc	CFAF	100 centimes	XAF 950	French franc (100.0)
Chad	franc	CFAF	100 centimes	XAF 950	French franc (100.0)
Chile	peso	Ch$	100 centavos	CLP 152	indicators
China	yuan renminbi	Y	10 jiao = 100 fen	CNY 156	m.float
Christmas Island	See Australia.				
Cocos (Keeling) Islands	See Australia.				
Colombia	peso	Col$	100 centavos	COP 170	m.float
Comoros	franc	CF	-none-	KMF 174	French franc (75.0)
Congo	franc	CFAF	100 centimes	XAF 950	French franc (100.0)
Congo, Dem. Rep. (former Zaire)	franc		100 centimes	CDF 180	U.S.-$ (2.50)

Country	Currency	Symbol	Subdivision	ISO-4217 Code	Regime
Congo, Dem. Rep. (2001–)	franc		100 centimes	CDF 976	float
Cook Islands	See New Zealand.				
Costa Rica	colon	slashed C	100 centimos	CRC 188	float
Côte d'Ivoire	franc	CFAF	100 centimes	XOF 952	French Franc (100.0)
Croatia	kuna	HRK	100 lipas	HRK 191	float
Cuba	peso	Cu$	100 centavos	CUP 192	U.S.-$ (1.0)
Cyprus	pound	£C	100 cents	CYP 196	1.7086 EUR/CYP +/– 2.25 percent
Cyprus (Northern)	See Turkey.				
Czechoslovakia	This split into Czech Republic and Slovak Republic on January 1, 1993.				
Czech Republic	koruna	Kc (with hacek on c)	100 haleru	CZK 203	float
Denmark	krone (pl. kroner)	Dkr	100 øre	DKK 208	EMU
Djibouti	franc	DF	100 centimes	DJF 262	U.S.-$ (177.72)
Dominica	dollar	EC$	100 cents	XCD 951	U.S.-$ (2.7)
Dominican Rep.	peso	RD$	100 centavos	DOP 214	m.float
Dronning Maud Land	See Norway.				
East Timor	See Indonesia.				
Ecuador	sucre	S/	100 centavos	ECS 218	m.float
Ecuador (September 15, 2002–)	Country has adopted the U.S. dollar.				
Egypt	pound	£E	100 piasters or 1,000 milliemes	EGP 818	m.float
El Salvador	colon	¢	100 centavos	SVC 222	float

287

Country	Currency	Symbol	Subdivision	ISO-4217 Code	Regime
Equatorial Guinea	franc	CFAF	100 centimos	GQE 226	French franc (100.0)
Eritrea	nakfa	Nfa	100 cents	ERN 232	
Estonia	kroon (pl. krooni)	KR	100 senti	EEK 233	German mark (8.0)
Ethiopia	birr	Br	100 cents	ETB 230	float
European Union (–1998)	European Currency Unit	ecu		XEU 954	
European Union (1999–)	euro	(insert graphic)	100 euro-cents	EUR 978	
Faeroe Islands (Føroyar)	See Denmark.				
Falkland Islands	pound	£F	100 pence	FKP 238	British pound (1.0)
Fiji	dollar	F$	100 cents	FJD 242	composite
Finland (–1998)	markka (pl. markkaa)	mk	100 penniä	FIM 246 (sg. penni)	euro—5.94573
Finland (1999–)	See European Union.				
France (–1998)	franc	F	100 centimes	FRF 250	euro—6.55957
France (1999–)	See European Union.				
French Guiana	See France.				
French Polynesia	franc	CFPF	100 centimes	XPF 953	French franc (18.18)
Gabon	franc	CFAF	100 centimes	XAF 950	French franc (100.0)
Gambia	dalasi	D	100 butut	GMD 270	float
Gaza	See Israel and Jordan.				
Georgia	lari		100 tetri	GEL 981	float
Germany (–1998)	deutsche mark	DM	100 pfennig	DEM 276	euro—1.95583
Germany (1999–)	See European Union.				
Ghana	new cedi	¢	100 psewas	GHC 288	float

Country	Currency	Symbol	Subdivision	ISO-4217 Code	Regime
Gibraltar	pound	£G	100 pence	GIP 292	British pound (1.0)
Great Britain	See United Kingdom.				
Greece (–2000)	drachma	Dr	100 lepta (sg. lepton)	GRD 300	euro—340.750
Greece (2001–)	See European Union.				
Greenland	See Denmark.				
Grenada	dollar	EC$	100 cents	XCD 951	U.S.-$ (2.7)
Guadeloupe	See France.				
Guam	See the United States.				
Guatemala	quetzal	Q	100 centavos	GTQ 320	float
Guernsey	See United Kingdom.				
Guinea-Bissau (–April 1997)	peso	PG	100 centavos	GWP 624	m.float
Guinea-Bissau (May1997–)	franc	CFAF	100 centimes	XOF 952	French franc (100.0)
Guinea	syli	FG	10 francs, 1 franc = 100 centimes	GNS 324	m.float
Guinea	franc			GNF 324	
Guyana	dollar	G$	100 cents	GYD 328	float
Haiti	gourde	G	100 centimes	HTG 332	float
Heard and McDonald Islands	See Australia.				
Honduras	lempira	L	100 centavos	HNL 340	m.float
Hong Kong	dollar	HK$	100 cents	HKD 344	U.S.-$ (7.73 central parity)
Hungary	forint	Ft	-none-	HUF 348	composite
Iceland	króna	IKr	100 aurar (sg. aur)	ISK 352	composite

Country	Currency	Symbol	Subdivision	ISO-4217 Code	Regime
India	rupee	Rs	100 paise	INR 356	float
Indonesia	rupiah	Rp	100 sen (no longer used)	IDR 360	m.float
International Monetary Fund	Special Drawing Right	SDR		XDR 960	
Iran	rial	Rls	10 rials = 1 toman	IRR 364	U.S.-$ (4750)
Iraq	dinar	ID	1,000 fils	IQD 368	U.S.-$ (0.3109)
Ireland (–1998)	punt or pound	IR£	100 pingin or pence	IEP 372	euro—0.787564
Ireland (1999–)	See European Union.				
Isle of Man	See United Kingdom.				
Israel	new shekel	NIS	100 new agorot	ILS 376	m.float
Italy (–1998)	lira (pl. lire)	Lit	-none-	ITL 380	euro—1936.27
Italy (1999–)	See European Union.				
Ivory Coast	See Côte d'Ivoire.				
Jamaica	dollar	J$	100 cents	JMD 388	float
Japan	yen	¥	100 sen (not used)	JPY 392	float
Jersey	See United Kingdom.				
Johnston Island	See United States.				
Jordan	dinar	JD	1,000 fils	JOD 400	composite
Kampuchea	See Cambodia.				
Kazakhstan	tenge		100 tiyn	KZT 398	float
Kenya	shilling	K Sh	100 cents	KES 404	float
Kiribati	See Australia.				
Korea, North	won	Wn	100 chon	KPW 408	
Korea, South	won	W	100 chon	KRW 410	float

Country	Currency	Symbol	Subdivision	ISO-4217 Code	Regime
Kuwait	dinar	KD	1,000 fils	KWD 414	composite
Kyrgyzstan	som		100 tyyn	KGS 417	float
Laos	new kip	KN	100 at	LAK 418	m.float
Latvia	lat	Ls	100 santims	LVL 428	SDR
Lebanon	pound (livre)	L.L.	100 piastres	LBP 422	float
Lesotho	loti, (pl. maloti)	L, pl., M	100 lisente	LSL 426	South African rand (1.0)
Liberia	dollar	$	100 cents	LRD 430	U.S.-$ (1.0)
Libya	dinar	LD	1,000 dirhams	LYD 434	SDR (8.5085)
Liechtenstein	See Switzerland.				
Lithuania	litas, (pl. litai)		100 centu	LTL 440	U.S.-$ (4.0)
Luxembourg (–1998)	franc	LuxF	100 centimes	LUF 442	euro—40.3399
Luxembourg (1999–)	See European Union.				
Macao (Macau)	pataca	P	100 avos	MOP 446	HK-$ (1.03)
Macedonia (Former Yug. Rep.)	denar	MKD	100 deni	MKD 807	composite
Madagascar	ariayry = 5 francs	FMG	1 francs = 100 centimes	MGF 450	float
Malawi	kwacha	MK	100 tambala	MWK 454	float
Malaysia	ringgit	RM	100 sen	MYR 458	m.float
Maldives	rufiyaa	Rf	100 lari	MVR 462	m.float
Mali	franc	CFAF	100 centimes	XOF 952	French franc (100.0)
Malta	lira (pl. liri)	Lm	100 cents	MTL 470	composite
Martinique	See France.				
Mauritania	ouguiya	UM	5 khoums	MRO 478	composite
Mauritius	rupee	Mau Rs	100 cents	MUR 480	composite

Country	Currency	Symbol	Subdivision	ISO-4217 Code	Regime
Micronesia	See the United States.				
Midway Islands	See the United States.				
Mexico	peso	Mex$	100 centavos	MXN 484	float
Moldova	leu, pl., lei			MDL 498	float
Monaco	See France.				
Mongolia	tugrik (tughrik?)	Tug	100 mongos	MNT 496	float
Montserrat	dollar	EC$	100 cents	XCD 951	U.S.-$ (2.7)
Morocco	dirham	DH	100 centimes	MAD 504	composite
Mozambique	metical	Mt	100 centavos	MZM 508	float
Myanmar	kyat	K	100 pyas	MMK 104	U.S.-$ (5.86of, 200–300bm)
Nauru	See Australia.				
Namibia	dollar	N$	100 cents	NAD 516	South African rand (1.0)
Nepal	rupee	NRs	100 paise	NPR 524	composite
Netherlands Antilles	guilder (aka florin or gulden)	Ant.f. or NAf.	100 cents	ANG 532	U.S.-$ (1.79)
Netherlands (–1998)	guilder (aka florin or gulden)	f.	100 cents	NLG 528	euro—2.20371
Netherlands (1999–)	See European Union.				
New Caledonia	franc	CFPF	100 centimes	XPF 953	French franc (18.18)
New Zealand	dollar	NZ$	100 cents	NZD 554	float
Nicaragua	gold cordoba	C$	100 centavos	NIC 558	indicators
Niger	franc	CFAF	100 centimes	XOF 952	French Franc (100.0)
Nigeria	naira	double-dashed N	100 kobo	NGN 566	U.S.-$ ((82.0))
Niue	See New Zealand.				

Country	Currency	Symbol	Subdivision	ISO-4217 Code	Regime
Norfolk Island	See Australia.				
Norway	krone (pl. kroner)	NKr	100 øre	NOK 578	float
Oman	rial	RO	1,000 baizas	OMR 512	U.S.-$ (1/2.6)
Pakistan	rupee	Rs	100 paisa	PKR 586	m.float
Palau	See the United States.				
Panama	balboa	B	100 centesimos	PAB 590	U.S.-$ (1.0)
Panama Canal Zone	See the United States.				
Papua New Guinea	kina	K	100 toeas	PGK 598	composite
Paraguay	guarani	slashed G	100 centimos	PYG 600	float
Peru	inti		100 centimos	PEI	(replaced)
Peru	new sol	S/.	100 centimos	PEN 604	float
Philippines	peso	dashed P	100 centavos	PHP 608	float
Pitcairn Island	See New Zealand.				
Poland	zloty	z dashed l	100 groszy	PLN 985	m.float
Portugal (–1998)	escudo	Esc	100 centavos	PTE 620	euro—200.482
Portugal (1999–)	See European Union.				
Puerto Rico	See the United States.				
Qatar	riyal	QR	100 dirhams	QAR 634	U.S.-$ (lim.flex.)
Reunion	See France.				
Romania	leu (pl. lei)	L	100 bani	ROL 642	float
Russia (–1997)	ruble	R	100 kopecks	RUR 810	(replaced, $^{1000}/_1$)
Russia (1998–)	ruble	R	100 kopecks	RUB 810	float
Rwanda	franc	RF	100 centimes	RWF 646	SDR (201.8?)
Samoa (Western)	See Western Samoa.				

Country	Currency	Symbol	Subdivision	ISO-4217 Code	Regime
Samoa (America)	See the United States.				
San Marino	See Italy.				
Sao Tome and Principe	dobra	Db	100 centimos	STD 678	m.float
Saudi Arabia	riyal	SRls	100 halalat	SAR 682	US-$ (lim.flex.)
Senegal	franc	CFAF	100 centimes	XOF 952	French franc (100.0)
Serbia	See Yugoslavia.				
Seychelles	rupee	SR	100 cents	SCR 690	SDR (7.2345)
Sierra Leone	leone	Le	100 cents	SLL 694	float
Singapore	dollar	S$	100 cents	SGD 702	m.float
Slovakia	koruna	Sk	100 haliers (halierov?)	SKK 703	composite
Slovenia	tolar	SIT	100 stotinov (stotins)	SIT 705	m.float
Solomon Island	dollar	SI$	100 cents	SBD 090	composite
Somalia	shilling	So. Sh.	100 centesimi	SOS 706	float
South Africa	rand	R	100 cents	ZAR 710	float
Spain (–1998)	peseta	Ptas	100 centimos	ESP 724	euro—166.386
Spain (1999–)	See European Union.				
Sri Lanka	rupee	SLRs	100 cents	LKR 144	m.float
St. Helena	pound	£S	100 new pence	SHP 654	GBP (1.0)
St. Kitts and Nevis	dollar	EC$	100 cents	XCD 951	U.S.-$ (2.7)
St. Lucia	dollar	EC$	100 cents	XCD 951	U.S.-$ (2.7)
St. Vincent and the Grenadines	dollar	EC$	100 cents	XCD 951	U.S.-$ (2.7)
Sudan (–1992)	pound		100 piastres	SDP 736	m.float
Sudan (1992–)	dinar		100 piastres	SDP 736	m.float

Country	Currency	Symbol	Subdivision	ISO-4217 Code	Regime
Suriname	guilder (aka florin or gulden)	Sur.f. or Sf.	100 cents	SRG 740	m.float
Svalbard and Jan Mayen Islands	See Norway.				
Swaziland	lilangeni (pl. emalangeni)	L, pl., E	100 cents	SZL 748	South African rand (1.0)
Sweden	krona (pl. kronor)	Sk	100 öre	SEK 752	m.float
Switzerland	franc	SwF	100 rappen/centimes	CHF 756	float
Syria	pound	£S	100 piasters	SYP 760	U.S.-$ (11.225)
Tahiti	See French Polynesia.				
Taiwan	new dollar	NT$	100 cents	TWD 901	
Tajikistan (–5- November 5, 2000)	ruble			TJR 762	replaced, 1000 TJR = 1 TJS
Tajikistan (November 6,2000–)	somoni	100 dirams		TJS 762	
Tanzania	shilling	TSh	100 cents	TZS 834	float
Thailand	baht	Bht or Bt	100 stang	THB 764	float
Togo	franc	CFAF	100 centimes	XOF 952	French franc (100.0)
Tokelau	See New Zealand.				
Tonga	pa'anga	PT or T$	100 seniti	TOP 776	composite
Trinidad and Tobago	dollar	TT$	100 cents	TTD 780	float
Tunisia	dinar	TD	1,000 millimes	TND 788	m.float (1.0)
Turkey	lira	TL	100 kurus	TRL 792	m.float
Turkmenistan	manat		100 tenga	TMM 795	U.S.-$ (10.0,230.0)

Country	Currency	Symbol	Subdivision	ISO-4217 Code	Regime
Turks and Caicos Islands	See the United States.				
Tuvalu	See Australia.				
Uganda	shilling	USh	100 cents	UGS	(replaced)
Uganda	shilling	USh	100 cents	UGX 800	float
Ukraine	Hryvnia		100 kopiykas	UAH 980	float
United Arab Emirates	dirham	Dh	100 fils	AED 784	U.S.-$ (lim.flex.)
United Kingdom	pound	£	100 pence	GBP 826	float
United States of America	dollar	$	100 cents	USD 840	float
Upper Volta	This is now Burkina Faso.				
Uruguay (–1975)	peso	Ur$	100 centésimos	UYP	(replaced)
Uruguay (1975–1993)	new peso	NUr$	100 centésimos	UYN	(replaced)
Uruguay (1993–)	peso uruguayo	$U	100 centésimos	UYU 858	m.float
Uzbekistan	som		100 tiyin	UZS 860	
Vanuatu	vatu	VT	100 centimes	VUV 548	composite
Vatican	See Italy.				
Venezuela	bolívar	Bs	100 centimos	VEB 862	float
Vietnam	new dong	D	10 hao or 100 xu	VND 704	m.float
Virgin Islands	See the United States.				
Wake Island	See the United States.				
Wallis and Futuna Islands	franc	CFPF	100 centimes	XPF 953	French franc (18.18)
Western Sahara	See Spain, Mauritania, and Morocco.				

296

Country	Currency	Symbol	Subdivision	ISO-4217 Code	Regime
Western Samoa	tala	WS$	100 sene	WST 882	composite
Yemen	rial	YRls	100 fils	YER 886	float
Yugoslavia	dinar	Din	100 paras	YUM 891	
Zaïre (November 1994–)	zaire	Z	100 makuta		(replaced)
Zaïre (–1997)	new zaire	NZ	100 new makuta	ZRN 180	float
Zaïre	Country was renamed in 1997 to Democratic Republic of Congo.				
Zambia	kwacha	ZK	100 ngwee	ZMK 894	float
Zimbabwe	dollar	Z$	100 cents	ZWD 716	float

INDEX